3

Civil Society, Philanthropy,
and the Fate of the Commons

CIVIL SOCIETY:
Historical and Contemporary Perspectives

Series Editors:
Virginia Hodgkinson: Public Policy Institute, Georgetown University
Kent E. Portney: Department of Political Science, Tufts University
John C. Schneider: Department of History, Tufts University

For a complete list of books that are available in the series, visit www.upne.com.

Civil Society, Philanthropy,
and the
Fate of the Commons

Bruce R. Sievers

TUFTS UNIVERSITY PRESS
Medford, Massachusetts

Published by University Press of New England
Hanover and London

TUFTS UNIVERSITY PRESS
Published by University Press of New England
One Court Street, Lebanon NH 03766
www.upne.com

Manufactured in the United States of America
Designed by Doug Tifft
Typeset in Minion Pro and Scala Sans by Michelle Grald

University Press of New England is a member of the
Green Press Initiative. The paper used in this book
meets their minimum requirement for recycled paper.

For permission to reproduce any of the material in this
book, contact Permissions, University Press of New England,
One Court Street, Lebanon NH 03766; or visit www.upne.com

Library of Congress Cataloging-in-Publication Data
Sievers, Bruce R.
Civil society, philanthropy, and the fate of the commons /
Bruce R. Sievers.
    p. cm.—(Civil society, historical and contemporary
perspectives)
Includes bibliographical references and index.
ISBN 978-1-58465-851-1 (cloth: alk. paper)
ISBN 978-1-58465-895-5 (pbk.: alk. paper)
1. Civil society. 2. Civil society—History. 3. Common good.
4. Social service. I. Title.
JC337.S555   2010
300—dc22   2009045127

5 4 3 2 1

To the memory of my parents
DOROTHY AND ED SIEVERS,
humanistic engineers

Contents

Preface

O ne advantage of taking a long time to complete a book is that it allows incorporation of new research and information on events that occur along the way. That has certainly been the case with this project. It began in the form of a monograph, "Can Philanthropy Solve the Problems of Civil Society?" published in 1995 in an Occasional Papers series of the Indiana University Center on Philanthropy. At the time, a colleague optimistically suggested that the essay might be easily turned into a short book. That was nearly fifteen years ago.

The original question remains at the heart of this book, but the route to answering it has taken many twists and turns. The question presumes a single understanding of civil society, but, of course, there is not one but many. So the first task was to arrive at a defensible concept of civil society out of the great body of literature on the subject. This in turn led to the development of the idea of seven constitutive elements, and consequently, the need to follow the seven threads into their particular traditions in the history of ideas. The second task was to trace the time and place at which these seven became fused into the first coherent manifestation of the civil society idea. Somewhat surprisingly, the course of my research increasingly led to an unlikely candidate for the title of the first civil society: the golden age of the Dutch republic in the seventeenth century. The evidence for this conclusion is compelling, and I present this argument in chapter 4.

At the same time, it became apparent that the evolution of civil society was intimately related to the development of liberal democracy and its efforts to deal with problems of the commons. Thus, the concluding chapters of the book take up the historical legacy of the development of civil society and the need for philanthropic attention to its contemporary deficiencies, particularly in light of the pressing need to address the contemporary problem of the commons. The writing emerges from a perspective of political theory and the history of ideas, reflecting the roots of my own intellectual orientation, but also from a career informed by more than thirty years spent working professionally in philanthropy.

Over the decade and a half during which this book evolved, much has taken place that has shaped both the worlds of practice and of scholarship on civil society and philanthropy. A huge wave of new nonprofits and foundations have joined the ranks of civil society in the late 1990s and early 2000s, followed by an era of great belt-tightening in the latter part of the first decade of the twenty-first century. Among the new foundations appeared the largest in history, the Bill and Melinda Gates Foundation. Around the world, the visible presence of civil society has grown dramatically, to the point that civil society is now considered an essential player, along with government and business, in addressing national and international problems. Scholarship on civil society, philanthropy, and the nonprofit sector has proliferated in a stream of new articles, books, and journals on important but previously little-studied aspects of the field and in the creation of important new centers of research on civil society and philanthropy (for one of which, the Stanford Center on Philanthropy and Civil Society, I serve as an adviser). While attempting to keep up with this expanding universe of civil society activity has been a challenge, this book has benefited greatly from the taking into account of recent events and scholarship.

Another advantage of an extended writing process is the ability to gain valuable insights and critical feedback from friends in the field. The advice on both substance and style offered by many colleagues and critics over the past decade has been enormously helpful. Of course, I take full responsibility for the final product and its deficiencies, but the work has been improved greatly by the thoughtful commentary of both scholars and practitioners who have been willing to take the time to read portions of the manuscript. I am particularly grateful for the commentary and support from my colleagues at the PACS Center, Rob Reich, Woody Powell, and Deb Meyerson; James Allen Smith at The Rockefeller Archive Center; Bob Payton and Les Lenkowsky at the Indiana University Center on Philanthropy; David Mathews and John Dedrick at the Kettering Foundation; Deborah Rhode at the Stanford Center for the Legal Profession; Bill Schambra at the Bradley Center for Philanthropy and Civic Renewal; Perla Ni and Eric Nee at the Stanford Social Innovation Review; Michael O'Neill at the University of San Francisco; Ginny Esposito at the National Center for Family Philanthropy; Doug Bauer at Rockefeller Philanthropy Advisors; Peter Shiras at Independent Sector; and David Myers at the UCLA Center for Jewish Studies.

A special note of gratitude goes to John Schneider, Series Editor at Tufts University Press, for his continuing encouragement, helpful feedback, and endless patience while waiting for the manuscript, to the other team members at University Press of New England, and to David Chu, for the application of his excellent editing skills. Another special word of thanks is owed to Anne Focke, a longtime friend, cheerleader, and superb editor, who published an earlier version of chapter 1 in the *Grantmakers for the Arts Reader*. And, to my most important source of ongoing inspiration, tough editing, and emotional support over the long gestation of the book, my wife, Cynthia Perry, my deep sense of appreciation goes beyond words in a preface.

Many others have provided helpful inspiration and feedback along the way: Paul Brest, Susan R. Clark, Susan S. Clark, Charles Drekmeier, Uri Herscher, Jim Joseph, Stan Katz, Malka Kopell, John Kreidler, Tom Layton, Kathy McCarthy, Craig McGarvey, Martin Paley, Frances Phillips, Jim Quay, Ted Smith, Ike Sofaer, Sterling Speirn, Steve Toben, Lauren Wechsler, Steve Weiland, and my bright and engaged students over the past seven years of teaching "Theories of Civil Society, Philanthropy, and the Nonprofit Sector" at Stanford.

Of course, institutional resources are critical to any research effort, and I am deeply grateful to Stanford's Haas Center for Public Service for hosting me as a Visiting Scholar over the past years and for affording me the fabulous resources at Stanford, especially the great Stanford Library. Suzanne Abel has been a rock of support and good advice. Thanks also to the foundations with which I have been privileged to be associated during my professional life, the Walter and Elise Haas Fund and the Skirball Foundation. The Kettering Foundation's ongoing series on "civil investing" under David Mathews's inspired leadership has also been a great source of ideas and encouragement.

This book is written in the hope that it might contribute in some small way to the solution of the problems of the commons that will, above all, affect the lives of future generations, represented now in my own life by new grandson Bannin.

Introduction

Beneath many of the great challenges facing humanity in the twenty-first century—threats to the environment, public health, and global security among them—lurks a single underlying dilemma: How do we solve the perplexing problem of the commons? The problem of the commons is an ancient one: the seemingly irresolvable conflict between individual interests and collective needs. But it has enormous consequences for the modern world. It is a problem that is woven into the fabric of modern social life in a way that makes it universal and virtually unseen. And yet it is so fundamentally important that it may determine the outcome of other, more immediately apparent issues of our time and those of future generations.

This book argues that a key to understanding and engaging with the problem of the commons lies in civil society, and that an essential resource for civil society to do this work is to be found in philanthropy. For it is in the birth of modern civil society (and of philanthropy with it) that the tension between individual and collective interests becomes a central feature of political life, and it is there that it is first understood that the solution to the most profound political and economic problems depends upon a satisfactory resolution of the underlying tension between private and public aims.

To explore these themes—why they are so important, how they are intertwined with the historical development of civil society, and how this development shapes our choices today—is the central intention of this book. Its aim is to examine the fundamental question: How does society balance the public and private sides of modern life in order to realize the ideal of individual freedom and, at the same time, make possible the achievement of collective aims? In pursuing the answer to this question, the book analyzes the construct of civil society, traces its historical development and its legacy for modern political life, explores the challenges confronting contemporary civil society in aiding or impeding our pursuit of solutions to public problems, and suggests specific steps modern philanthropy can take to strengthen civil society.

These are big themes. They involve interpretations of diverse traditions of political and social history and analysis of complex problems of producing public goods in the modern world. This exploration draws upon a range of disciplines and historical accounts, including the history of ideas, political theory, philosophy of social science, historical narratives, economic theory, and contemporary analytical approaches to the study of the nonprofit sector and philanthropy. Accordingly, I owe a great debt of gratitude to the theoretical and empirical analyses of many writers whose work is cited in the text and upon whose insights this study is based.

Chapter 1 begins with definitional issues. A vast amount has been written in recent years about the concept of civil society—how it is to be defined, what social space it occupies, where to seek its historical origins, whether it is a liberal or conservative concept, how it relates to cultural context, and how to understand its relationship to democracy. The conceptual thread pursued here draws upon the interconnectedness of a range of definitions, borrowing from Ludwig Wittgenstein's notion of "family resemblance" among meanings in a web of relationships. Together, a family of concepts grouped under the same encompassing rubric—in this case, "civil society"—shares interwoven meanings in such a way that there is not "some one fiber [that] runs through its whole length, but in the overlapping of many fibers."[1]

The focus here is explicitly on the Western cultural and political tradition and the emergence of civil society within that tradition. Although a highly fruitful exploration of the relationship of the Western tradition to concepts of civil society in non-Western cultures has been underway in recent years, the primary purpose of the present work is to examine the philosophical and historical background of civil society, with its essentially Western roots, as it shapes contemporary public life in the United States.[2] To explore the broader issues as to whether the concept of civil society is primarily an idea rooted in Western thought, is a culturally relative phenomenon, or is a universal concept that transcends particular traditions, would be a productive enterprise but unfortunately exceeds the scope of the present work.

Accordingly, amidst a plethora of factors that emerge from theorists' diverse descriptions of civil society, I propose seven core elements as the constitutive elements of a definition of civil society. Although there is legitimate debate about the exact requirements for this definition, there are compelling arguments, on both historical and logical grounds, for understanding these seven elements as its necessary components. The seven appear frequently in the large body of civil society literature, and, by incorporating essential institutional and normative factors, these seven supply the necessary and sufficient conditions for a coherent contemporary theory. Understanding civil society in these terms provides the platform for an analysis in the concluding chapters of this study of contemporary civil society's weaknesses and possible responses to them.

Chapters 2 and 3 explore these seven elements in depth, beginning with an examination of the institutional structures that have evolved through the course of Western history to become the extra-state framework of modern civil society. These institutions rely on embedded norms but take concrete form as organizational structures that endure over time. Two sorts of institutions—philanthropic and legal institutions—have persisted over more than two millennia, while two others—private associations and a system of free expression—have evolved in later eras. Similarly, three normative elements—commitments to the common good, individual rights, and tolerance—have appeared sequentially through a long developmental process.

Although each of the seven elements emerged from an independent course of historical development, they gradually became woven together into the fabric of civil society in the early modern era. Chapter 4 describes the first appearance of this interconnected pattern in the early Dutch republic in what is dubbed here as the "first civil society." An unusual convergence of historical forces and ideas took place in the sixteenth and seventeenth centuries in that tiny country in the northwestern corner of Europe, producing novel political and social forms. The fundamentally new social construct was that of a politically decentralized republic that accommodated diverse religious groups and promoted the free flow of ideas. The Dutch republic became a political and social experiment that served as a magnet for leading thinkers, new ideas, and publications flowing in from throughout Europe, and it provided a supportive environment for the creation of many of the great works—by Hugo Grotius, René Descartes, Benedict Spinoza, and John Locke, among others—that shaped the early formation of civil society. The seven constitutive elements created the essential social framework for the political and cultural life that flourished during that unique period, the golden age of the Dutch republic.

The body of ideas that emerged from this productive time became a foundation for early Enlightenment thought that was to spread throughout Europe in the eighteenth century. Included in the newly forming worldview was a new conception of society as a collection of rights-bearing individuals existing separately from the state—a conception variously expressed as "*société civile*," "civil society," or "*bürgerliche Gesellschaft*" in its several French, English, and German manifestations. The challenge posed by this emerging concept of civil society was to reconcile the fragmenting individualism of private interest–seeking social actors with the traditional understanding of community as the locus of the pursuit of collective ends. Exacerbating the tension between the two modes of social decision making was the growth of the absolutist state. Civil society was increasingly seen as a bastion against the ominous and growing power of the state.

Chapters 5 and 6 trace the development of this tension in Enlightenment thought and its infusion into the newly forming American republic. As Alexis de Tocqueville observed early on, the United States was born in an age of tension between private and public interests, and the development of its institutions has reflected that tension since colonial days. The unfolding of individual rights of expression, belief, and association, and the flowering of private associations and private philanthropy (turning into what later was called the nonprofit sector) in the United States, are manifestations of the commitment to individualist ideals, while the recurring themes of the rule of law and the pursuit of the common good reflect an assumed, underlying sense of common purpose. The ability of civil society to balance these two tendencies—private and public—is the primary source of its strength in providing a platform for the development of the liberal democratic state.

In the contemporary era, and at least since the 1950s, the United States and much of the rest of the world have experienced a new, expanded wave of privatization ("hyperindividualism," as some have called it) in cultural, economic, and political life.[3] In chapters 7 and 8, I argue that this trend poses a new challenge to societies worldwide in their efforts to produce public goods. It has become difficult for democratic, market societies to solve major problems that affect the entire community—the problems of the commons, such as global climate change, allocation of taxation burdens, provision of health care, and alleviation of poverty—because the needed remedies are not well provided for by market mechanisms or by political approaches that view members of the community as customers rather than as citizens.[4] Economists and political scientists treat the "problem of public goods" as a central dilemma of public choice in modern societies, and they seek solutions to this dilemma in improved regulatory mechanisms and a strengthened disposition toward civic commitment (an increase in the level of "generalized reciprocity" in Robert Putnam's apt phrase). But attempts to improve regulation or to increase civic affinity must swim against a powerful tide of market triumphalism.[5]

Civil society, as it has evolved over the past four centuries, has managed to maintain a delicate balance between the public and private dimensions of social life. In fact, both are incorporated in the underlying institutional and normative structures of civil society. In recent decades, however, this balance has been gradually eroded by the increasingly powerful privatizing forces that play out in the market dynamics of economic, political, and cultural life at the expense of a commitment to the pursuit of public goods and to protection of the commons.

One might look to philanthropy, an institution dedicated to the pursuit of public benefit and guided in part by the norm of the common good, to help restore the balance in civil society in favor of a public mission. Yet, because the modern rebirth of both philanthropy and nonprofit organizations occurred at a time of assertion of the private against the public, they have developed an ambiguous relationship to the powerful economic and ideological forces of the market. It has thus become a perplexing challenge for them as *private* institutions to claim to speak and act on behalf of the public. Yet, as I argue in the concluding portion of this book, philanthropy and nonprofit organizations can do much to champion the renewal of public norms and institutions. Indeed, the fundamental problems of the commons will not be solved without them.

1   The Concept of Civil Society

The concept of *civil society*, like that of democracy, has come to have worldwide resonance. But what exactly is civil society?

The idea has ancient roots. From the earliest times, human communities required cooperative behavior for survival, and ancient patterns of social coordination imprinted institutional practices and beliefs that still shape our contemporary world. Recent decades have witnessed a great surge of new interest in civil society. Scholars, commentators, and political actors of all stripes have debated the concept, universally acknowledging its centrality to the rise of modern democracy while disputing its definition and function. It remains a contested and elusive idea, simultaneously animating and complicating contemporary debates about the nature of political life and the best paths toward solutions to social problems.

One fact is a given. We are all members of civil society. Just as citizens relate to the state and family members relate to domestic life, we all connect to each other in society through a network of values and institutions that define us as actors in the civil sphere. The quality of our participation in private and public life is in fact closely intertwined with the character of our actions in civil society.

In the economic world, we think and act as producers, consumers, and investors; in the political world, we play the roles of voters, lawmakers, and public administrators. In the world of civil society, we become community members, volunteers, and civic actors. Pluralism, distinctive social values, and a creative tension between individual interests and the common good particularly characterize this world. It is the sphere in which privatized visions of the public good play out and intersect with one another to shape the social agenda. Participating in civil society involves the pursuit of a mixture of public and private goals, of social problem solving and individual expression.

Theorists invoke the term "civil society" in a variety of different ways, depending on particular theoretical assumptions. It is used variously to describe a mediating realm between the individual and the state, the worlds of nonprofit associations and philanthropy, the network of international NGOS, social relations of mutual respect, and many other phenomena.[1] Common to all of these meanings, however, are two central ideas: pluralism and social benefit. Together these ideas reflect the myriad interests and identities present in contemporary society and the task of working to improve conditions in the world. In a social environment increasingly beset by intolerance, threats to freedom of belief and action, and an inability to pursue common goods, the prospect of strengthening civil society suggests a ray of hope in an otherwise dishearteningly bleak picture.

This hope is justified, I believe, not just because the mores of civility suggest an aspiration toward more harmonious social relations, but also because the historical development of civil society has been a vital force in the creation of modern liberal democracy. It continues to play that role today. Civil society's complex framework of freedoms, rights, common commitments, and procedures for peaceful dispute resolution is the source of its promise for the future.

While civil society provides an enabling framework for democracy, at the same time it contains an intrinsic tension, a fragile balance between private and public interests. Maintaining this balance is essential to finding solutions to vital challenges in modern democracies that demand public resolution, challenges such as environmental degradation, deficient educational systems, ethnic and religious strife, and deterioration of public decision-making processes. These are often described as issues of *the commons*, the resolution of which will determine the future of humankind.

The concept of the commons is key to understanding civil society. It refers to a central tradition in Western thought: the shared sphere of communal life where collective goods reside. These goods include not only air and water, but also such public-benefit ideals as social justice and civic commitment, which cannot be achieved by individual decision-making processes alone. Rather, they are created and sustained by common action and by the frameworks of institutions and norms that make such action possible. The commons are critical to the well-being and ultimately the survival of the community.[2]

For the purposes of this book I use a minimalist definition of the commons offered by Charlotte Hess and Elinor Ostrom: "a resource shared by a group of people that is subject to social dilemmas."[3] This definition encompasses the vast range of problem areas related to the commons, ranging from local land use to scientific research, but it is specifically applied here to the kind of large-scale public problems such as global warming that seem consistently to defy solution by markets or governments.

Following the publication of two landmark works, Mancur Olson's *The Logic of Collective Action* (in 1965) and Garrett Hardin's "The Tragedy of the Commons" (in 1968), a vast outpouring of research has explored many complex dimensions of the commons—definitional issues, conditions for long-term survival, economic and political analyses, and application to new fields such as the information commons. The central insight on which all of this work centers is contained in Hardin's memorable warning: "Ruin is the destination to which all men rush, each pursuing his own best interest in a society that believes in the freedom of the commons. Freedom in a commons brings ruin to all."[4] Whether civil society, by escaping the limitations of markets and governments, has the capacity to help the public avoid this ruin is the question at the heart of this book.

In exploring this question, I focus especially on the normative ideal of the common good. As discussed below, the common good is stipulated as one of the constitutive elements of civil society. Strong commitment to this norm is a necessary precondition, along with the presence of six other constitutive elements, for civil society's ability to contribute to the solution of problems of the commons. As I will argue in the concluding chapters, strengthening civil society's normative commitment to the common good, while posing special challenges, takes on extraordinary importance in today's world.

While a significant portion of the following discussion is devoted to analyzing the particular path of the historical development of civil society, the ultimate purpose of the narrative is to describe how the modern construct of civil society contains an inherent tension that, paradoxically, can both increase the difficulty of solving the problems of the commons and at the same time contribute to their solution. The concluding chapters of this book explore the contemporary challenges and opportunities facing philanthropy in its tasks of strengthening civil society and, consequently, enhancing society's ability to make progress toward solving the daunting problems of the commons.

Defining Civil Society—Seven Key Concepts

The modern evolution of the civil society idea is an extraordinarily complex story. It is a story that has profound importance for the future of social and political change and, ultimately, for democracy itself. The story emerges from the gradual intermingling of seven threads of historical development in the world of ideas and from the evolution of institutions and norms that surfaced in early modern Europe. Roughly from the beginning of the sixteenth century, these threads became woven into the fabric of a new social form that spanned national and intellectual frontiers.

Each of the seven strands in this story is complex in its own right and has its own theoretical justification. Four reflect institutional structures that have evolved through the course of Western history to form the structural framework of modern civil society. Two of these organizational structures—philanthropic and legal institutions—have existed throughout the past two millennia, while the other two—private associations and a system of free expression—have evolved in later eras. The other three strands reflect social norms—commitments to the common good, to individual rights, and to tolerance—that appeared sequentially through a long developmental process.

This conception of civil society, as a constellation of seven defining elements, draws upon the work of many contemporary scholars and theorists. Indeed, most contemporary works on civil society begin, not surprisingly, with questions of definition. These thinkers reflect diverse cultural and philosophical traditions, and their analyses of the nature and dynamics of civil society draw on distinctive traditions of social thought. Although we find among them broad agreement on the idea of civil society at an abstract level, when we probe further into their content we find significant differences. Nevertheless, it is useful to explore the areas of intersection between diverse theoretical perspectives and to understand them in relationship to historical developments. What follows, then, is a brief summary of the seven strands as identified by contemporary theorists.

Philanthropy

From quite different theoretical perspectives, Robert Payton and Kathleen McCarthy argue for the critical significance of philanthropic values and practices to the constitution of civil society. Closely related to the tradition emphasizing individual action on behalf of the common good, philanthropy becomes an essential vehicle for realizing this intention. Payton views philanthropy as the central value of civil society, and McCarthy describes how a wide range of groups animated by a philanthropic impulse shaped the emergence of American civil society in the eighteenth and nineteenth centuries. From a sociological perspective, Peter Halfpenny suggests a close albeit complex relationship between charity (and by extension philanthropy), social trust, and civil society.[5]

The common good

A parallel and equally ancient stream of thought is the conceptual tradition of the common good. Modern theorists who stress the significance of this component include Helmut Anheier, Michael Walzer, Charles Taylor, and Amitai Etzioni, all of whom emphasize the central importance of civic norms directed toward achieving communal ends. Anheier's definition of civil society adopted by CIVICUS places central emphasis on the "advance of common interests." Walzer views various civil society traditions as sharing a commitment to the solution of problems in the public realm. Taylor describes the importance of the "Montesquieu stream" of civil society thinking, which views civil society as an extension of the public realm and as a complement to the state, versus the "Locke stream," which emphasizes the protection of individual rights.[6]

The rule of law

Inextricably connected to both the pursuit of the common good and the protection of philanthropy is the "rule of law." Ralf Dahrendorf in particular has described the rule of law as a defining characteristic of civil society, in its capacity to establish fair and predictable rules for the exercise of public authority. Although laws are enacted and enforced by governmental bodies, they require a pre-political legitimacy that inheres in civil society and transcends the authority of a given regime. As Dahrendorf and others suggest, the rule of law provides an essential guarantee that other elements of civil society, especially individual rights, are protected from the arbitrary exercise of power.[7] Gerhard Luf similarly emphasizes the degree to which the culture of the law and civil society are intertwined, the law acting as a protector of autonomy of action in civil society and as a vehicle for implementing the maximum feasible subsidiarity of state power.[8]

Nonprofit and voluntary institutions

A widely shared view identifies civil society with the set of nonprofit (the primary term used in the United States) or nongovernmental (the term used worldwide) organizations. As suggested by Lester Salamon, Michael O'Neill, and Brian O'Connell, this tradition reflects a long history of social theory viewed in institutional terms.[9] Private voluntary associations have, since ancient times, played a vital role in achieving social purposes. The contemporary "nonprofit sector" refers to the part of society populated by such voluntary organizations, in contrast to both public sector, governmental entities and for-profit, private sector businesses. Especially in the United States and Western Europe, there is a well-grounded body of law that establishes the status of entities in each of these three sectors, and the structure and behavior of nonprofit organizations can be described in terms that are specific and legally defined. Despite the clarity and concreteness of such an associational definition of civil society, however, its descriptive and analytical power is limited. As explained in the following two chapters, equating civil society with the nonprofit sector excludes important institutional and normative dimensions that are of fundamental importance to understanding civil society's central role in political and social life.

Individual rights

A fifth thread of broad agreement among contemporary theorists focuses on the rise of the individual and of individual rights as a distinctive characteristic of civil society. For example, John Keane, Adam Seligman, and Ernest Gellner view civil society as anchored primarily in the growth of a sphere of private action and individual rights defended against the state. Keane, in particular, in his classic study of the development of civil society thinking since the seventeenth century, emphasizes the gradual separation of civil society from the state. Seligman describes the emergence of "the autonomous and agentic individual upon which the idea of civil society rests in the West." Gellner describes the growth of civil society in the West as a correlate of the growth of individual freedom and pluralism, in contrast to the authoritarianism of traditional or "segmentary" societies.[10]

Free expression

The concept of free public communication has flowed into the stream of the development of civil society since the early modern period. This concept, most notably articulated by Jürgen Habermas in his notion of the "public sphere," describes the free formation of public opinion that becomes a precondition for the effective functioning of civil society in that it makes possible the emergence of a "reasoning public." Charles Taylor similarly emphasizes the emergence of a system of free expression as a definitive characteristic of early modern civil society, and John Keane stresses the critical importance of "publicity" as a prerequisite for a functioning civil society. Michael Edwards views the public sphere as central to one of three alternative definitions of civil society.[11]

Tolerance

Not as frequently invoked but nevertheless widely understood as essential to the gestation of the civil society idea is the norm of tolerance. An outcome, albeit unintended, of the religious wars of sixteenth- and seventeenth-century Europe, this normative element is implicit in the growth of the idea of civility. Dominique Colas brings tolerance to center stage in the development of civil society (contrasted with "fanaticism"), describing its emergence in seventeenth-century philosophical theories as "the essential, defining virtue of civil society." The notion of tolerance is also an essential feature of descriptions of civil society in John Hall's explication of cultural adaptation to "multi-polar pluralism," Ernest Gellner's "modular man," and Edward Shils's concept of "civility."[12]

Synthesizing the Seven Strands

As suggested above, these seven strands appear in various constellations in the work of many contemporary theorists.[13] My central argument is that they are constitutive and interactive components that together create the necessary and sufficient conditions for the successful functioning of modern civil society. They are mutually supportive and interdependent.

Indeed, it is the argument here that these seven themes in fact define modern civil society. As described in the following chapters, they serve as the foundational institutional elements and key norms that have enabled civil society to become a major force in the post-sixteenth-century world by creating a platform for the formation of the liberal democratic state. The institutional elements that constitute the structure of civil society—organized philanthropy, the rule of law, private associations, and a system of free expression—are the primary vehicles outside the state through which citizens interact and collaborate to achieve common purposes. The three normative elements—commitments to the common good, individual rights, and tolerance—are the values animating these institutions.

This approach views civil society as a singular social construct, comprising both institutions and norms that evolved historically through the seven conceptual streams. The brief definition that best captures these integrated elements is one proposed by Helmut Anheier as a modified version of the definition employed by CIVICUS in its Global Survey of the State of Civil Society:

> Civil society is the arena outside family, government, and market where
> people voluntarily associate to advance common interests based on civility.[14]

The seven constitutive elements complement and reinforce each other in the operation of civil society. The development of the rule of law, for example, is a precondition for the protection of individual rights and the trust necessary for the pursuit of the common good. The evolution of the tradition of toleration performs an essential function as a mediating norm between the defense of individual rights and the pursuit of communal ends. Private associations depend upon individual rights (specifically the rights to associate and to freely advocate points of view), legal protection of those rights, dedication to common purposes, philanthropy, and tolerance of coexisting associations as they carry out their purposes.[15]

Similarly, a system of free expression requires legally sanctioned individual rights and an ethic of tolerating diverse points of view. Philanthropic institutions rely on a commitment to the pursuit of the common good (interpreted in individualized terms), the right to express that commitment through the contribution of money and time, a legal guaranty that a philanthropic purpose will be carried out, tolerance for differing and even opposing philanthropic purposes, and the ability to create private organizations to carry out philanthropic missions. The historical development of these elements and their growing interconnectedness in Western thought and political development are the themes of the next three chapters.

Most evident in the interaction of the seven elements is the centrally important relationship among the three constitutive norms. Given civil society's equally significant commitments to individual rights and to the common good—a dualism that can create fundamental tension between individual and communal impulses—what allows these two value systems to achieve congruence in the form of a coherent social agenda? As elaborated in chapters 3, 4, and 5, the norm of tolerance has become the link that allows competing individual visions of the public good to coexist and reconciles the private and the public in civil society, albeit always provisionally.

Civil Society and Democracy

The development of modern civil society is inextricably linked to the development of liberal democracy. Robert Post and Nancy Rosenblum describe a consensus among contemporary theorists:

> that democracy depends on the particularist, self-determining associations of civil society, where independent commitments, interests, and voices, are developed . . . [C]ivil society is the precondition for democratic decision making, whether democracy is conceived as deliberation or as interest group pluralism, and this is true even if the goal of democracy is to transcend particularism and arrive at uncoerced agreement or a common will.[16]

This close interconnection between civil society and the democratic state is historically rooted in the fact that the concepts of the individual and of individual rights emerged at the very time when the idea of government itself was being radically reconceived in the early tug-of-war between democratic and absolutist theories of the state.

In the seventeenth century, James Harrington famously described this evolving complex of ideas when he advanced an idea of government that was beginning to appear in the works of nontraditional political writers: "Government . . . is an art whereby a civil society of men is instituted upon the common foundation of common right or interest, or (to follow Aristotle and Livy) it is the empire of laws and not of men."[17] Similarly, John Locke viewed the formation of civil society through the act of consent as the creation of the founding framework of government.[18] Harrington and Locke were in the forefront of those developing the new theory in which government was grounded in civil society, as defined by the rule of law and an accompanying commitment to individual rights. These, in effect, became the founding pillars of the newly emergent liberal democratic state.

Contained in the new vision of a rights-based polity, however, is an inherent tension—between the defense of individual rights (in the forms of private association, free expression, and other freedoms), on the one hand, and the power of the state to pursue its mandate to achieve the well-being of the community, on the other. For Locke and his contemporaries, civil society was the arena in which this tension played out. It was there that individuals came together through civil interactions based on trust, tolerance, and a shared sense of public purpose, to form a natural community of common interest to pursue collective purposes. Radically different spiritual or political ideals could coexist in this arena, where the free play of ideas produced public consensus that in turn produced the ultimate basis for action by the state. Civil society organizations could propose, but only the state could dispose.

Contemporary theories of liberal democracy have been strongly imprinted by that historically determined structure in which civil society and the modern democratic state became mutually interdependent. Fred Miller Jr., for example, provides one comprehensive statement of the required conditions of civil society:

> In order for civil society to exist and thrive, certain preconditions must be met. First, there must be toleration of a diversity of views: religious, cultural, scientific, aesthetic, and so forth. Second, there must be protection of private property and contracts to enable individuals to cooperate in a variety of different associations and to coexist peacefully as they pursue their respective goals. Third, and most importantly, there must be the rule of law, so that governmental officials as well as private individuals are restrained by objectively defined laws that prevent them from doing whatever they please.[19]

To sustain these conditions, civil society requires the protection of governmental authority and law, and, conversely, liberal democratic government requires a balancing of private and public purposes that is the product of a robust civil society.

Theorists have highlighted two essential features of the concept of liberal democracy: It is a mode of social decision making that flows from the popular will, and it limits the scope of government by protecting individual rights and pluralism. Contemporary political theorist William Galston further defines what is protected through the limitation of government by introducing three key concepts: "political pluralism" (multiple sources of political authority), "value pluralism" (qualitatively different goods that cannot be ranked), and "expressive liberty" (freedom for individuals and groups to lead lives they choose). The challenge for liberal democracy, then, is to reconcile these forms of pluralism with the legitimate exercise of public power. The more diverse and differentiated a society is, the greater the challenge.[20]

Liberal democracy inevitably gives rise to conflict between the protected domains of private belief and action on the one hand, and the state's need to achieve goods that benefit the entire community on the other. Galston finds that, in a society that accepts and even promotes diversity and pluralism, the norm of tolerance is elevated to "a core attribute of liberal pluralist citizenship." Civil society becomes the primary arena for fostering institutions and values through which conflict can be resolved, a place where "a variety of conceptions of the good—including many that deviate widely from the beliefs of the mainstream majority—may be freely enacted."[21] To perform this task, civil society relies upon the seven elements elaborated above: the norms of individual rights, the common good, and tolerance, and the institutions of free associations, a system of free expression, the rule of law, and philanthropy.[22]

A major concern today is that the very impulse to protect and invigorate individual preferences may diminish a broader sense of social bonds and trust necessary for collective action. The growth of exaggerated individualism in civil society becomes one of the preeminent public concerns of liberal democracy. The tendency in Western societies to accentuate the satisfaction of wants over civic formation threatens the pursuit of public goods.[23] The financier and philanthropist George Soros expresses this concern when he warns of the increasing dominance of the market values of self-interest: "Market values express only what one participant is willing to pay another in free exchange and do not give expression to their collective interests."[24]

To the degree that civil society's ability to balance the pursuit of private interest with public well-being is diminished, liberal democracy is endangered. The health and further evolution of civil society are thus profoundly important for the unfolding of political life in the twenty-first century.

2 Institutional Structures

The institutional structures of modern civil society evolved from a long sequence of historical developments that have their beginnings in the classical formulations of civic life in ancient Greece. The polis, the city-state, in its ideal form provided a vehicle for the collective determination of essential civic norms and behaviors, but it did not recognize a significant distinction between the community composed of individual citizens and the community as a whole. Purely private matters of domestic life, the *oikos*, were treated as household concerns, separate from the matters of the city. Throughout the next two millennia, however, a gradual process of differentiation occurred, resulting in the creation of new institutions to address the increasingly complex relationship between society and the state.

From this process emerged the core institutions of civil society: philanthropy, a system of the rule of law, a network of private associations, and institutions of free expression. This chapter provides a brief overview of the development of these institutions as they began to blend into the foundations of the civil society construct.

Philanthropy

The allocation of private resources to important public needs is an idea deeply grounded in human history. The seemingly universal tradition of giving aimed at benefiting those beyond oneself or one's immediate family has appeared in almost all cultures. Among the multiple motivations for such giving described by historians and anthropologists, two emerge as common characteristics of philanthropic behavior in most ancient civilizations: a sense of obligation for the general betterment of the community and honor accorded the donor through his or her act of giving.[1] Thus, from its early history, philanthropy has contained a blend of private and public purposes.

Beginning in the West, in ancient Greece, such giving primarily took the form of philanthropic benefactions for communal purposes, such as hospitals, public baths, schools, and food distribution. From the earliest appearance of the concept of philanthropy, the term contained a sense of reciprocity: benefit to the community connected to honor for the benefactor. For Aristotle, this reciprocity blends into a combined sense of personal and communal good, implying that philanthropy, properly administered, is part of the virtue that defines the character of both the good person and the good community.

The practical expression of philanthropy through private giving in both Greece and Rome provided the major source of support for institutions serving the public. To carry out these philanthropic aims in practice, however, two institutional requirements had to be met: the creation of an enduring legal personality for donated funds, and a means of supervising the allocation of these funds over the generations. The former had been solved by the early Middle Ages; indeed, by the second century, the Romans had already begun to develop the legal concept of the permanently endowed gift.[2] The latter, however, proved to be a fundamental challenge for philanthropy dedicated to serving a specific purpose over multiple generations.

The advent of Christianity introduced a new conceptual element into the understanding of philanthropy. In the early Christian era, the concept of *caritas* (caring as a form of Christian love) became a central theme in discussions of philanthropic practice, reflecting a movement from personal honor accorded by the community for good works directed toward the general public to an understanding of the intrinsic value (divinely recognized) of charitable actions, especially of giving for the benefit of the poor, the sick, and travelers in need. Scott Davis observes that an additional transformation in the accepted meaning of philanthropy occurred with St. Augustine's view that charitable action is the expression of God's law of universal love rather than of more self-interested motivations such as personal salvation. Indeed, for Christian Europe, charity came to be seen as "the highest theological virtue."[3]

The hospital, one of the earliest institutional forms of philanthropy, reflected these blended motives that were embedded in philanthropic good works. Originally founded to fulfill religious obligations of charity by providing aid to the poor and care for the sick, hospitals took multiple forms from ancient times through the Middle Ages. The primarily medical function of hospitals emerged in Byzantium, where they first became known for providing specialized medical treatment and care outside the home. Timothy Miller describes both the advanced medical care provided by Byzantine hospitals and their strong connections to the philanthropia of Eastern Christianity, especially through their sponsorship of "public physicians." The functions of hospitals evolved over time, adapting to the needs of the societies in which hospitals emerged. In medieval Europe, hospitals became identified with a wide spectrum of charitable services, including leper houses, institutions for the non-leper sick, and almshouses. In some cases, hospitals began to serve fee-paying clients through the practice of "d'corrody," a form of pension involving the regular allocation of food and clothing to a designated group of recipients.[4]

From the widespread charitable funds and practices scattered throughout medieval Europe, a set of institutions with similar characteristics began to emerge: They were endowed, more or less self-governing under a framework of some form of governmental oversight, typically but not universally based in a religious community, and dedicated either to some general public purpose, such as the construction of a bridge or fountain, or to a particular group in need, such as the poor, the sick, widows, orphans, indigent scholars, or travelers. Thus hospitals, almshouses, universities, orphanages, and other social institutions that had ancient origins proliferated from the twelfth through the sixteenth centuries with the financial backing of charitable funds. Such a fund was described in different languages as a foundation, trust, *Stiftung, fondacion, fundacao, saatio,* or other term denoting a private fund dedicated to some public purpose over an extended period of time.[5]

The greatest challenge to sustaining the initial mission of such a charitable fund was the uncertainty whether those charged with its supervision in successive generations would faithfully carry out or, in the longer term, even adequately understand the donor's original intent. Funds might be diverted to other purposes, or the original purpose could be made moot through changed social circumstances. An increasingly common solution to these dilemmas was to create a dual oversight process through which a governmental entity shared responsibility with the governing body of the foundation for determining whether the funds were being spent in accordance with the original intent. Because of the increasing demands on their resources from the rising numbers of urban and vagrant poor, governments had a strong incentive to gain greater control over charitable endowments.[6]

Although at the beginning of the High Middle Ages, in about the eleventh century, charitable funds for public purposes such as aid to the poor and the sick were closely tied to religious purposes and administered largely through the Church (including the monasteries), by the late thirteenth and fourteenth centuries a long tug-of-war began between the religious and secular authorities over the control of these important funds. For example, the Italian confraternities, financed through personal donations, became primary sources of aid to the poor in cities such as Florence and Milan from the twelfth through the fifteenth centuries, but their work over time was increasingly intertwined with the state's activity and regulation in addressing the needs of the poor.[7]

As such charitable resources gradually moved from the centralized administration of the Church into separately administered funds, they became vulnerable to disputes over control. Along with the dramatic changes in economic and political life at the end of the medieval period, charitable institutions became increasingly subject to a struggle between religious and public entities, leading to ongoing disputes between the named overseers of foundations and the secular authorities. Frank Rexroth describes a case in the sixteenth century of the city of Nuremberg's assuming control of a foundation originally established by Sigmund Oertel to keep the city's churches free of stray dogs. After this designated purpose had been neglected for several decades, the city council determined that the foundation's proceeds would be better used for the support of a hospital. Rexroth offers this case as an illustration of the general movement toward adapting idiosyncratic donor intentions to the public authorities' sense of the need to fulfill communal needs, such as hospitals, bridges, universities, and the care of the poor.[8] Many foundation charters included similar residual delegations of oversight to a municipal body in case the donor's original intent was no longer relevant or feasible.

The delegation of such dual authority, however, led to many disputes over interpretation and governance of private charitable funds. One example is the conflict that arose over a foundation established in 1479 by the Vöhlin family of Memmingen in southern Germany to underwrite the position of a minister whose duties included celebrating a mass annually in the family's name in a chapel that they had donated. Seven decades later, the Reformation had radically altered religious practices in the community, and the mayor and city council of Memmingen took control of the foundation away from the family heir, Erhard Vöhlin, and redirected the funds to the poor of the city, even excluding a family representative from the distribution ceremony. Benjamin Scheller cites this as an example of the "foundation paradox," in which a donor's intent to carry out a specific purpose in perpetuity becomes problematic because of changed social circumstances. The conflict between the private rights of donors and the public supervision of foundations thus has a long history.[9]

A similar gradual evolution in the motivation and purposes of charitable activity occurred in Italy. Shifting from a traditional emphasis on the virtue of charity as an expression of Christianity's seven works of corporeal mercy, which demonstrated the love of God through serving the poor, aid to the poor began to take on a newer, more communal character from the fifteenth to the seventeenth centuries. This transition is particularly visible in the *monte di pietà*, an institution that began as a religiously inspired, pawning-based loan fund for the poor but gradually evolved into a quasi-public loan fund to respond to health emergencies and other communal needs.[10]

Yet a further aspect of the combination of public and private purposes of philanthropy appeared in the turbulent times of the Dutch Republic. In accordance with the wide variation in communal governance structures, cities in the Netherlands adopted radically different approaches to the administration of charitable funds for the poor. In Amsterdam, the Calvinist church and city magistrates operated parallel systems of support for indigents, which kept religious and municipal authorities separately responsible for their respective constituencies. In Leiden, on the other hand, the city assumed a dominant role in poor relief, requiring all donations to be placed in a common fund administered without regard to religious affiliation. This combination of secular and religious purposes is also reflected in the motivations of the donors, exemplified by the donative behavior of the Portuguese business community in sixteenth-century Antwerp. The Portuguese residents of Antwerp, primarily converted Jews (*conversos*), were active philanthropic donors who directed their gifts to a variety of causes, including the construction of church buildings, the celebration of masses in memory of the donors, and distributions to the poor. As with much of the history of philanthropic activity, these benefactions served multiple purposes: enhancement of the reputation of the donor (in this case, by conferring legitimacy within the Christian community), long-term stability for religious institutions, aid to the poor, and maintenance of the social order.[11]

The philanthropic and communal practices in England during the fourteenth and fifteenth centuries reflected a similar blend of purposes. At a time of great social disruption—episodes of the plague, starvation, religious strife, and economic boom and bust—secular and religious authorities faced growing challenges in addressing the pressing needs of growing numbers of the rural and urban poor and in keeping order in the community. A study of charitable practices in the town of Cambridge in this period reveals a "shift from communal and cooperative forms of charitable organizations towards a more personal and individual search for religious and social benefits." The Cambridge case illustrates the complex ambiguities contained in the concept of charity as an overriding principle in the lives of late medieval men and women: insuring the salvation of donors in contrast to benefiting the community, assisting the needy versus keeping the poor under firm control, and sustaining religious institutions as opposed to transferring their endowments to preferred charitable purposes.[12]

Early-sixteenth-century Europe witnessed a dramatic growth in charitable institutions of all kinds—hospitals, homes for the aged, orphanages, and food distribution programs—in response to widespread economic crises and a corresponding explosion in the numbers of the impoverished. At the same time, the spread of the Reformation challenged the Catholic Church's dominance in the provision of charitable aid. The result was increasing state intervention in the regulation of charity, signaling a growing process of secularization and a transition from an individual to a communal sense of responsibility for meeting social needs.[13]

A prominent example of the growing public commitment to aiding the most vulnerable was the increasing number and quality of orphanages throughout Europe, with the Dutch Republic leading the way. Almost every Dutch city had an orphanage by 1600, and many were well endowed and administered as joint public-private partnerships. The orphanages had a legal status allowing them to hold real estate and to operate endowments in order to generate a reliable income stream. Although they started out as selective "citizen orphanages" (*burgerweeshuis*), by the middle of the seventeenth century they had expanded to admit all orphans regardless of birth, and the quality of these institutions was a matter of civic pride. The orphanages became the explicit model for one of the most celebrated of such institutions in Europe, the Orphanage of Halle.[14]

England's famous Statute of Charitable Uses, promulgated by Queen Elizabeth in 1601, both embodied and advanced the movement toward secular purposes and state control of charity. Precipitated in part by Henry VIII's earlier expropriation of Catholic holdings and the consequent elimination of church-sponsored charitable support for the steadily increasing number of rural migrants, the passage of the Statute and the accompanying Poor Laws represented the state's assumption of a new role in dealing with the poor. The statutes gave full legal sanction to the allocation of private charitable resources to a wide range of secular public purposes, stimulating an unprecedented increase in charitable donations to causes ranging from "seabankes" (protective sea walls) to hospitals. Indeed, as W. K. Jordan points out, the only mention of religious purposes in the 1601 Statute is a reference to the "repair of churches": Otherwise, the list of uses for charity is entirely secular. Jordan also notes that the timing of the Statute coincided with a transition in the pattern of charitable giving away from individual alms to endowments for broader purposes.[15]

The 1601 Statute thus marks the definitive emergence of the new role of philanthropy in the birth of civil society. By the early seventeenth century, the guiding principle of charitable giving had changed from an emphasis on personal salvation to a focus on addressing broad social needs. This transition, guided by the Tudors, reflected a gradual assumption by the state during the sixteenth century of responsibility for insuring that the needs of the indigent were met, displacing the traditional role of the Church and establishing a new sense of public obligation for creating the basis for a compassionate and orderly society.[16] At the same time, this obligation was considered to be appropriately fulfilled through the direction of private resources to independent institutions such as hospitals, schools, orphanages, and almshouses, for the sustenance of those in need. And the newly wealthy in England responded with a dramatic outpouring of wealth for these purposes through the more than six thousand trusts that came into existence in this period.[17]

This entire development posed a new, centrally important question to those concerned with the changing nature of the civil order: To what degree was the burden of meeting public needs primarily a private versus a public responsibility? Hugo Grotius, and Samuel Pufendorf after him, had already distinguished between the requirements of justice ("perfect rights") and the moral duties implied by the virtue of charitable love ("imperfect rights"). It is the voluntary exercise of the latter, Pufendorf argued, that creates social solidarity. John Locke took this argument further, suggesting a strong obligation beyond voluntary charity to assist those in desperate need. The debate about the appropriate location of the boundary between voluntary charitable acts and the mandates of public policy has continued to characterize discussions of civil society and government to the present day.

The Rule of Law

A fundamental requirement for the creation of peace and stability in any community is agreement to a body of rules providing an accepted framework for the resolution of disputes and the pursuit of common social aims. The establishment of the rule of law, therefore, stands as one of the most ancient features of organized societies. While the earliest legal systems are associated with the dictates of lawgivers, such as Hammurabi, Moses, and Solon, the concept of legal rules as determined by society as a whole, through a mixture of religious and secular sources, gradually gained acceptance throughout the Western world. In classical Greece, for example, law was considered to consist of the rules generated and enforced by the polis in pursuit of the common good.[18] Roman law became distinguished for being written, first through the medium of the famous "twelve tables," and later in its broad application throughout the Roman Empire. This led to a new body of scholarship and analysis in formal jurisprudence. By the thirteenth century, a highly differentiated legal structure had evolved, explicated through the theological writings of Thomas Aquinas in terms of graduated levels of universality: human, natural, divine, and eternal.

While Aquinas sought to unify legal thinking into an all-encompassing theological system, a parallel course of development had begun to shape legal thinking in the eleventh and twelfth centuries, with profound consequences for the Western legal tradition. The Investiture Contest, beginning in the period around 1100, signaled the emergence of a duality of legal legitimacy, resulting in a continuing balancing act between religious and secular authorities in governing jurisdictions throughout Europe. Brian Tierney summarizes this tension:

> There was never just one structure of government, presided over by an unchallenged theocratic head, but always two structures, ecclesiastical and secular, always jealous of each other's authority, always preventing medieval society from congealing into a single monolithic theocracy. Ecclesiastical authority diminished the aura of divine right surrounding kingship; royal power opposed the temporal claims of the papacy. Each hierarchy limited the authority of the other. It is not difficult to see how such a situation could be conducive to a growth of human freedom.[19]

Yet a third element entered into this complex interchange between ecclesiastical and secular authorities in a way that shaped the emergence of constitutional thought in the West: the proliferation of corporate bodies. These entities, represented most notably by confraternities and guilds (described in greater detail below), served as vehicles in which the forces of religious and secular power played out in practice. The result of the tripartite division of legal authority and practice was a blended system of law that ingrained the principles of autonomy and decentralization into the foundations of the Western legal system.

By the late Middle Ages, this framework created the foundation for the historically new phenomenon of constitutional law. The new system combined three distinct elements: the ancient concept of law as grounded in the community, the later Roman idea of sovereign power exercised by a central authority, and the medieval notion of the juridical personality of the corporate body (*universitas*). Together these concepts formed the basis of the developing theory of constitutional law, a theory that balanced the sovereignty of the people with the effective authority of the ruler, along with a binding set of legal principles that overrode the personal prerogatives of particular holders of power. Implicit in this system was an assumption of the consent of the community and a recognition of a fundamental line of demarcation between an underlying set of social norms and rules that establish the framework for rule-making and the particular laws that evolve over time. In the early development of constitutionalism, as Francis Sejersted notes, "constitutionalists had to create their own master—the law. The main distinction between the rule of Man and the rule of Law was the abolition of arbitrariness and consequently the ensuring of predictability and of 'justice as regularity.'"[20]

The subsequent emergence of refined bodies of law in Continental Europe and England laid the groundwork for the modern system of uniform procedures, legitimate jurisdiction, and fair administration of justice. In particular, the development of English common law represented the codification of rules that were grounded in tradition and social practice and that furthered the integration of legal norms into the course of community life. Inherent in all legal systems were the notions of predictability, fairness, equality (at least within social strata), enforceability, and a sense that social rules were founded on external authority, whether a spiritual source, custom, or legitimate governmental body. Moreover, as Tierney notes, the old tensions between church and state and among diverse religious persuasions required a neutral system of law that could negotiate between centralized and decentralized authorities.[21]

The next stage in the evolution of legal theory appears first in the works of Hugo Grotius and then in those of Thomas Hobbes. Grotius and Hobbes sought to embrace seventeenth-century doctrines of individual interest in a manner compatible with the tradition of communal sovereignty. Their common goal, pursued from radically different theoretical perspectives, was to legitimize the exercise of uniform legal authority in the face of fundamentally differing religious and political forces. Both thinkers, reflecting the growing attention accorded by seventeenth-century thought to individual agency, began with the concept of an individual natural right to self-preservation that defined the human condition and argued that, through a process of transference, community members gained the security of a uniformly enforced set of laws in exchange for giving up a measure of personal autonomy.

It is generally agreed that Grotius marked a pivotal turning point in the history of jurisprudence. As secular forces gained ascendancy, a new grounding of legal legitimacy was needed, and the compelling argument of the law of nature, articulated by Grotius, filled that need.[22] Searching for a new basis of obligation that relied neither on heavenly commandments nor on Aristotelian communal precepts, Grotius found that basis in a rational analysis of the preconditions for survival in society and in what he suggests was the model (even when understood as hypothetical) of the ancient constitution of the Batavian Republic, in which the people freely elected their leader. The natural right to survival implied a natural law to this same end, and both became the basis for allegiance to a system of law for nations as well as individuals.

Hobbes proceeded from a like starting point—individualistic and secular—to argue for a binding legal system based on covenant, but a system with strikingly different consequences from those of Grotius's system for the exercise of public authority. In both cases, individuals consented to the creation of a system of laws that secured peace and security in the face of increasingly fragmented societies. Grotius, however, invoked the additional human qualities of love, honor, and duty to establish the bonds that held society together in peaceful coexistence. For Hobbes, only the all-powerful Leviathan was capable of exerting the indisputable force necessary to maintain a peaceful existence.

In many ways, Hobbes represents the first theorist to formulate a comprehensive legal system based on the radical new vision of a society consisting of self-interested, rights-bearing individuals who inhabit a state unfettered by the control of traditional religious doctrine. He devoted much of Leviathan and De Cive to the argument for the separation of church and state and the absolute priority of the latter in matters of security and governance. The logical result of this austere vision was the requirement for an all-powerful sovereign whose edicts were the only source of law and who brooked no bodies intervening between the individual and the state— hence Hobbes's famous dismissal of corporations in the commonwealth as the equivalent of "worms in the entrails of a natural man." While this system raised the specter of the exercise of arbitrary power inherent in absolutism, Hobbes was actually making the case for unchallengeable power expressed in the supreme force of law issued by the sovereign, whether the sovereign power took the form of monarchy, aristocracy, or democracy.[23]

In the subsequent development of European law, post-Hobbesian concepts of sovereign authority came to coexist with more ancient notions of common law that accommodated other sources of authority and the legitimacy of intermediary bodies.[24] The new legal framework that eventually constituted the emerging systems of both England and the Continent blended notions of individual consent with older medieval corporatist philosophies, producing an amalgamation of justifications for allegiance to the law as a neutral sphere for the adjudication of social conflicts independent of particular officeholders, religious orthodoxies, or political philosophies.

Even as the modern democratic state began to appear, the rule of law was seen as something prior, a norm that both facilitated and limited the growth of the democratic form. Deeply embedded in civil society, the rule of law became the basis for constitution-making, "directed against the power of the state, no matter who held power—a king or democratically elected assembly."[25] The result was a widely accepted concept of the rule of law that became an essential element in the birth of modern civil society.

Private Associations

The rise of associational life coincides with the rise of human society. Otto von Gierke, the German historian of ideas who devoted much of his work to analyzing the cultural origins of corporate bodies, opens his definitive book with the observation, "Man owes what he is to his union with his fellow man." He then proceeds to trace the origins of the modern nation-state through five historical periods, revealing a progressive amalgamation of different forms of associational life defined as "fellowships" and "limited communities."[26]

Specific predecessors of the modern private association are to be found in the Roman collegia and later in medieval corporate bodies. The most direct modern antecedents were the emergent guilds in the Germanic settlements of Northern Europe, appearing most commonly in Germania, Frisia, and the Low Countries. Antony Black describes the important functions of these early associations as:

> mutual support groups, an alternative to feudal relations in an age of acute instability when something more than family bonds was required . . . Their functions were now extended to all kinds of mutual protection: burial funds, support for poor members or dependents of deceased members, an insurance service in case of fire or shipwreck. Their ties were expressed as "brotherhood" or "friendship."[27]

During the medieval period the guilds, sometimes referred to as "confraternities," took on an increasingly religious character in advancing pious and charitable causes. They assumed both social and economic functions, especially the protection and regulation of trades, but also the celebration of the communal rites of religious brotherhood, representing a "mixture of public spirit and self-interest."[28] Their essential character was defined by their voluntary nature, commitment to a common ethos, provision of mutual support, defense of the rights of members, and legitimization by the state.

Legally, the guilds were recognized as quasi-autonomous bodies in the form of corporations or "colleges." While they were often officially sanctioned as part of a city's life, their primary legitimacy derived from the tradition of self-authorizing customary groups. Thus, the corporate body was established through the voluntary acts of its members, ordained its own rules and regulations, elected its leaders, disposed of its common goods, and represented its members to public authorities. Indeed, as Black notes, "in many instances guild authority rivaled or complemented state authority."[29] Guilds served as a link between the private realm of the family and the higher order of governing bodies, playing a vital role in the medieval hierarchy.

The combined spiritual and political functions of the guilds were directly relevant to the evolution of civil society. Serving the communal purposes of their members and founded on voluntary consent, the guilds also represented the members' rights and interests in the wider community. Johannes Althusius, a German theologian strongly influenced by Dutch thought, articulated a comprehensive theory of the nature of the guild and its role in society. He began his *Systematic Analysis of Politics* with a discussion of *consociatio*, the fundamental concept of association. *Consociatio* could be found in various private and public forms, but the essential mediating body between the family and public bodies was the *consociatio collegarum*, the guild and similar forms of private association.[30] In this analysis of the structure of social life, Althusius "combined the 'medieval' ideas of a collegiate, organic polity federated under the rule of law with 'modern' emphasis upon contract" and thus became the exemplary transitional thinker between the ancient and modern notions of private association.[31]

The organization that best exemplifies the fusion by emergent private associations of medieval collegiality, mutual support, and moral purposes with modern contractual relations and private activity for public benefit is Freemasonry. Originating as a guild of stonemasons in the Middle Ages, over time the Freemasons grew into an organization with exceptional influence in European intellectual and political life. By the seventeenth century, the Freemasons had evolved from a trade guild closely identified with Catholicism into an association of gentlemen and intellectuals that endorsed religious toleration and ecumenical moral principles. Organized into "lodges" (essentially private social clubs), the association spread from England and Scotland to the Continent and the American colonies, attracting to its membership leading figures in political, economic, and intellectual life. Over time these luminaries included George Washington, Benjamin Franklin, Wolfgang Amadeus Mozart, Friedrich Schiller, Winston Churchill, and Franklin Delano Roosevelt. Operating with secret dictates and rituals, Freemasonry generated widespread suspicion from conspiracy-minded critics over the years, but the organization has functioned essentially as a private fellowship championing the ideals of tolerance, brotherhood, knowledge, and charity, which are among the essential values and institutional characteristics of civil society.

In another respect as well, the Freemasons represented an archetypal organization for the birth of modern civil society. As Margaret Jacob has documented, the Masonic lodge became a kind of school for democratic citizenship, putting into practice the ideas of written constitutions, elected officers, majority rule, government by laws, religious toleration, taxation, and equality of participation. Jacob observes that the lodges left "the most remarkable records we possess for tracing the prehistory of nationally identified formal institutions of representative government, most of which emerged throughout continental Europe only late in the eighteenth or early nineteenth century."[32] Here we have an early indication of civil society's emerging role as a platform for democratic government.

As new modes of understanding the world surfaced in Enlightenment thinking in the seventeenth and eighteenth centuries, private associations such as the Freemasons increasingly were seen as contractually based groups through which citizens could come together to pursue common aims. At the same time, they retained the older notions of friendship and solidarity that transcended the individual interests of members. Associations of all sorts—religious, scientific, literary, professional, charitable—flourished throughout Europe and the New World. In London alone, more than two thousand clubs and other societies met regularly in the early eighteenth century for purposes of self-improvement, debate, the arts, science, religion, and politics.[33] Such associations formed a basis for the exchange of ideas and the formulation of social agendas apart from the corridors of officialdom.

A prominent example of such influential associations was the Select Society of Edinburgh, a debating club founded in 1754 by fifteen Scottish luminaries, including Adam Smith, David Hume, and Adam Ferguson, dedicated to the exploration of various scientific, political, and philosophical issues of the day. The group soon expanded to include over one hundred members and became a defining force in the Scottish Enlightenment, as described in chapter 5.

As offshoots of their parent bodies in Europe, collegial organizations flourished in the American colonies, although with a peculiarly New World twist. Benjamin Franklin's Junto was the American version of the English club, but it had a characteristically American emphasis on egalitarian structure and self-help. The Junto's combination of community purpose, philanthropy, professional advancement, literary discussion, and fellowship provided the model of the activist private association in the emerging American polity. The proliferation of these associations led to the early network of private, voluntary organizations that began to define the public-private relationship in the new American Republic.

Alexis de Tocqueville found this network of private associations so impressive that he authored the first comprehensive analysis of the role and importance of private associations in America. He thereby became the preeminent commentator on the role of associational life in the emerging democratic state. Tocqueville's famous description of the role of associations in the young American polity stands as the definitive statement of the ways in which private citizens join together to achieve public aims:

> Americans of all ages, all conditions, and all dispositions constantly
> form associations. They have not only commercial and manufacturing
> companies, in which all take part, but associations of a thousand other
> kinds, religious, moral, serious, futile, general or restricted, enormous or
> diminutive. The Americans make associations to give entertainments, to
> found seminaries, to build inns, to construct churches, to diffuse books, to
> send missionaries to the antipodes; in this manner they found hospitals,
> prisons, and schools. If it is proposed to inculcate some truth or to foster
> some feeling by the encouragement of a great example, they form a society.
> Whenever at the head of some new undertaking you see the government
> in France, or a man of rank in England, in the United States you will be
> sure to find an association. . . . Thus, the most democratic country on
> the face of the earth is that in which men have, in our time, carried to
> the highest perfection the art of pursuing in common the object of their

common desires and have applied this new science to the greatest number of purposes.[34]

In articulating the character of such associations in the life of the new democracy, Tocqueville identified a central element in the rise of civil society in America: the proliferation of private bodies in which citizens freely associate to achieve common purposes, creating that "close tie that unites private to general interest."[35] The distinctiveness of such associations, even in comparison with their European predecessors, lay in their emphasis on mutual self-help, on achievement rather than status. The importance of private associational life continued to grow in the course of American development, and private associations formed a pillar of the liberal democratic system in the United States.

A System of Free Expression

Open communication has explicitly defined participation in social life since at least the golden age of ancient Greece. The specific term used in Athens to describe this phenomenon was *isegoria*—the equal right to speak in the public forum—and it was considered an intrinsic element of citizenship. Indeed, by the fifth century BC, isegoria came to be identified with the essential character of the democratic polity. The ability of any Athenian citizen to speak freely in the assembly and to present matters for public deliberation was taken to be the distinctive quality of Athenian democracy. To subject one's arguments to the test of reason and the counterarguments of opponents was to fulfill one's civic role in shaping the nature of the polity.

Thus speech is deeply entwined with the origins of the democratic idea. In the Greek polity, however, this took the form of oral arguments delivered in open public debate in the face-to-face arena of the forum. Although political communication took place in various forms (in face-to-face discussion and in written correspondence) throughout the Middle Ages, it was not until the mid-sixteenth century in Europe that the full effects of the invention of the printing press in the previous century and the rapid dissemination of printed information generated dramatically new forms of public debate on issues facing the community. The radical transformation of public discourse brought about by the innovation of printing has been thoroughly documented. During this period the dissemination of information on matters of essential public importance migrated from the reading of royal proclamations by the town crier to hand-copied bulletins and ultimately to placards, handbills, pamphlets, and the first newspapers.

With the dramatic expansion of the availability of information about political, religious, and social issues, there immediately arose a struggle for control of the flow of public information between the central authorities, especially royal governments, and the array of private parties who wished to champion their causes before influential elites and the public at large. Paul Starr describes this struggle as the critical period of an alignment of forces that started the development of the world of modern media, reflected in initial state control of the new networks of communication (post offices in the first phase), attempts by states to license or censor all publications, and the gradual erosion of state control.[36]

In France, for example, near the end of the sixteenth century Henry IV instituted a process of issuing official proclamations through the office of the Prevost of Paris, a process which later evolved into a central censorship agency requiring printers to submit manuscripts for approval before they could be published. This agency was countered by the expanding press of the French opposition operating in the Dutch Republic and Switzerland. In England, both the Tudor and Stuart monarchies exerted stringent control over the press through licensing, precensorship, and, in some cases, outright bans. However, these efforts were opposed by the centrifugal forces leading up to the dramatic political and theological divisions of the English Civil War. In every European country, attempts by the state authorities to maintain control of information were systematically undermined by the inherently decentralized nature of information and the new technologies that aided that decentralization.

In fact, it was the flood of pamphlets filled with heated rhetoric about religious positions that led to the unprecedented growth in public involvement in concerns once limited to church and state elites. In the early-seventeenth-century Dutch Republic, for example, pamphleteers increasingly focused their brief vernacular publications on the important political and religious issues of the day—the debate over the Remonstrants, the growing resistance to Spanish authority, the situations in England and France. These pamphleteers directed these publications toward "everyman" (*gemeente*). The growth in this pamphlet culture was dramatic, from an estimated 50,000 pamphlets per year in the 1570s to 200,000 per year in the 1640s.[37] Over time, these publications evolved from ponderous reports by the government or opposition partisans into increasingly entertaining formats, including allegedly intercepted letters, dialogues, rhymed texts, and canal boat conversations, complete with creative illustrations.

Both the Thirty Years' War on the Continent and the English Civil War gave enormous impetus to the demand for information about the outcomes of battles and campaigns and to the circulation of tracts about disputed religious doctrines. The explosive growth of all forms of political publications—pamphlets, newspapers, broadsides, books—met a growing demand for news about conflicts and doctrinal disputes from a growing spectrum of the public. Although readership was still primarily limited to the elite, the appetite for news was expanding rapidly throughout the population. This public hunger for the latest information about the state of the world became the butt of ridicule among some writers as the "horrible curiosity of certain people to read and hear new things."[38]

From the pamphlet culture sprang the new phenomenon of regularly published newsletters and newspapers. Although such printed newsletters had already begun to appear in Europe in the late sixteenth century, a vast expansion of these publications occurred in the first half of the seventeenth century. Described by one author as the "political information business," the proliferation of regularly issued publications about local politics, religious disputes, war, parliamentary debates, and all manner of political and social issues began to reach all classes and groups in European society.[39] Regularly published newspapers also began to appear in the early seventeenth century, the first of which was the *Avisa Relation oder Zeitung* of Strasbourg in 1609, followed quickly by a number of newspapers (known as *corantos*) in the Dutch Republic.[40] Translated into English, the *corantos* became the first English newspapers.

All of this put great pressure on official censors, to the point that censorship of English publications declined significantly during the Civil War. It was in opposition to the reinstatement of prepublication censorship through the Licensing Act of 1643, at the height of the Civil War, that John Milton wrote his famous work *Areopagitica*, in which he defended the free flow of information and argued that only free thought arrives at the truth. (Parliament largely ignored him.) Indeed, the overall movement of ideas away from the centralized control of the state and toward the increased expression of diverse views through the diffusion of print media became a kind of ironic countercurrent in an age when absolutism was on the rise.

The new sense of public engagement made possible by the proliferation of cheap and easily produced printed matter created the platform for what Jürgen Habermas describes as the emergent "public sphere." As elaborated in the following chapters, the private individual emerged in the eighteenth century as both a consumer of and a participant in discussions of political and social matters. Habermas describes this as a historically new phenomenon—an arena in which private persons come together to form a public through the creation of a realm of public opinion that mediates between state and society. He links the appearance of this political public sphere directly to the emergence of modern civil society, understood as "the domain of private autonomy that stood opposed to the state."[41] The central challenge to this emergent construct, and the source of its later transformation, was the difficulty of rationally resolving the competition of private interests in the modern democratic state.

By the mid-seventeenth century, the essential structural elements for the creation of modern civil society were clearly established throughout Europe: growing philanthropic institutions, accepted legal systems, proliferating private associations, and rapidly expanding communications outlets. All were the products of a long process of historical development, but each took on new forms through engagement with the commercially driven, fractionated forces of the early modern era. Each arena faced the central questions of the individual's role in the newly powerful state and of the secular role of the state itself in a world rife with religious conflict. This was the challenge that confronted the newly emergent civil society.

3 Normative Traditions

L ike the institutional elements, the three normative strands that are central to the constitution of civil society emerged from a long history of moral argument and social change. They represent the value commitments that underlie the institutional structures of modern civil society. How these normative elements evolved and were woven into the fabric of the modern democratic state is the subject of this chapter.

The Common Good

In the context of the modern liberal democratic state, the concept of the common good seems almost anachronistic. Indeed, to the degree that contemporary market theorists even entertain the notion of common values and goods, they are usually viewed merely as the maximization of summed self-interests.

Yet the idea of the common good as a social value counterpoised against private interests has an ancient and venerable history in Western social thought. In a sense, it is the most ancient topic of social inquiry—an exploration of the assumptions behind the idea of the good community and what is required to achieve it. Commentary on the idea of the common good and the nature of the ideal social order preceded the discussion of individual rights by almost two millennia. As Guido Kirner notes: "The question of what constitutes good for all in a community provides the starting point for political thinking in the broadest sense, the forms of which begin in the ancients and continue to shape thinking into the modern era."[1]

The well-being of the community as the highest aspiration of social life is a central feature of classical Greek thought. Indeed, a wide spectrum of Greek statesmen and thinkers were concerned with the structure and purpose of community in the form of the polis. The pursuit of the greatest good in human life through an ideal form of community is frequently featured in commentary by Thucydides, Pericles, and Demosthenes, among many others.[2] Plato elevates the concept of the common good as realized through the actions of elite leadership to a primary position in his system, and Aristotle's concept of the common good becomes a defining quality of the good life, intimately connected to the other virtues of justice, friendship, and respect for law. As Kirner observes, both Plato and Aristotle posit the concept of the common good as a generalized standard by which the normative structure of the political order is to be judged.[3]

Plato presupposed a unity of the good of the community and its members such that human achievement was unthinkable except through the polis, and the *Republic* is largely dedicated to demonstrating this view of the human condition. The republic embodies the objective good of the community, to which the interests of individual members are subordinated, and it is the duty of the philosopher-king to maintain this order and thereby to insure the realization of the good.

By contrast, Aristotle allows for a distinction between individual goods and the common good and deliberates on the merits of each. In the end, the good life requires a balance between the two: "[M]en, even when they do not require one another's help, desire to live together; not but that they are also brought together by their common interests in proportion as they severally attain to any measure of well-being. This is certainly the chief end, both of individuals and of states."[4] For Aristotle, the state is a kind of partnership: Whatever ultimately produces the good of the polis by definition produces the greatest good of its members. In this formulation, the common good synthesizes ethical and practical ends and at the same time reconciles individual and communal interests. Ultimately, the common good is reflected in *eudaemonia*, the notion of the highest ethical aspiration of the community.[5] Aristotle's transformation and further elaboration of this concept of the ultimate goal of the polis was to shape thinking on the topic into the period of the Renaissance.

Prior to the reemergence of Aristotle's legacy in the early Renaissance, however, the intellectual journey of the common good continues in the Roman Republic as exemplified in the writings of Cicero. Cicero's discussion of the *res publica* moves the concept from the transcendent, ethical realm to that of the concrete, well-ordered republic. For Cicero, the common good of the polity is expressed through a system that secures the combined well-being of all citizens.

A later but independent tradition of thinking about the nature of the good community grew out of the Germanic experience of communal life as expressed in the ideas of the *Gemein* (commons) and the *Genossenschaft* (brotherhood) that solidified relationships within towns and guilds during the Middle Ages. This tradition was based on a concept of authority that emerged through a process of self-organizing communities. These communities, although fundamentally religious in character, were not dependent on the authority of the pope or emperor.[6] Otto Gerhard Oexle describes the core of this social structure as "mutual protection and mutual help—*mutuum consilium et auxilium*—a specifically constituted, group-connected, common good."[7] The corporate character of life in medieval communities generated a strong sense of communal identity, both protecting against the outside world and supporting the internal, organic social order of the village or town.

The rediscovery of Aristotle by the thirteenth-century Scholastics reintroduced discussion of concepts of the natural, political community into to what had become an essentially theological understanding of the human condition. In traditional medieval thought, as Walter Ullmann and others have observed, church and state were closely enmeshed, both as a locus of authority and as a vehicle for the exercise of power.[8] However, with the introduction of Aristotelian thought into Scholastic discussions of law, power, and the good in human community, commentators such as Albertus Magnus, Thomas Aquinas, William of Ockham, Giles of Rome, and Marsilius of Padua elaborated new understandings of the relationships between the individual and the state and between secular and sacred authority.[9] M. S. Kempshall argues that the influence of Aristotle allowed for a new synthesis of a secular concept of the common good (justified through Aristotle's clear hierarchy that placed the "good of the polis" at the peak of the moral order) with a traditional, theological understanding of the common good as a transcendent virtue representing the realization of the divine will on earth.[10] St. Thomas Aquinas in particular integrated the Christian notion of divine law with the idea of the earthly legal order through the concept of the *bonum commune*, ultimately anchored in the *summum bonum*. The blending of religious and political ends introduced a new level of complexity to the understanding of the good of the community: For Thomas, the well-ordered community was a manifestation of both divine justice and peaceful human existence. Thus began the movement toward the secularization of the political community, even as thinkers continued to express a deeply religious understanding of the social order.

Therefore, the three elements that define the evolution of the concept of the common good in the later history of Western thought were already present in thirteenth-century thinking: a transcendent moral concept (the *summum bonum*) expressed as an ethical, initially religious, ideal; the notion of a good political order that provides peace and other benefits of a well-functioning community; and the first glimmerings (especially in Marsilius of Padua) of the idea of the maximization of benefit to a collection of individuals. All three of these ideas contributed to the emergent concept of the common good as a constitutive element of civil society.

Amidst the growing importance of the guild and the town and the first stirrings of republican ideas of governance, the evolution of the concept of the common good began to take on an increasingly secular cast during the late Middle Ages. Corporate entities, particularly the guilds and fraternities, had been founded upon an underlying commitment to the common good of the group. The challenge was to integrate these fractionalized corporate entities into the larger political community and also to define the nature of communal goals that might be distinct from those of specifically religious purposes.

With the advent of Martin Luther, the decisive turn occurs: Individual salvation becomes distinguished sharply from the regulation of communal life, and the princes are charged primarily with the well-being of the latter. As Francis Oakley describes this stark separation of spiritual and temporal realms, "Luther saw them as distinct and, in a sense, parallel—concerned with different aspects of man's existence, exerting different modalities of authority, resorting to different instrumentalities of persuasion."[11]

The idea that those who were charged with governing the public realm, whether king or local council, had responsibility for the well-being of the community, and that the community's well-being transcended the needs of individuals, was a fundament of political thinking until well into the seventeenth century. Only with the rise of new forms of individualism, rooted both in the Reformation and in the rapidly emerging commercial economy, did the idea of common utility as the maximized benefits of individuals begin to compete with the traditional notion of the common good. But a notion of communal well-being that transcended particular interests remained, for example, in cases in which the maximization of economic output might work to the disadvantage of some individuals but to the greater benefit of the entire community.

This duality—between the idea of the collective good and the idea of summed individual goods—became inseparably linked to the emergent concept of civil society. Indeed, the tension between public and private definitions of communal well-being signaled a decisive moment in the gestation of the civil society idea. A related parallel transformation influenced the concept of "republic" during the same period. As David Wootton has observed, the idea of a republic moved down two distinct paths from the late sixteenth century onward—one emphasizing the natural rights tradition (in resistance to despotic power) from Locke through Paine, and the other emphasizing the common good of the civic humanist tradition from Machiavelli through John Adams.[12] In both cases, the goal is the exercise of public power for the benefit of the broad political community (*res publica*), but the former understands the collectivity as the sum of individuals, while the latter understands it as a transcendent entity representing the good of all. In its modern use, the concept of republic has retained this ambiguity of meaning.

As explored later in chapter 5, the duality of summed individual goods and supervening communal goods moved to the center of the newly developing tradition of social thought in the early Enlightenment. The influential *Fable of the Bees* by Bernard Mandeville, a Dutch physician living in London, expressed the new view most dramatically: Like the bees, human beings pursuing their individual aims worked together in a coherent but undirected way to create the greatest social benefit. Many tracts on economics and society, particularly those of the Scottish Enlightenment, explored this apparent paradox. The most notable statement of this paradox, of course, appeared in Adam Smith's idea of the "invisible hand," whereby individuals in the market were supposed to produce the maximum social benefit, although their own motivations were self-interested and narrowly economic. As a product of this era, modern civil society would be inextricably identified with the challenge of reconciling the pluralism of individual interests with the common good.

Rights

One characteristic agreed upon by both contemporary and historical theorists as central to the definition of civil society is its protection of the realm of private action from the state. In the sixteenth and seventeenth centuries, this protection was becoming increasingly important as state power grew and wars over religion spread throughout Europe. The defense of a domain in which the private exercise of belief could take place became a paradigm for the new arena of the exercise of individual, natural rights.

The history of the development of individual rights is embedded in a long historical evolution of ideas, including the more general history of the development of law and the concept of the just allocation of goods.[13] But the modern notion of rights as attributes of individuals can be traced to an ideological transformation occurring in the sixteenth century, specifically to debates about the nature of subjective right that took place in the Dominican school of Salamanca in Spain. Annabel Brett points to the work of Fernando Vázquez as central to the creation of what became a dominant new legal tradition. This tradition conceived of rights within a voluntaristic framework that broke free of the Aristotelian and medieval concept of right as the object of justice, that is, "the just portion that is due between persons," which had defined the concept of objective right from its appearance as the Roman *ius* through the late medieval period. The new notion of rights drew upon Renaissance language of human agency and individual liberty, as stated by Vázquez: "The primary right of people dictates that all men should share a common liberty."[14]

Richard Dagger shares this general view of the timing of the transition from premodern to modern concepts of rights but points to a slightly different aspect of the transformation in the meaning of rights. He notes that although

> intimations, anticipations, or glimpses of the concept are as old as legal and political thinking . . . the concept of rights itself is not fully present until sometime in the later middle ages. After that, emphasis shifts from the notion of *right* as a standard for conduct to the notion of *rights* as possessions, a kind of personal property.[15]

The combined notions of individual liberty and personal possession set the theoretical course for the evolution of the idea of individual rights that culminated in the seventeenth-century work of Hugo Grotius, John Selden,

Thomas Hobbes, and, ultimately, John Locke. The simultaneous emergence of absolutist state monarchies, devastating conflicts between groups with opposing religious doctrines, skepticism borne of the new learning, and the concept of the individual led to a search for a new formulation of the constitutive elements of the social order. The contemporaries Grotius, Selden, and Hobbes began to elaborate a new theoretical foundation based on the premise that individuals who are guided by an ultimate right of self-preservation come together and create a social contract to insure safety and provide the benefits of collective action.

The right of the individual to self-defense thus became the cornerstone of a broad framework of social contract theory positing individual rights as a new foundation for social cooperation and coordinated action. Although this theory was vehemently opposed both by traditional defenders of a society grounded in religious doctrine and by contemporary champions of the absolutist state, its gradual diffusion through European culture shaped the development of legal and political structures from the seventeenth century onward. The momentous events of the Civil War in England, the regicide of Charles I, and the Glorious Revolution (with its Declaration of Rights) exemplify the degree to which these new theories molded social thought and action in the seventeenth century.

Writing in the first decades of the century, Hugo Grotius became the key conceptualizer of a new theory of republican liberty.[16] This theory synthesized the ideas of natural rights, sovereignty derived from consenting citizens, and a federal structure of governance, with the concept of republican virtue as the moral glue for the edifice. This new formulation of the basic bonds of social life became the foundation for the nascent concept of civil society.

As an adviser to the moderate Dutch leader Johan van Oldenbarnevelt, Grotius served as a practical political force and as an intellectual leader in the creation of the golden-age Dutch Republic that became a model for liberal state builders throughout Europe. In his final work, *The Law of War and Peace*, he moved this conceptual framework to the international plane, extrapolating to nations the same requirements for a common moral basis of agreement in order to insure peaceful coexistence as for consenting individuals in order to create a harmonious social order.

Grotius's idea of an original, absolute natural right was adopted by both Selden and Hobbes, who constructed theories based on the notion that individuals yield initial rights in order to gain the benefits of a society in which "private well-being is subordinate to public well-being."[17] Selden and Hobbes, however, took this theory in dramatically different directions. Deeply engaged in the fateful struggle between parliament and the king, the two provided theoretical justifications for the opposing sides in the controversy. Selden reserved to citizens the right to withdraw their consent in accordance with their residual rights, thus supporting the parliamentary cause, while Hobbes initially defended the monarchy by famously delegating all power to the sovereign. In adopting this stance, Hobbes left unresolved the conundrum about what individuals were to do in extreme cases in which the sovereign threatened their own lives.

By the mid-seventeenth century, much of the debate about the exercise of public power was cast in terms of rights and the moral basis of sovereign authority, a theoretical shift of fundamental importance for the development of the idea of civil society. If the old foundation of the divinely ordered state was disintegrating, what was to replace it? The new thinking of Grotius and his followers had posited an original, self-evident right to self-defense as the platform for the construction of the social order, and Hobbes took this argument to an extreme in *Leviathan*. But many rejected this move, objecting both to Hobbes's atheism and to his statism while still holding to the rights-based concept of social theory.

Entering this intellectual ferment in the 1660s, Locke took the argument in a different direction. Disagreeing with Hobbes's derivation of individual rights from a basis of pure self-interest, Locke spent much of his intellectual career working out a new theoretical grounding of "civil or political society" (he did not distinguish between the two) premised on a broader framework of private rights ultimately guaranteed by divinely inspired reason. In his early works, Locke had declared a fundamental right of religious belief, but it was only in the *Second Treatise on Government*, strongly influenced by his colleague James Tyrell, that he postulated a number of "inalienable" rights to be exercised outside of the control of the state, including the famous list of rights to life, liberty, and property.

With Locke, then, the reconstruction of the new social order reaches its full formulation. Beginning from the premise that man, enjoying liberty in a state of nature, possesses certain inalienable rights, Locke derives civil society as created through consent: "The only way whereby any one divests himself of his natural liberty, and puts on the bonds of civil society, is by agreeing with other men to join and unite into a community, for their comfortable, safe, and peaceable living one amongst another in a secure enjoyment of their properties, and a greater security against any that are not of it."[18] The individual's fundamental right to judge the legitimacy of a political system, and to resist if necessary, lies at the heart of this structure.

Locke was, of course, not writing a purely theoretical discourse. Having come of age during the English Civil War, he was immersed in the life-altering politics of his day, particularly the struggle between parliament and the king that culminated in the Glorious Revolution of 1688. He was forced to take refuge in the Netherlands during the period of 1683–89 because of his increasingly critical views of royal power and his close association with some of those who were actively plotting against the king. His later works, the two *Treatises* and the *Letter Concerning Toleration*, make practical arguments for the protection of a private realm of action and belief from the overpowering might of the state. These principles gain practical expression in the Declaration of Rights, the guiding statement of the tenets of the Glorious Revolution.

Individual rights thus become a normative cornerstone of the emerging concept of civil society, and central to those rights is the notion of the right to a free exercise of conscience. It is to this topic that we now turn.

Tolerance

Early manifestations of the norm of tolerance were already present in the ancient world in such customs as Roman acceptance of diverse religious and cultural practices within the Empire as long as ultimate allegiance was sworn to Roman authority. The acceptance of coexisting belief systems was in fact present in many civilizations. The distinctive pattern that emerged in the West, however, was a long process, beginning in the Middle Ages, of the separation of religious from political authority, which had profound implications for the protection of private belief. In particular, the demarcation of separate domains of the exercise of authority, symbolized by the Augustinian doctrine of the Two Cities, began an extended development of thought culminating in the recognition much later of the civil power's role as arbiter among coexisting spiritual communities.

In *Civil Society and Fanaticism*, Dominique Colas traces the etymological evolution of the term civil society (in its Latin form of *societas civilis*) within the tradition inaugurated by St. Augustine's formulation of a sharp division between the City of God and the City of Man.[19] Augustine's clear articulation of the fundamental distinction between the spheres of the sacred and the secular set the course for the conceptualization of the balance of authority between church and state in the Western tradition.

Two later medieval exponents of arguments related to the growth of toleration, Anselm and Abelard, were primarily responsible for popularizing the tradition of dialogue among representatives of conflicting religious views. Still not defenses of tolerance for its own sake, these arguments championed the mutual engagement of conflicting views for the sake of the truth they would ultimately elucidate about Christianity. The arguments did, however, encourage openness to conflicting worldviews that were legitimized through the dialogic form of argumentation and thereby set the stage for the later elaboration of theories of tolerance.

Colas observes that Aristotle's term *koinonia politike* was first translated into Latin as *societas civilis* in 1279 by the Augustinian monk Giles of Rome. In advancing his argument for the superiority of papal over royal authority, Giles first invoked the concept of the *societas civilis* to describe the arena of worldly and therefore inferior power, namely, the realm of secular power. However, the term *societas civilis* did not come into general circulation until it was revived in 1416 by the Renaissance humanist Leonardo Bruni, who invoked the concept to champion a rigorous separation of the two spheres. In so doing, Bruni explicitly criticized Giles for his unconditional subordination of civil society to church authority.

The polarity between the Two Cities that characterized medieval thinking moved into a dramatic new phase with the emergence of Reformation ideas about the individual's relationship to God. The Reformation became the defining moment in the evolution not only of the modern idea of the separation of civil and religious authority, but also of the acceptance, often from sheer exhaustion among warring religious groups, of the coexistence of fundamentally differing communities of belief.

Colas names Philipp Melanchthon, a close friend and adviser to Luther, as the first author to use the term "civil society" in a strictly modern sense, that is, in direct opposition to religious fanaticism. Colas then argues that civil society's modern beginnings appear in the context of a dual relationship with the forces of intolerance and ideological repression. In a commentary on Aristotle from 1529, Melanchthon contrasts *societas civilis* with fanaticism by championing the autonomy of social and political life as legitimate spheres of human activity that are not to be subjected to attempts (by the Anabaptists, for example) to establish a divine kingdom on earth.[20]

By the time of the intense early-sixteenth-century battles over religious doctrine, a sharp dividing line becomes quite clear, between the concept of society as a secular state coexisting with officially sanctioned religion, and that of society as a chiliastic kingdom, advocated by those who would implement their version of a City of God. In the war of ideas, *societas civilis*, now translated into the vernacular (*société civile* in the French translation of Melanchthon's text and *bürgerliche Gesellschaft* as first introduced by Kant and Fichte), comes to stand for a place that is separate from religious zeal, in contrast to totalistic communities of belief in which a single doctrine is ordained for all believers and nonbelievers are treated as profane. In this phase, civil society becomes the concept opposed to that of a society controlled by religious doctrine, whether that doctrine arises from papal authority or from the divine inspiration of other sectarian leaders. It represents a reformulation and partial reversal of the historic Catholic argument that the City of Man is to be subsumed under the dominant authority of the City of God.

Lutheranism marks the definitive break with the older tradition that viewed the theological and political realm as unitary, in its condemnation of corrupt religious institutions, maintenance of the secular authority of civil society, and avoidance of the trap of establishing countertotalistic institutions advocated by many dissident religious movements (although Luther's critics accused him of despotic tendencies of his own). In this context, civil society becomes a public sphere that is insulated from direct control by ecclesiastical forces and is defended against those driven by "fanatical" visions. A series of sixteenth- and seventeenth-century writers, including Jean Bodin, Hugo Grotius, John Milton, Adriaan van Paets, Pierre Bayle, and Benedict Spinoza, wrote texts criticizing intolerance and particularly the use of state power to force individuals to conform to doctrine that violated their personal confessional beliefs. A common thread throughout these writings was the defense of the fundamental right of personal religious belief, as long as that commitment did not disrupt or endanger civil order.

As noted by Dominique Colas, the contrast between civil society and fanaticism, first articulated by Melanchthon, represents a critical moment in the development of the former and marks an important inflection point in the modern process of secularization. It required, however, yet an additional evolution of thought in the next century to produce a conception of civil society as separate not only from religious extremism but also from all forms of intolerant worldviews. In this phase, exemplified above all by the work of Spinoza, civil society becomes the arena in which diverse religious views and confessions can coexist, a sphere that champions tolerance and that mediates among conflicting religious doctrines.

With the rise of the idea of individual conscience as a challenge to a single, state-imposed belief system, toleration became a way of reconciling radically divergent concepts of human community. As a moderating force, it served as a brake on the tendency of visionary doctrines of social change and transformation to devolve into fanaticism. Civil society, when viewed through this lens, became the ordered political community that supervised and moderated the realm of worldly affairs, providing a neutral space of secular social life in which worldly purposes could be acted out and peaceful coexistence could occur among spiritual kingdoms of ultimate ends.

Spinoza's discussion of the essential nature of freedom of belief initiated a new stream of social thinking that increasingly emphasized the fundamental role of tolerance in establishing the well-ordered, free, and just society. Through the subsequent development of this idea in the works of Pufendorf, Leibniz, Locke, Mill, Voltaire, and many other writers (see chapters 4 and 5), tolerance becomes a central concept in the development of liberal democracy.

In structural terms, through a historical development from the Reformation onward, tolerance comes to perform the role of a mediating value between a commitment to individual rights and a commitment to communal goods. Toleration allows for the balancing of fundamentally opposed visions of human ends. On the one hand, there exists a primary commitment to the free exercise of rights by individuals. (In its radical form, this becomes anarchic libertarianism.) On the other hand, there exists a pursuit of authoritatively established, communal goods. (In its extreme form, this becomes authoritarian collectivism.) Tolerance permits these essentially contradictory elements of modern liberal democracy to coexist within a common political framework, creating a balance that holds an otherwise fragmentary system together. It thereby establishes a metastructure both for the autonomous development of ideas and for free exchange and deliberation concerning those ideas, if tolerance is supported by institutional vehicles of free expression.

The norm of tolerance is an often-overlooked but essential pillar of modern liberal democracy. With respect to the American polity, Michael Walzer states the case succinctly: "Political principles, maxims of toleration: these constitute our only stable and common commitment. Democracy and liberty fix the limits and set the ground rules for American pluralism." He generalizes the principle in describing the role of tolerance in all modern democracies: "Tolerating and being tolerated is a little like Aristotle's ruling and being ruled: it is the work of democratic citizens . . . Toleration makes difference possible; difference makes toleration necessary." Tolerance allows competing worldviews to be expressed in society, permitting them to vie for broader electoral validation while avoiding violence in their translation into social policy.[21]

The Three Normative Prerequisites

Normative components, often overlooked in definitional discussions, are essential constitutive elements of civil society. The three norms described above, each the product of a long process of independent historical development, together constitute the value fundaments of modern civil society. The ancient concept of the common good has persisted as a central tenet of political and social life through the millennia and across the entire spectrum of governmental systems. It remains a sine qua non for organized society. The idea of individual rights, which arose later, became the guiding principle for the emergence of the liberal democratic idea during the early Enlightenment. The resulting tension between these two principles—the advancement of collective action on behalf of the common good, on the one hand, and the pursuit of individual rights and interests (with associated centrifugal implications), on the other—required a third principle to mediate between the first two. That principle is the norm of tolerance that emerged from the religious conflicts of sixteenth- and seventeenth-century Europe.

These three normative elements constitute the value platform for civil society, both as normative features and as prerequisites for the institutional structures described in chapter 2. Thus, the modern legal system, philanthropic institutions, and private associations presuppose the norms of the common good and individual rights; and a system of free expression requires acceptance both of the norm of tolerance and the right of free speech. We now turn to the historical era in which these norms and institutions became integrated into the first instance of modern civil society.

4 The Emergence of Civil Society in the Dutch Republic

The streams of philosophical and social development that predated modern civil society flowed in parallel currents from the classical period into the early modern era of sixteenth-century Europe. In the seventeenth century, these streams met in a new historical construct—what we have now come to recognize as the earliest instance of modern civil society—that was being shaped by new intellectual and social forces.[1] The focal point of this convergence was the Dutch Republic during its golden age, and it was the Dutch philosopher Benedict Spinoza who provided the first comprehensive conceptualization of this new vision of society.

Although religious belief and authority were still dominant influences in familial and political life at the advent of the seventeenth century, new voices and ideas were beginning to be heard in the home, pew, and chambers of state. The dramatic impact of the rise of Protestantism in the previous century had already transformed belief systems throughout Europe and had begun to alter the role of religion in public life by introducing, for Protestants, a new concept of a personal relationship with the divine. This in turn had led to a weakening of the traditional power of institutions over spiritual life and to fundamental cleavages between confessional groups, reflecting a progressive disintegration of the organic unities of medieval life. Concurrently, the new discoveries of science and medicine, the rapid spread of printing, and pervasive economic changes were transforming worldviews and the practical realities of social life. Cumulatively these social and ideological forces were the defining elements of what later came to be understood as a radical transformation of the social and intellectual climate of Europe.

Convergent Threads in the Dutch Republic

Nowhere was this transformation more evident than in the emergent Dutch Republic. In 1579, reacting to a threat of invasion by forces of the Habsburg Empire, the separate political regions of the Netherlands banded together under the Union of Utrecht to form the United Provinces. This unprecedented step was the result of more than two decades of debate, negotiation, and political maneuvering among the provinces. What began as a defensive military and economic alliance, however, soon manifested the characteristics of a new kind of social and political entity. The inherent tension between a centralized, quasi-monarchical authority in the person of the Prince of Orange and independent centers of authority in the provincial governing bodies was to create, almost inadvertently, a balance of power within a larger state structure that was novel to the European experience. Contributing to this emerging pluralism were the religious differences between the strong Calvinism represented by Orange, the reformed Calvinism of Holland and other provinces, and the traditional Catholicism of the south.

The proliferation of tracts and pamphlets in the provinces between 1555 and 1590 provides insight into the way this new kind of political structure was theoretically justified. Four basic principles appeared as constant threads in this resistance literature: the defense of ancient liberties, the preservation of privileges, the autonomy of the states, and, of overriding importance, a striving for the common good.[2] Together, these founding tenets of the Dutch Republic formed a kind of constitutional framework for a new, hybrid entity on the European scene, a coalition of quasi-independent states bound together in a national political body under centralized leadership, represented by the authority of the stadtholder.[3] Along with repeated emphasis on the pursuit of the common good as the transcendent purpose of a political community, there was increasingly strident condemnation of the ruler (Philip II of Spain) who violated this purpose. Furthermore, since the defense of liberty entailed the defense of the right of religious belief, there emerged a strong theme of toleration in the foundational literature as well. Cumulatively, the fundamental precepts of the Dutch revolt against Spanish rule were woven together in the late sixteenth century into a historically new statement of principles for a liberal republic. The striking similarity in tone and theme between these arguments and those used to justify the American War of Independence two hundred years later is worthy of note.

It is the argument here that the ideas originally articulated in this formative period of the Dutch Republic were elaborated over the next century into a unique blend of Dutch ideas and institutions that became the first modern civil society. E. H. Kossmann describes this novel configuration of ideas and institutions:

> From the late sixteenth century onwards the Dutch had developed a set of ideas and worked out a set of ways to implement them that were eminently practical and, though unsystematic, nonetheless not incoherent. This is the astonishing aspect of the Dutch seventeenth century.... Although we know that freedom in the sense of independence, of provincial sovereignty or particularism, of a non-monarchical, republican form of government and religious and intellectual freedom are different conceptions not necessarily belonging together, it is as if in the Dutch seventeenth century they are quite naturally united in an organic whole.[4]

The history of the development of toleration in the Dutch Republic is a complex and fascinating thread in this story. From early suggestions of openness on some religious issues in Erasmian humanism and Pieter de Zuttere's defense of freedom of belief in Dutch Reformed thought to a full philosophical rationale for toleration in the works of Spinoza, the idea of tolerance grew from a suggested non-persecution for differences of secondary religious importance to a full-blown philosophical argument about the role of the conflict of ideas in the pursuit of truth.

Diverse schools of thought framed these developments over the course of the seventeenth century. Jonathan Israel divides them into four primary camps that define thinking on toleration in this period: radical theologians, moderate republicans, radical Cartesians, and Remonstrants.[5]

From these differing perspectives, writers including Guy de Bray, Dirck Volckertzoon Coornhert, Adriaen Paets, Pieter de la Court, Franciscus van dan Enden, Simon Episcopius, Pierre Bayle, Benedict Spinoza, and, of course, John Locke (while in exile in Holland), formulated increasingly sophisticated defenses of the moral and religious foundations of toleration. Embedded in this growing body of tolerationist thought was an increasing emphasis on the separation of the realms of spiritual belief and state action: The state should not seek to dictate one's personal relationship to God nor should private religious commitments control the state. The arguments were both theoretical (that truth could only emerge out of the free exchange of ideas) and practical (that a healthy economic life could only grow out of an environment that allowed for the peaceful expression of differences and supported freedom of thought).

To say that the Dutch Republic was the home of the most advanced discussion and practice of toleration in seventeenth-century Europe, however, is not to say that the process was a smooth, uncontested unfolding of progressive ideas. In fact, there were frequently bitter and often violent confrontations over doctrinal matters and the power of authorities to enforce them at the local, provincial, and national levels. Already in the 1560s, public statements such as the *Declaration of the Church or Community of God* were proclaiming the right of resistance to governmental authority in the name of conscience, and the Synod of Antwerp raised the stakes further by declaring that armed resistance to religious oppression was justified.[6]

Beyond their widely shared opposition to the practices of the Inquisition, political and religious leaders engaged the central authorities and each other in almost constant battles over the rights to believe, practice, preach, and publish on matters of religious and philosophical doctrine. There were frequent clashes between Catholics and Protestants, strict Calvinists and Remonstrants, Arminians and Gomarists, Voetians and Cocceians, and many other religious confessions. An early victim of this religious strife was Johan van Oldenbarnevelt, a prominent leader of the States of Holland, who was overthrown by Maurits of Nassau, the contemporary Prince of Orange, in 1619 and condemned to death, in part for his tolerationist views. Later in the century, among the many examples of censorship and punishment for espousal of unapproved doctrine was the notorious case of Adriaen Koerbagh, a follower of Spinoza, who was arrested and imprisoned in 1668 for publishing two books critical of the accepted tenets of Christianity. He died in prison.

Nevertheless, in comparison to residents of other countries of the time, inhabitants of the Dutch Republic enjoyed an unprecedented degree of freedom of belief. Indeed, the most striking fact about the Dutch experience with toleration was the widespread acceptance of the right of believers with diverse perspectives to coexist. The Dutch states exhibited a previously unknown blend of established religion and permissive practice in their day-to-day, lived experience. Contemporary commentators often pointed to the Dutch Republic as a haven of toleration in Europe. Although historians differ over the sources of the pragmatic acceptance of religious toleration in the Dutch Republic, there is widespread consensus in the view that the Republic manifested "a measure of freedom more generous than anywhere in the world of that time."[7]

A primary factor contributing to this emerging ethos of toleration in the Dutch Republic was the explosive growth of printing. Early in the seventeenth century, the ongoing controversy between the Gomarists and the Arminians led to a flurry of publications arguing their respective cases. In 1670 Spinoza published his *Tractatus Theologico-Politicus*, in which he articulated a strong theory of freedom of conscience. Pierre Bayle, residing in Rotterdam, later wrote a critique of the *Tractatus* while simultaneously championing the idea of toleration from a skeptical perspective. Near the end of the century, Locke composed and published his famous *Letters on Toleration* in the Dutch Republic, where he had taken refuge prior to the Glorious Revolution in England. The development of a mainstream of philosophical writing on toleration went hand in hand with the extraordinary opportunities for the publication and distribution of books in the Dutch Republic.

Enhanced by an unprecedented latitude of expression and growing Dutch prosperity, commercial printing began a period of dramatic expansion in several cities of the Low Countries. The preeminence of Dutch universities, particularly Leiden and Utrecht, which were becoming known throughout Europe as tolerant centers of learning, also contributed to the proliferation of publications in the United Provinces. While in today's terms still far from an environment that allowed full-blown free expression on political and religious issues, the atmosphere in the Dutch Republic, especially when compared to the rest of Europe, fostered widespread public dissemination of philosophical and scientific questions. These ideas found rapid expression through the thriving Dutch printing industry, the most prolific in Europe during the seventeenth century. J. L. Price observes that

> In the seventeenth century Holland was probably the greatest centre of
> book production in the whole of Europe, and it was particularly important
> as a place where books could legally be published which would have been,
> or had been, banned elsewhere.[8]

Historians of printing point to the special role that Dutch publishers and printers played in European letters:

> The history of the book trade in Holland is astonishing. . . . The book trade was peculiarly suited to the temperament of the Dutch merchants, who were keen for liberty and connoisseurs of the arts. . . . Men of learning thronged to the cities and engaged in correspondence with their equals in foreign countries.[9]

This thriving book trade was the product of contemporary Dutch economic success, extraordinarily high literacy rates (among the highest in Europe, according to Margaret Spufford), and the decentralized power structure of the provinces, which limited repressive censorship.[10] The synergy of these factors led to the pride of place held by the Dutch Republic in the exchange of ideas across Europe during the early Enlightenment. Moreover, this ferment of ideas was not limited to intellectual elites, as Jonathan Israel observes: "The man on the street was aware of developments, being ceaselessly bombarded with anonymous pamphlets, and hearing politics and theology discussed in taverns, and on passenger barges."[11]

Indeed, both Craig Harline and Jeremy Popkin have argued that the proliferation of pamphlets, books, tracts, and all forms of publication played an important role in the development of the unique character of political discussion in the Dutch Republic. According to Harline, pamphlets not only conveyed political ideas, but "were themselves representative of the idea that the opinions of interested subjects had to be considered in government."[12] The rapid spread of pamphleteering after 1565, and particularly after 1607, is remarkable both in the range of subjects covered—religious, political, social—and in the diverse audiences to which pamphlets were addressed. Harline estimates that by the 1640s two hundred thousand pamphlets were circulating annually in a country of fewer than two million people and that "major events and controversies were almost always accompanied by a flood of pamphlets."[13] These pamphlets were directed toward a variety of audiences, including a large portion directed not toward elites but toward the common reader. The first Dutch newspapers appeared in 1618, preceded by handwritten news bulletins at least as far back as the late 1580s, and they came to play an influential and often hotly debated role in public affairs.[14]

This unusual flowering of freedom of expression through books, pamphlets, and newspapers was not limited to toleration of religious belief; it

also extended to and was supported by the relative political freedom characterized by the continued negotiation between the stadtholder and the states
and, ultimately, by the new phenomenon of a republican form of government.[15] While the struggle for power between centralized and local sources
of authority was not unique to the Dutch Republic—it had deep roots in
medieval Europe—it reached a new level of importance and a new degree of
complexity in the Netherlands.[16] This new republican model, as it achieved
particular expression in the Dutch Republic, combined the older sense of
a government founded on a civic ethos with the novel elements of limited
monarchical power and the protection of the domains of religious belief
and private activity from state interference.[17] J. L. Price observes that Dutch
republicanism can "be summed up in the formulation that Dutch burghers
were citizens not subjects. The political system was seen as protecting individual freedoms and property against arbitrary acts of government and
especially against taxation without consent."[18] The division of power inherent in this model created space for the realm of the private to grow and to
develop within the public sphere.

The practical manifestation of this unique blend of freedom and decentralized authority was found in nearly every sphere of Dutch society. The
rapid expansion of economic life led to a continuously evolving mixture of
classes, cultures, lifestyles, and foreign influences. The multiplicity of authority structures (guild, town, confession, province, nobility, Estates General, and stadtholder) created a freedom to maneuver among competing
institutional allegiances and, unlike most other societies of the era, generally precluded domination by a single belief system. In intellectual life,
the Dutch Republic of the seventeenth century produced an extraordinary
outpouring of diverse artistic, scientific, and philosophical theories and
discoveries.

This high level of pluralism and differentiation of authority in Dutch
culture expressed itself not only in the expansion of tolerance and free expression, but also in a broad philosophical commitment to the protection
of individual rights. When Hugo Grotius surveyed the diversity of moral
doctrines and normative claims operating in the international arena and
in the provinces of his own republic, he concluded that a universal feature
lay behind the multiplicity of claims, a feature that allowed society to come
together around a common principle. For Grotius, this was the principle
of natural law and with it the fundamental right of each individual to self-

preservation, along with the need for mutual recognition of that right by all members of society. This fundamental right, in turn, led to the recognition of other basic rights, such as the rights to property, security, and belief, and created an obligation for both individuals and the state to respect those rights. The ability to recognize the natural law lay in human beings' natural rationality and sociability, capacities that prevented them from becoming just a collection of disconnected individuals (*dissociata multitudo*).[19] Thus, Grotius's *De Jure Belli ac Pacis* established a universal platform for social obligation based on a natural sociability rooted in the rights of the individual.

While the work of Grotius played a key role in establishing the modern conceptual foundation for individual rights, it was the practical exercise of these rights in daily life—the assertion and defense of rights to confessional belief, publication of ideas, and local self-governance—that truly distinguished the Dutch Republic. The historical origins of the widespread recognition of rights in the Republic lay in the zealously defended autonomies of villages, towns, provinces, and religious bodies (the "privileges" and "freedoms" so often referred to in resistance literature) that evolved within the highly variegated authority structure of the Netherlands. This was by no means a harmonious, conflict-free process; indeed, many of the intense and sometimes savage disputes among religious groups, government entities, and partisan factions in the provinces led to repression and censorship that crushed the rights claims of opposing groups. However, the upshot was a balance of interests and in many cases mutual acceptance of the rights of opposing entities to determine their ways of life and allegiances.

Freedom of conscience thus became a de facto reality and an acquiescence to, if not unqualified acceptance of, the idea of coexistence. Public authorities, such as Johan van Oldenbarnevelt and Johan de Witt, continually sought to find ways to balance an acceptance of freedom of conscience with some core set of publicly acknowledged central tenets of belief. Writers such as Uytenhage de Mist published tracts declaring that the essential interest of the Republic was to defend "freedom of life and conscience, and, especially, of religion."[20] Outside observers in Europe were either awed or dismayed, depending on their philosophical orientations, at the latitude in the exercise of rights that was allowed in the Dutch Republic. Locke, in particular, was impressed as much by the practical respect for rights in the

Netherlands as by the overall atmosphere of toleration he experienced during his six-year refuge there.

The multilayered social structure and growing accommodation of a plurality of belief systems in the Republic was accompanied by a corresponding expansion of private associations. Although the proliferation of religious groups adhering to diverse confessions created a constant source of social strife, their increasing ability to find ways to coexist provided at the same time a de facto validation of the freedom to organize privately in pursuit of religious, philosophical, and social ends. One of the best known of these groups was the Collegiants, a circle of intellectuals, mostly liberal Arminians, who began to meet in the 1620s in Rijnsburg to worship in a nondogmatic way and to discuss theological and philosophical issues. Spinoza was a member, as were other influential members of Dutch society, such as Adriaen Paets and Coenraad van Beuningen.

But such associations were not limited to religious groups; they extended into many private organizations oriented to communal purposes— scientific societies, hospitals, orphanages, associations for local security (the oft-portrayed civic guards of golden-age paintings), old-age homes, and private schools. By the mid-sixteenth century, these private institutions were sprouting up throughout Europe, and the Dutch Republic stood at the forefront of this development. The combination of the increased wealth and thriving civic cultures of the Dutch cities and towns led to an extraordinary expansion of civic organizations.

Probably the most comprehensive analyst of the role of the private association in the emerging modern state was the German Calvinist Johannes Althusius. During the latter part of his career, Althusius, writing from his residence near the Dutch border, was deeply affected by events in the Netherlands, and he in turn exercised a strong influence on the evolution of Dutch political thought. Althusius developed a comprehensive theory of the social order that joined the medieval concept of the college, *consociatio collegarum*, with the modern idea of the contractual state in a federated system that emphasized decentralized power checked by communal groups. Although communal bonds also characterized public bodies, such as villages or provinces, Althusius directed most of his attention toward the personal bonds created in private associations, such as guilds, religious societies, and learned associations. These associations provided the building blocks of mutual aid and social support that created a stable state. In Althusius's system

> [T]he college is precisely not a natural but a "civil" association, formed, like all civil associations, by human will and design in response to human need and utility. Collegiate membership is the first step towards citizenship.[21]

Supporting these private communal bodies, both for their mutual assistance programs and for their assistance to outside causes in the community, became an important social obligation for many Dutch citizens. One example is the proliferation of Dutch orphanages, which became a model for Europe. August Hermann Francke, A leader of the German Pietist movement, sent two of his associates to the Dutch Republic to study the renowned *burgerweeshuizen* and to develop a model for what became the famed orphanage Francke built in Halle. They were particularly interested in the financing arrangements for the Dutch orphanages, which, unlike those elsewhere in Europe, survived mostly on local, private support and on shrewd investment strategies. Dutch orphanages were symbols of communal wealth and benevolence and became "an expression of civic pride."[22]

In their success, these institutions were emblematic of the channeling of private efforts into collective purposes. The Amsterdam orphanages performed a vital public function of building private social connections through their conferring of prestige and civic position on those who provided funds and served as regents.[23] At the same time, the orphanages demonstrated the capacity of private institutions to perform an important public function of caring for the city's orphaned children, particularly children of the "middling" class who were trained in these institutions to become much-needed members of the workforce.

Tension between Pluralism and Unity

These pluralistic threads of tolerance, individual rights, and private organizational activity, particularly associated with the rise of the Dutch Republic, represented the leading edge of two powerful forces that shaped the entire seventeenth century: the rise of the individual and the decentralization of political and social authority. Alongside these pressures toward fragmentation, however, were the seeds of their opposite: the drive toward reintegration and cohesiveness. Ever-present practical problems demanding collective action, such as external threats to security and economic disturbance, made it necessary for members of every level of society continually to confront serious issues of allegiance and identity. It is therefore not surprising that the pervasive need for cooperative effort in many areas of social life in the Netherlands produced some of the most advanced European thinking about questions of the common good.

Embedded in these normative and institutional developments in the Dutch Republic of the sixteenth and seventeenth centuries was one overarching aspiration: to retain, or in many cases to create, a sense of common social purpose in a world that was rapidly fragmenting into a multiplicity of individual and group interests. The most obvious manifestation of this aspiration was the immediate need to defend the Republic against the ever-threatening forces first of the Habsburg Empire and later of France and England. The Dutch Republic was in many ways the product of a defensive alliance. However, the pursuit of a sense of the common good among the provinces began to extend far beyond security interests. Earlier, the need to regulate and integrate management of the waterways of low-lying areas had already fostered widespread cooperation among these communities. In the seventeenth century, the explosion of commercial life in the Dutch Republic required a set of norms and institutions allowing for efficient and trustworthy transactions for the acknowledged benefit of an expanded economy. Finally, as religious and political conflicts intensified, the desire for peaceful relations among competing factions generated a strong drive toward shared norms of coexistence.

The most influential early philosophical statement in the Netherlands concerning the central significance of the common good in political and social life was Justus Lipsius's *Six Books on Political or Civil Doctrine*, published in 1589. As a classical philologist and humanist, Lipsius sought to blend Christianity and Stoicism into a powerful argument for reaching the highest aspiration of society, the *bonum publicum*, and for achieving "mutual commodity and profit, and common use of all."[24] Lipsius was deeply concerned about the socially destructive effects of religious conflict, which could be seen throughout Europe (the *publica mala* that defined the times), and he championed enlightened, centralized authority as the antidote to this evil. Probably the best-known political philosopher of his age, Lipsius exerted a strong influence on the development of political and social thinking in the young Dutch Republic and in the wider intellectual circles of Europe.

Lipsius's work, however, already contained a polarity that would characterize Dutch religious and intellectual life throughout the seventeenth century: the tension between the desire for a centralized authority structure to maintain order (he was a strong advocate of princely rule) and the ideal of creating a decentralized, procedure-based social system (*vita civilis*) that advanced individual freedom, especially freedom of conscience. As one of the first writers to address this tension, Lipsius invoked the ancient ideals of Stoicism as a means of reconciling the pluralism of individual desires with the political community's need for cohesion. The solution was to cultivate the application of reason and self-restraint to individual conduct so that members of society could realize their natural sense of community. His definition of the *vita civilis* synthesized prudence and virtue in pursuit of a harmonious life in political community. Above all he emphasized the absolute imperative to avoid destructive religious conflict of the kind he witnessed throughout the Europe of his day.[25]

Spinoza: The First Philosopher of Civil Society

The pursuit of the common good as the highest aim of society, whether through an enlightened leader or through the reasoned actions of the populace, remained a constant theme of Dutch intellectual and political life throughout the seventeenth century. At the same time, the defense of the liberty of individual belief became an equally honored tenet of Dutch civic thinking. These themes converged most comprehensively in the work of Benedict Spinoza, a thinker who might be described as the founding philosopher of civil society.

Spinoza articulated a novel and consequential formulation of the relationship between these topics in three works: *Theologico-Political Treatise*, *Ethics*, and *Political Treatise*. In these works he argued for a new relationship between the goals of seeking the highest good through community and accommodating individual differences of belief. He took the radical position that the highest public good can be achieved *only* by protecting the freedom of the individual to arrive at truth for himself.

As noted in chapter 3, this radical new construction of the nature of the common good marked a pivotal transition in European thinking about the relationship of the individual to the community. In Spinoza's system, there could be no conflict in the ideal state between individual freedom and the interests of the community; indeed, in the *Theologico-Political Treatise*, he states that "the true aim of government is liberty." This marks a major re-conceptualization of the highest goals of society, with a new focus on the individual. As Stuart Hampshire describes this centerpiece of Spinoza's thought: "Spinoza's philosophy can be construed as a metaphysical justifica-tion of individualism in ethics and politics."[26] The reason there is no conflict between individual liberty and order in the state is that, in this idealized community, citizens live in accordance with the "guidance of reason" and thus implicitly understand the requirements of harmonious coexistence.

Of course, this harmonious existence could be attained only if both individuals and the state were guided by a norm of toleration and if so-ciety provided the means of a maximum degree of free expression. Only through the free exchange of ideas about science, philosophy, religion, and politics could the mind reach its potential and comprehend the true nature of human existence. This would lead to the acceptance of the rule of law as a necessary requirement for maintaining the conditions of free inquiry. Spinoza's system delegates to the sovereign the ultimate authority to pre-serve peace and order, and in this he resembles Hobbes. But there is a funda-mental difference between the two theories. Spinoza, unlike Hobbes, holds democracy to be the best form of government to attain the end of preserv-ing peace and order, because democracy represents the best opportunity for preserving freedom while encouraging individual allegiance to com-munal purposes. For Spinoza, civil society manifests a corporate character that, when fully realized, protects freedom and achieves the transcendent public good, "the good that is common to all."[27] For civil society to function properly, its members must exercise a certain virtue through a respect for the law and a commitment to the commonweal, for "citizens are not born, but made."[28]

Spinoza's attempt to reconcile individual freedom and public authority was a radical innovation in its time, but the practical issues addressed in his work were evident at every level of Dutch society. The pragmatic challenges of security, economics, and governance faced by the Republic during the golden age kept the question of how best to pursue the collective good con-stantly at the center of politics. Whether the question concerned cooperat-ing to salvage land from the sea, providing for the common defense against threats from Spain, France, and England, resolving bitter internal religious divisions, resisting domination by the Princes of Orange, creating conditions for continued trade and economic growth, or maintaining the Dutch position of leadership in European science and culture, the citizens of the Netherlands had no choice but to address issues of their common interests as daily factors in their lives.

An essential vehicle for realizing these common purposes, as well as for protecting individual rights, was the institutional structure of the rule of law. As previously noted, Hugo Grotius played an important role in this domain, both in the Netherlands and in the larger European "Republic of Letters," by providing a new theoretical foundation for universal legal principles and by seeking to counterbalance the powerful forces of fragmentation and contestation with an equally strong conceptual framework of coherence and integration based on law. In addition to his groundbreaking theory of natural rights, Grotius provided a new formulation of the foundational principles of law based on universal human nature. This new foundational structure of the legal system came in part from Grotius's experience in the early decades of the seventeenth century with the emergence of the balance of power among authority structures in the provinces of the Netherlands and a similar balance of power among the nations of Europe. He responded to the chaotic interaction among the different legal systems on the international scene by articulating a novel concept of universal natural law that reflected the aspiration for a new connectedness in an increasingly pluralistic society.

Like his theory of natural rights, Grotius's theory of natural law had important practical consequences. *De Jure Belli ac Pacis* served as a foundation for the development of a secularized civil philosophy by Pufendorf and Thomasius, and the treatise served as a common reference work for judges and statesmen throughout Europe.[29] The example of the Dutch provinces coming to agreement with each other and the stadtholder, albeit slowly, on principles and institutions for dispute resolution demonstrated the success of a recognized, independent legal system in maintaining peace and order among social bodies with differing norms and allegiances. This was another case in which, almost unintentionally and out of necessity, the Dutch provinces worked out a practical system that proved a novel solution to problems arising from the transformed social relationships of the early modern era.

Moreover, continuous engagement with questions of communal wellbeing found expression in a very specific development in the Dutch Republic: the extraordinary phenomenon of Dutch charitable and civic welfare institutions, widely regarded as the most progressive in Europe:

> [F]ew aspects of the Dutch seventeenth and eighteenth centuries were more striking than the elaborate system of civic poor relief and charitable institutions. So exceptional, in European terms, were the conditions which gave rise to this system of civic charity that there was probably never much likelihood of its being emulated elsewhere. But its superiority over what one then found in the neighbouring countries was sufficiently obvious to be frequently acknowledged by foreign visitors.[30]

Coincident with the dramatic increase in urbanization and the growth of the economy, a consensus arose throughout the Dutch Republic on the communal obligation to make provision for those unable to take care of themselves. In most towns throughout the Republic, it was considered a civic duty to care for the poor, the infirm, and orphans. The high level and creativity of the Dutch commitment to these charitable institutions were unique in Europe, as evidenced by the amounts of funding and the sophistication of administrative practices.[31] Among the means used to generate support for civic causes was the innovation of the lottery, a mechanism that encouraged broad public participation especially in support of orphanages and homes for the aged. Dutch orphanages were particularly advanced for their day.

The most interesting aspect of this highly developed system of charitable support, beyond its sheer size, was its decentralized and pluralistic character.[32] The administration of these philanthropic entities in the sixteenth and seventeenth centuries illustrates in a particularly revealing way the complex interactions of religious, political, and social forces in the emerging Dutch Republic. Mirroring both the decentralization and the balancing of religious and political authorities, local charities were controlled variously by Calvinist clerics, city magistrates, and a combination of the two.[33] At stake were overlapping questions of responsibility for civic obligations, church-state relations, freedom of belief, and taxing authority. Philanthropy became the primary vehicle enabling private associations, under the aegis of civil authority, to fulfill public needs. As the charitable system evolved in the Dutch Republic, therefore, it exhibited the novel mix of decentralized public and private responsibilities for social purposes that characterized the overall development of the Republic.

Civil Society in the Dutch Republic as a Social Construct

The seven threads of the construction of civil society were thus clearly evident in the Dutch Republic from the sixteenth century onward, and together they created a new kind of social system that was, in the words of one contemporary observer, "the wonder of all their neighbours."[34] In a country distinguished by high levels of wealth, literacy, political and religious liberty, tolerance, and charity, the seven streams contained both new and old elements of philosophical thinking and institutional structures. However, the Dutch experience is unique not only because the seven streams of social development were present together during the emergence of the Dutch Republic, but also because their interaction with one another in this epoch created a new social construct. Indeed, it was the mutual reinforcement and counterbalancing of these elements that transformed the Dutch Republic into what I have suggested was the first modern civil society.

This can be seen in the interaction of each strand of development with the others. Willem Witteveen, for example, describes the emergence of the Dutch legal system in the form of the *rechtstaat* as "characterized by a strong preference for classical human rights, such as religious freedom and freedom of expression; this clearly builds on the republican heritage of tolerance and individual freedom."[35] Rights, in turn, are linked to the protective effects of private associations, because, as James Tracy points out, the strong "corporative principle of social organization"—urban guilds, shooting guilds, guilds of rhetoric, and similar bodies—became an anchor of the decentralized power structure, and this structure defended traditional rights and privileges: "[I]n the history of European political thought the twin principles of 'guild' (meaning fraternal solidarity within small groups) and 'civil society' (meaning the rights of individuals within the larger society) should be seen as complementary, not as antagonistic to each other."[36]

Private associations were also strongly tied to philanthropy in the Dutch Republic, reflecting, on the one hand, philanthropy's "pluriform and divided confessional structure," and, on the other hand, its expression of shared civic commitment arising from an understanding that "municipal residents constituted an organic spiritual and civic community."[37] And finally, the recurrent normative theme of the common good that appears throughout the political, religious, social, and philosophical literature of the Dutch Republic refers to each of the other six elements: as the desirable outcome of the protection of rights, free expression, and tolerance; as the purpose of the activity of private associations and charitable institutions; and as both a prerequisite for and a result of the rule of law.

Thus, it was a particular combination of normative and institutional factors that lay behind the emergence of civil society in the Dutch Republic.[38] Founded on a balance between centralized and decentralized authority structures, this combination was characterized at its core by a tension between its private and its public nature—between the Republic's private, decentralized, liberal character that championed rights, free expression, toleration, private associations, and philanthropy, and its public, institutional structure, rooted in the pursuit of common aims and a uniformly administered system of law, which was needed for the Republic's survival as a coherent state among other European states.

The civil society construct of the Dutch Republic not only served as the foundation for the enormous political and economic achievements of the Republic's golden age, but its influence extended far beyond the United Provinces. Beyond the national borders of what might seem like a small, outlier experiment on the margins of the European continent, this novel blend of ancient and modern norms and institutions exerted enormous influence on the development of social thought and practice throughout Europe and North America. Grotius's central role in the development of natural rights and legal theory, Spinoza's influential articulation of the role of freedom of expression in the founding principles of the liberal polity, Lipsius's widely read analysis of the exercise of political leadership for the common good, Locke's influential *Letters on Toleration*, and, later, Mandeville's controversial argument linking private and public interest all shaped the evolution of international thinking during the formation of the liberal democratic idea.

Nor was the Dutch influence limited to the power of ideas. By leading a massive invasion across the English Channel in 1688 and initiating what became the Glorious Revolution in England, William III started a process that not only transformed the government of Great Britain but also altered the entire civic and political culture of the West. William's Declaration, written to justify the invasion and circulated as he entered England, contained commitments to constitutionalism, respect for rights, and religious toleration that led directly to Parliament's Declaration of Rights and, in the spring of 1689, to the passage of the Toleration Act. These laws in turn had a momentous impact on the evolution of parliamentary democracy and the proclamation of rights in Europe and America.

The effects of the Glorious Revolution subsequently shifted from strengthening the British Parliament and the tolerationists to an increase in momentum for autonomy in Scotland, Ireland, and the American colonies. It ultimately became, in Jonathan Israel's phrase, "a pivotal constitutional and ideological turning point" in the West.[39] It provided fundamentally new validation for a contractual conception of government known as constitutionalism (under which the sovereign was obligated to operate within the rule of law and to respect ancient rights) and for toleration of diverse religious beliefs and practices.

In this, as in the larger legacy of Dutch thought, we can view the seeds of liberalism and the liberal democratic state. A complex of ideas found in its most coherent form in Spinoza became a precursor of the emergence of civil society: the primacy of the liberated self, a contractual model of civil association, freedom of belief and expression, defense of natural rights, and government as a vehicle for the advancement of private well-being.[40] Together these concepts established the framework for a new emphasis on the private character of social being and set the stage for the growing contest between private interests and communal goods that was to become explicit during the expansion of Enlightenment thought in the eighteenth century.

5 The Enlightenment Legacy

The conclusion of the Thirty Years' War in Continental Europe, the Civil War in England, and the Glorious Revolution marked points of radical historical transformation in Western culture, resulting in a new relationship between state and society. Opposing religious camps were forced to coexist, and competing political factions gradually eroded the absolute authority of monarchical power.

Underlying these changes in state and religious authority were the major intellectual currents that have been examined thus far. These currents culminated in a fundamentally new view of the human social condition that accepted a claim for rights as the foundation of political society, a modern formulation of toleration as a practical necessity as well as a philosophical ideal, a rational construction of cooperative social endeavor in place of a divinely mandated social hierarchy, a commitment to free expression initially based on the protection of religious beliefs and later extending to other areas of personal conviction, and a new respect for private philanthropy as an essential civic value. Together these values constituted core norms of the emerging era of the Enlightenment.

Complementary institutional structures provided the framework for the establishment of these philosophical values. These structures consisted of legal institutions, solidified as the widely accepted, legitimate means of adjudicating conflict and guaranteeing individual rights, and an emerging set of private associations separate from and, in later periods, often opposed to the state.

Realization of Enlightenment Ideals

The era was one of extraordinary intellectual and social ferment premised on a newfound faith in reason, a critical questioning of authority, and a celebration of individual freedom, which were collectively and self-consciously described by eighteenth-century commentators as "Enlightenment" ideals. The vast literature on the Enlightenment has fully documented its transformative power as it swept across late-seventeenth- and early-eighteenth-century Europe. Throughout this period in the Netherlands, England, France, Prussia, Scotland, and Russia, Enlightenment ideas began to pervade varied aspects of intellectual life: philosophy, law, science, literature, and economics. The universally accepted premise of this movement was an assumption that empirically grounded, critically tested, rational knowledge could provide a comprehensive explanation of the natural and social worlds. From this knowledge, humankind would progress toward a society composed of free, enlightened, and autonomous individuals pursuing the goals of mental and material well-being.

From the earliest appearance of the historical trends that eventually led to the Enlightenment, however, a fundamental conceptual divide emerged between those who viewed the Enlightenment as primarily grounded in the pluralism of cultural and social belief systems and associated institutional expressions—each with its own claims to the pursuit of truth and the good life—and those who viewed the Enlightenment as a single coherent intellectual enterprise, the goal of which was to give rational thought free rein in pursuit of higher truths about nature, humankind, and science. Ian Hunter describes this as a divergence between two opposing worldviews, between "civil" and "metaphysical" Enlightenments. In Hunter's terms, the civil Enlightenment was the philosophical movement led by Grotius, Thomasius, and Pufendorf that responded to the devastating consequences of the religious wars of the seventeenth century. For them, the preeminent goal of enlightened thinking was to desacralize politics—to separate politics and law from the private practice of religious belief and to sanction the state's role in insuring religious toleration. Civil Enlightenment aimed at creating the conditions for social peace while allowing the expression of radically different worldviews, thus accommodating difference while advancing freedom of belief.[1]

The opposing "intellectualist" thread of Enlightenment thought was advanced by thinkers in the tradition of Leibniz, Wolff, and Kant, who championed rational discourse by self-directing citizens as a means of pursuing higher truths and a unitary sense of the common good. Hunter describes this as an approach that envisioned the "moral renovation of . . . political governance through the figure of the rational community."[2] The culmination of this vision of rational Enlightenment appeared in Kant's famous essay "An Answer to the Question: What is Enlightenment?" Writing as a contributor to the increasingly animated discussion in late-eighteenth-century Germany of the meaning of the new concept of Enlightenment, Kant argued that private citizens can be organized as a public through the exercise of public reason. By freeing themselves from the yoke of self-imposed ignorance, individuals can thus collectively influence public authority while playing their role in civil society independently of the state. Implicit in this view was the notion of publicly achieved reason that constituted the basis of a truly enlightened society.[3]

These competing strains within Enlightenment thought—between pluralism and the defense of private belief, on the one hand, and the aspiration to a rationally achieved, common, civic life, on the other—produce the central tension in the origins of modern civil society. Both streams of thought champion free expression, tolerance, individual rights, law as a governing framework for peaceful coexistence, and the importance of private civic association. But the pluralist strain emphasizes the radical autonomy of the private sphere (the privatization of moral life, in Hunter's terms) and a corresponding sense of civil society as a realm of the free exercise of individual belief and action. The rationalist strain, by contrast, prioritizes the pursuit of common social ends through participation in rational discourse; in this view, civil society becomes a collective achievement and the only legitimate means of pursuing public goods in a democratic society. These two senses of Enlightenment together formed the defining influence on the character of modern civil society.[4]

In practice, the Enlightenment movement began with claims by early Enlightenment thinkers of the fundamental human rights of freethinking, liberty of religious practice, and freedom of expression but soon was championed as a new mode of citizens' relating to the state in political movements that swept across Europe from England to Poland. One of the first places where these ideas began to be realized in practice was, as has been seen, the Dutch Republic. The relatively free atmosphere for expression that prevailed there in comparison to other Continental countries provided an unusual opportunity for "a systematic philosophical radicalism" to flourish.[5] Moreover, with its leading universities, centers of European printing, economic prosperity, active religious competition, decentralized governmental structures, tradition of historically defended local rights, and proliferation of privately supported associations, the Dutch Republic became a petri dish of experimentation with Enlightenment ideals.

Roy Porter explores the way in which these ideas proliferated in post–Glorious Revolution England, which became the model for Europe in its ability not only to foster critical thinking in science and philosophy but also to put those ideas into practice in the press, politics, and religion. Porter traces the dissemination of Enlightenment ideas of individual rights, toleration, and free expression through all sectors of late-seventeenth- and early-eighteenth-century Britain: religion, science, the press, associations, politics, and education. "More like a communing of clubbable men than a clique or a conspiracy, the Enlightenment derived its currency in Britain largely from a shared currency of images and idioms—it was as much a language as a programme."[6] The changes depicted by Porter were particularly evident in the explosive growth in the eighteenth century of what Jürgen Habermas has termed the "public sphere." There occurred a dramatic expansion of venues where the exchange of ideas about social and political life took place—coffeehouses, clubs, societies, newspapers, pamphlets—accompanied by a growing sense of political efficacy on the part of those classes traditionally excluded from public life.[7] There was a wild profusion of these forms of expression as they appeared in Britain:

> Apart from traditional corporate forms, new bodies and groups now colonized public space. The formation of innumerable types of voluntary association has been counted as a leading feature of emerging civil society. (An eighteenth century contemporary has estimated that 20,000 Londoners met in various clubs each night.) If we single out such a city as Edinburgh . . . we notice that members of the learned professions (especially lawyers and clergy), literary folk, large and middling landlords, and later, physicians, practically minded farmers, and merchants assembled in a variety of clubs and societies for the improvement of all matters. All matters ranged from agriculture to commerce to vernacular culture to recreation and leisure time. Civic issues were certainly not neglected and scientific concerns were to be furthered. These voluntary associations went by the names of Philosophic Society, Musical Society, the Poker Club, the Select Society, Rankenian Club, The Honorable society of Improvers in the knowledge of Agriculture in Scotland, and dozens more.[8]

The new associational forms and the ideas behind them had their roots in a group of revolutionary thinkers and political activists in the late seventeenth and early eighteenth centuries. At stake was a newly evolving conceptualization of the relationship between the individual and the state.[9] Above all in the work of John Locke, this newly framed view defined the human condition as a composite of individual autonomy, basic rights, religious toleration, and freedom of conscience (and with it, freedom of expression). In a dramatic departure from the traditional view of the individual as a subordinate part of the great social body headed by the twin authorities of church and state, Locke championed the new importance of the individual as the centerpiece of the system.

In both the *Second Treatise of Government* and the *Letter on Toleration*, Locke exalts the idea of individual rights—beginning with the right to life and property and extending to the right of individual conscience—as the centerpiece of his system. While Locke was not the first to expound these views (he drew heavily on the tradition of Grotius and Pufendorf and explicitly on the work of his contemporary Tyrrell), he is credited with creating a new synthesis of a theory of knowledge and a theory of society anchored in the critical judgment of the rational individual.

This new synthesis had its origins not only in scholarly speculation but also in Locke's deep immersion in the dangerous political battles of late-seventeenth-century England. Indeed, four of his contemporaries— Lord William Russell, Thomas Coleman, Stephen Colledge, and Algernon Sidney—were executed in the 1680s for expressing similar views about political authority and belief, and Locke wrote a significant portion of his work while hiding in the Netherlands during this period. England experienced savage turmoil throughout the last half of the seventeenth century, with the beheading of Charles I, the Rye House plot, and the Glorious Revolution of 1688. Fueling these events were contested ideas about the status of the king, conflicting religious confessions, and the state's authority.

Locke's central aim was to develop a new philosophical foundation for social and political life that reconciled the growing claims of individual interests and rights, which he championed, with the preservation of a legitimate and peaceful political order. Against the fissiparous forces in this new system that permitted diverse religious affiliations and competing economic interests to coexist, it was necessary to have a source of binding connection that accommodated pluralism but kept the polity intact. One influence in

Locke's thinking on this subject was the work of Pierre Nicole, a French Jansenist who was one of the first thinkers to describe the unintended positive social consequences of the pursuit of individual gain.[10] Locke translated some of Nicole's *Moral Essays* for his own use and was clearly concerned with the same central question of the role of the individual in the commonweal. However, Locke's system ultimately posited the idea of the direct expression of divine forces at work in the form of trust and natural law. Locke's student Anthony Ashley Cooper, the Third Earl of Shaftsbury, took the notion of a harmoniously ordered system a step further—for him, humans had an innate moral sense that was part of a natural order and that consequently produced a culture of "politeness."[11]

While Lockean theory emphasized the moral, rights-based philosophy that became a central element of the liberal democratic state and that inspired many Enlightenment thinkers, including the founders of the American Republic, the contrarian writings of a Dutch expatriate in London, Bernard Mandeville, unearthed the core issue at the center of the Enlightenment debate about the animating forces of civil society. Mandeville's conception of human behavior, like that of Hobbes, presumed unbridled self-interest and competition. He explicitly rejected Shaftsbury's notion of the innate moral sense and natural sociability.[12] Expressed forcefully in the famous *The Fable of the Bees*, this view became as influential in the formative period of modern civil society as Locke's had been in the founding of contractarian democracy.

Mandeville's unorthodox theory came to occupy, in the words of one observer, a "central place in the moral imagination of Enlightenment Europe."[13] The publication of *The Fable* in 1723 created an immediate sensation. Dr. Johnson is reported to have said that "every young man had Mandeville's work in his shelf in the belief that it was a wicked book."[14] It marked a significant turning point in the description of the new form of society, one that sought to unmask the motivations of self-interested behavior. In doing so, it embraced the new understanding of social relations that had emerged from commercial society, namely the pursuit of pure economic self-interest. This view directly challenged the dominant social philosophy that had emerged from the civic humanist tradition, shared by Locke among many others, of a sense of divinely inspired benevolence and republican virtue that kept the potentially destructive forces of self-interest in check. Mandeville boldly asserted the opposite: that it was the unrestrained pursuit of material gain that led, albeit in an unintended way, to social productivity and peaceful relations.

Mandeville was widely attacked for his radical and irreverent views of the human condition. A grand jury in Middlesex charged that *The Fable* intended "to run down Religion and Virtue as prejudicial to Society, and detrimental to the State; and to recommend Luxury, Avarice, Pride, and all vices as being necessary to *Public Welfare*."[15] Mandeville responded in the press with an acerbic critique of what he described as the self-deceptive and outdated moralism of the intellectual elite, defending the benefits of the new economic behavior and egoistic morality. Even the traditional virtue of charity did not escape his biting criticism in his dismissal of the work of the charity schools as economically dysfunctional and socially destabilizing.[16] Throughout the furor generated by *The Fable* during the decade that followed, Mandeville further developed his argument for the advantages of a society governed by self-interest, expressing ironic praise for the hypocrisy of the ruling class, which he saw as usefully promoting the values of frugality while itself indulging in luxury.

The Scottish Enlightenment and the Hegelian Turn

The Fable stimulated a highly charged debate throughout the entire period of the Enlightenment about the role of self-interest and its sufficiency or insufficiency as a binding force in society. This debate achieved a special resonance in increasingly prosperous Scotland. That nation had experienced a dramatic transition as it moved into the second half of the eighteenth century, evolving from an intellectual and economic backwater into a leading source of Enlightenment thinking. James Buchan describes the particular role of the city of Edinburgh: "For near fifty years [1745–1789], a city that had for centuries been a byword for poverty, religious bigotry, violence and squalor laid the mental foundations for the modern world."[17] As it recovered from its latest conflict with England, Scotland began to prosper economically and became a catalyst for the most advanced Enlightenment thinking about the nature of commercially based civil society.

Interestingly, there are a number of striking similarities between the political, social, and economic conditions in the Dutch Republic during the seventeenth century and those in Scotland during the eighteenth. If the unusual circumstances of the Dutch Republic provided the necessary conditions for the birth of the practices of modern civil society, its theoretical foundations were fully elaborated in the next century in Scotland, another small country in northern Europe. A brilliant group of Scottish thinkers emerged in the second half of the eighteenth century to delineate a new view of the relationship between the individual and society. Their collective work became the source of the famed Scottish Enlightenment that, in the words of Buchan, for a half century "ruled the Western intellect."[18] As the Netherlands had, Scotland was experiencing divided political authority, dramatic economic growth, competing religious confessions, the rapid expansion of literacy and publications, and the appearance of a remarkable group of intellectual leaders. Although both countries faced external enemies, they managed to retain sufficient internal order to accommodate highly pluralistic domestic societies. Despite important differences, the developments that occurred in both environments suggest that the existence of decentralized authority structures within a larger framework of legal legitimacy contributed to the flourishing of pluralistic private activities that permitted the emergence of modern civil societies.

One of the intellectual leaders of this era, Francis Hutcheson, became one of Mandeville's leading critics. Hutcheson, holder of the chair of moral philosophy at the University of Glasgow, criticized Mandeville and his adherents for seeking to reduce all human behavior to the single motivating force of self-interest. In place of that reductionist view, Hutcheson saw a blending of motivations, including a benign "calm desire of wealth." Simple observation of human behavior revealed this blend of compassion, sympathies, and desires that kept civil society intact. Following Shaftsbury, he accepted the notion of a moral sense natural to the human condition that was the source of benevolent impulses. However, he disagreed with Shaftsbury's view that the natural moral sense was adequate to hold together the artifice of civil society. What were needed in addition were the compelling obligations of legal rules that accompanied the concept of rights. Modern society thus embodied a complex mixture of benevolence, social comity, competition, and contractual obligations, all leading to the creation of the social bonds that formed the glue of a society that was characterized more by interests rather than by traditional fellowship.[19]

Hutcheson's most famous student was Adam Smith. Born in 1723, at a time when the new forces of commercial capitalism were beginning to overwhelm traditional norms and social bonds in Scotland, Smith was steeped in a culture that was facing, in both practice and theory, the problematic relationship between private interest and the public welfare. Educated in the classics with an original orientation toward a career in the church, Smith soon redirected his interests toward literature and philosophy, studying under Hutcheson and eventually succeeding to the chair of moral philosophy at the University of Glasgow.

Although the vexing question of the role of self-interest in the new society became a primary theme in Smith's work, he was dissatisfied with the traditional abstract treatments of that question. Smith, like his colleagues, had much more empirical interests, and he framed the existing philosophical debate in terms of the realities of the socioeconomic world of the latter half of the eighteenth century.[20] Smith devoted his efforts to exploring, both empirically and analytically, the central paradox of Enlightenment society: A society founded on the exercise of individual rights and freedoms—the famous "society of strangers"—soon encounters the problem of cohesion. What will continue to hold it together once traditional authority and custom have been undermined by a culture of rationalism?

Contrary to the common misunderstanding of his work as a single-minded promotion of free-market economics, Smith was acutely aware of this tension. Both of his celebrated works, *The Theory of Moral Sentiments* and *An Inquiry into the Nature and Causes of the Wealth of Nations*, address this tension and seek to resolve it. Written seventeen years before *The Wealth of Nations*, *The Theory of Moral Sentiments* develops an elaborate ethical analysis based on Smith's concepts of "the impartial spectator" and "sympathy." Smith argues that the two curbs on what otherwise would be a world of unrestrained egoism that would "crumble into nothing" are: (1) the subtle and somewhat ironic work of "the invisible hand" (a concept that first appears in *The Theory of Moral Sentiments*) that converts the pursuit of individual betterment into broad social benefit and (2) the inculcation of moral education.

For Smith, the two limiting factors are equally important, because the pursuit of pure self-aggrandizement (which is popularly but inaccurately understood to be Smith's idea of the working of the market economy) cannot alone sustain a society. While it does contribute to the engine of economic growth, it must be supplemented by a strong internal sense of other-regarding ethical concern and "public spirit." These are rooted in a basic human capacity for psychological identification with the passions of others, resulting in the "sympathy" that provides the ultimate connecting link. Unlike Locke, Smith does not anchor this ethical orientation in religious belief; rather it is a self-constituted value underlying the coherent operation of market society. It is through the "natural principles" of human behavior, involving sympathetic understanding and "self-command," that individuals who pursue their own private ends create a set of social relationships that are beneficial to all.

To the end of his life (through six editions of *The Theory of Moral Sentiments*), Smith continued explicitly to engage the core issue initially posed by Mandeville of how to reconcile the self-seeking behavior of the modern individual with the well-being of society. He sought his solution not in the natural benevolence imputed by Shaftsbury and Hutcheson, but in empirical analysis of the hidden but efficient causes of human behavior, a kind of Newtonian approach to the study of human action. To what degree "sympathy" and moral education can produce all the positive benefits for society required of the "invisible hand" has remained the unanswered question of the Smithian legacy.

Dugwald Stewart, Smith's biographer, points to the powerful influence Smith's ideas exerted on both thought and practice in the contemporary world when he observes that Smith's genius served "to enlighten and reform the commercial policy of Europe."[21] One vehicle by which this influence was extended was Smith's active membership in the Select Society of Edinburgh. A classic expression of the Scottish Enlightenment, the Select Society was a debating group that convened the best minds from religious, academic, and government life to address the pressing intellectual and social issues of the day. David Hume was its first host, Adam Smith was one of its first presidents, and its membership included many others from the Scottish intellectual and political elites, including Adam Ferguson, Lord Kames, and Alexander Wedderburn. As one commentator has noted, such "institutional connection of the literati with the Law and the Church" gave the Scottish Enlightenment its special character.[22]

David Hume was a longtime friend and mentor of Smith, and the similarity of their approaches to the study of the social world is clearly evident. Already in his *Treatise of Human Nature* (1740), Hume suggested that the forces that determine human behavior were to be discovered through an experimental method like that of Newton. Hume was particularly interested in one such force animating human behavior, the "love of gain," which he regarded as a central feature of the human condition. There was a need to counterbalance this force in order to "render men fit members of society," but the only thing capable of doing this ("benevolence to strangers is too weak for this purpose") was the redirection of the love of gain in a socially beneficial direction.[23] An anticipation of the "invisible hand" is quite plain here.

Also like Smith, Hume had an aversion to abstractions, and his skepticism and empiricism became increasingly apparent in his essays of later years. He was deeply critical of religious doctrine, especially religious fanaticism, and championed the free flow of ideas. Above all, he was interested in the actual workings of society—what guided behavior as opposed to what he considered empty, moralistic rationalizations of conduct. And when Hume looked at Scottish society in the mid-eighteenth century, he saw a positive picture of a commercially successful community and observed that the more it developed in this direction, "the more sociable men become."[24]

Another contemporary of Hume, Adam Ferguson, had a fundamentally different view of the direction Scottish society was taking. Ferguson was deeply distressed about the dark underside of an increasingly commercial society. While he acknowledged the liberating aspects of this new social form, he expressed great concern about its tendency to fragment and undermine traditional collective norms:

> The commercial and lucrative arts may continue to prosper, but they gain an ascendancy at the expense of other pursuits. The desire of profit stifles the love of perfection. Interest cools the imagination and hardens the heart.
> . . . as commerce advances . . . [it] serves, in some measure, to break the bands of society.[25]

The forces of specialization and commercialization were responsible for breaking these bands, and the result was that a "society is made to consist of parts, of which none is animated with the spirit of society itself."[26] What Ferguson is lamenting here is the loss of the connection and fellowship that characterized the pre-commercial world, one with which he had direct experience in the traditional communities of the Scottish Highlands.

Thus, while Hume and Smith celebrate the growth of material well-being, improved education, the greater flow of ideas, and the general liberation of the individual in the new civil society and express confidence in that society's ability to enhance the public welfare through the proper direction of the forces of self-interest, Ferguson is acutely aware of the deficiencies of this new social system, especially the loss of social solidarity. This is the central theme in his now-famous work of 1767, *An Essay on the History of Civil Society*, the first publication in English devoted to the history and analysis of the "new" civil society.

Up to this point, the term "civil society" had been used ambiguously, even by other Enlightenment writers such as Locke, Hume, and Smith, to refer to the blended social, economic, and political dimensions of the life of human communities, as in the title of chapter 7 of Locke's *Second Treatise of Government*: "Of Political or Civil Society."[27] While eighteenth-century thinkers, as previously discussed, were increasingly describing the new, de facto social world that was characterized by autonomous economic, intellectual, and associational activity and partially detached from the official public realm, no one had as yet devoted a work exclusively to the analysis of this new phenomenon. Ferguson, who had grown up in the Scottish Highlands and had served as a military chaplain with the Black Watch, had personally experienced the transition from the old to the new social forms. Even as he later came to hold the chairs first of natural philosophy and then of moral philosophy at the University of Edinburgh, he remained focused on the gains and losses from the emergence of the newly defined "civil society."

Although Ferguson still does not make a sharp conceptual distinction between the realm of the state and the realm of civil society, he takes another step toward conceiving of the latter as an autonomous sphere of interaction between newly liberated individuals. Modern civil society, as he sees it, operates under the laws and jurisdiction of the centralized, constitutional state that provides the security and efficient administration necessary for the maintenance of the rights and prosperity of its inhabitants. But the state, in his analysis, recedes farther and farther into the background as a necessary but not primary factor in shaping the contemporary human condition. The primary influence is the increasing power of the civilizing force itself, which comprises politeness, mutually beneficial commercial relations, the restrained pursuit of self-interest, and abstract social bonds. The gains in personal liberty and prosperity in civil society, however, come at a high cost: the loss of a sense of public spirit, communal bonds, and honor that defined the character of traditional communities. In the chapter "Of the Consequences that result from the Advance of the Civil and Commercial

Arts," Ferguson laments that the very specialization that creates modern prosperity tends "to dismember the human character, and to destroy the very arts we mean to improve."[28] Clearly, Ferguson does not share the optimism of Smith or Hume about the felicitous, behind-the-scenes working of laws of behavior to insure social cohesion in the new civil society.

Ferguson did, however, place some hope in one possible solution to the civil society dilemma. His longstanding appreciation of the value of communal organizations became the focus of his interest in reviving social cohesion in the modern world. He had great faith in the ability of all forms of associational activity to generate a civic spirit and a sense of social solidarity. Undoubtedly, his active involvement with Scotland's thriving intellectual clubs, particularly the Select Society and the Poker Club, reinforced this optimism about the positive effects of private associational life.[29] As John Keane observes in his influential essay on the developmental phases of civil society, "Ferguson comes close to saying that the survival and progress of modern society require the development of independent social associations—the development of a civil society within a civil society."[30] However, Keane also notes that Ferguson's classical assumptions caused him to stop short of making that strong a claim for the redemptive power of private associations within civil society. So, for Ferguson, the fate of civil society remained an open question.

Two German philosophers at the beginning of the next century brought the Scottish Enlightenment's conception of civil society to its logical conclusion. Norbert Waszek has documented the strong influence of the Scottish Enlightenment on the development of German thought during the late eighteenth and early nineteenth centuries, especially on the philosophies of Immanuel Kant and Georg Wilhelm Friedrich Hegel.[31] Kant, who acknowledged Hume's influence as "awakening him from his dogmatic slumber," sought to reconcile the notion of freely acting individuals pursuing their private affairs with that of an ideal "public" whose members pursued common purposes in the realm of public reason. For Kant, this task is accomplished by civil society, which he views as a "mediating institution between universal standards and practical politics."[32] A key attribute of this civil society is its creation of a setting for the free formation of public opinion—the sphere of *Publizität*. It is in this realm that private individuals become organized as a public and develop freely held, collective views, including pluralistic religious views, which may exert influence on state policy. Thus, freedom of expression, especially freedom of religious expression that is independent of the state, becomes the defining quality of civil society.

Hegel took a significant further step in delineating the distinctiveness of civil society and its clear separation from the state. He had read Hutcheson, Smith, Hume, Ferguson, and James Steuart and drew heavily on their ideas when developing the portions of *Philosophy of Right* that discuss civil society. He was particularly taken with the concept of a social system that develops separately from the state and in which free individuals pursue their economic and other private needs, thereby producing a network of interdependent legal, financial, and ethical elements. Hegel incorporated this theme, which, as previously noted, is a central feature of the Scottish works, into his much more comprehensive vision in which "civil society" (*bürgerliche Gesellschaft*) becomes one of the four constitutive elements of his world-historical system.

Hegel's complete separation of civil society from the state moves beyond the position of the Scottish Enlightenment thinkers, who sought to sustain the traditional integration of the civil and political elements of public life even as they implicitly acknowledged the diminishing role of the state. Hegel by contrast posits a sharp division between a civil society that is composed of independent competitive individuals (whose common bonds are their shared interests rather than a higher connection of citizenship or civic obligation) and the supreme authority of the state that represents and advances the universal ethical good of the entire community. The two can in fact oppose each other, as when the private interests and antagonisms of civil society threaten the common good, in which case it is the role of the state to intervene and exert control over a malfunctioning civil society.

This opposition was anticipated by the Scottish thinkers, particularly in the case of what we now term "market failure." Both Smith and Steuart acknowledged the importance of government as an intervener and regulator in cases where the market breaks down, and Hume stated the potential opposition in more general terms:

> In all governments there is a perpetual intestine struggle, open or secret, between Authority and Liberty, and neither of them can absolutely prevail in the contest. . . . In this sense it must be owned that liberty is the perfection of civil society, but still authority must be acknowledged essential to its very existence.[33]

Hegel, however, in conceiving of civil society as a wholly autonomous sphere of private action set apart from the state but needing to be controlled by it, signals a decisive break with the traditional understanding of civil society. In *The Philosophy of Right*, he develops the tripartite distinction between family, state, and civil society, with the last serving as the transitional vehicle for moving from purely private, domestic concerns to the general, civic concerns of the state. It is the complex task of civil society to create a conscious relationship between the role of its members (*Bürger*) as private persons pursuing their own private interests (both material and spiritual) and their role as citizens of the larger polity.

In an insightful essay James Schmidt describes this transition: "In the mad jostle of Hegel's uncivil society, the *bourgeois* somehow learns to be a *citoyen*." For Hegel, this is accomplished through a process of education (*Bildung*), but the *Bürger* who populate civil society cannot aspire to attain anything like classical Greek citizenship; rather, they become members of society who adapt to the challenges of the market and accept the order imposed by the state. Schmidt points to this underlying tension animating much of Hegel's work as a pivotal, unresolved question in Enlightenment thought: "How could the classical ideal of the citizen, an individual willing to risk his life for the survival of the polity, be reconciled with the modern *bourgeois*, the private individual who is concerned, above all else, with the satisfaction of his own material needs?"[34]

The question recalls the question raised most incisively by Bernard Mandeville at the beginning of the eighteenth century, as to whether a society can reconcile the unfettered pursuit of self-interest with the public welfare, as well as Mandeville's answer, that it is precisely the natural laws underlying social behavior that create, in unintended ways, the desired public benefit (but not necessarily public virtue). Other writers, rejecting Mandeville's reductionist naturalism, sought answers in ethically based human impulses: Hutcheson's "natural benevolence," Smith's "sympathy" that guided the invisible hand, and Hume's "natural affection and public spirit," among others. But as Hegel's dichotomy, still unresolved at the beginning of the nineteenth century, demonstrates, "the specter haunting Enlightenment understanding" remained the inability of the proposed solutions, whether naturalistic or philosophical, to overcome the polarity between competitive private interests and the well-being of the community as a whole.[35]

A New Construct of Civil Society

This tension is reflected in all phases of Enlightenment thought, including several of the strands that have been highlighted previously as the constitutive elements of civil society. During this period, the new intellectual paradigm envisioning society as a collection of individuals who pursue particularized interests and rights transformed the meaning of concepts traditionally understood in collective terms—the common good, the rule of law, philanthropy, and communal associations—into products representing aggregated individual interests. For example, discussion of the nature of the common good moved from the Aristotelian notion of a transcendent good representing a universal ethical plane to a notion of maximum mutual benefit for the collection of individuals who compose society. The ultimate outcome of this transformation in thinking was early utilitarianism as it began to appear in the works of William Paley and William Godwin at the end of the eighteenth century.[36] Hegel's contrast of an interest-maximizing civil society with the universal pursuits of the state clearly demonstrates the overt difference between the two modes of pursuing the common good.

The traditional role of law as an expression of combined royal, customary, and ecclesiastical authority encountered a new challenge in the Enlightenment's emphasis on law as arising from contractual agreement. While the traditional sources of central authority continued to govern criminal justice and public policy, the growing influence of the market and civil matters ushered in a newly developed body of "civil law" that regulated commerce and contracted and enforced rights. This "law from below" was a signature of the Enlightenment:

> [B]oth Hegel and the Scottish philosophers . . . stress the need which
> modern commercial society has for an elaborate system of *private law*
> (especially laws of contract), and the proper administration of it, though
> Hegel, in comparison with the explicit statements of Adam Smith, for
> example, makes the point more implicitly.[37]

This form of law, administered efficiently by a neutral state, is essential to the maintenance of harmonious relations among the free and equal members of the new civil society.[38]

Charity in the Enlightenment took on a new character as well, influenced both by a growing acceptance of doctrines of individual rights and a quite different impulse on the part of elites to guide social development

in a way that maintained order and security. In this movement, the allocation of surplus wealth to the poor became a matter not of religious duty but
rather of justice and a growing pragmatism. As previously noted, Locke had
already moved toward such a position. Godwin took this view to its logical
conclusion when he castigated the purported generosity of the wealthy by
describing it as "a system of clemency and charity, instead of a system of
justice."[39] Charitable giving thus changed from the fulfillment of a religious
duty to a means of guiding and managing society, both to meet the sense of
obligation associated with surplus wealth and to maintain social order.

A leading force in this transition was the philanthropic movement initiated by August Hermann Francke in Prussia in the late seventeenth century. As noted in chapter 3, Francke developed his first orphanage after
an extensive study of Dutch institutions, which were considered to be the
most advanced in Europe at the time. Francke was a truly transitional figure, combining the religious reform of the German Pietist movement with
a new approach of creating well-managed, economically viable institutions.
Following August Hermann Francke's death in 1727, the work of the Francke
Foundations was carried on by his son Gotthilf August Francke, expanding to include a house for widows, schools, a hospital, and a mail-order
pharmaceutical business. This last endeavor was of particular importance
because the foundation leaders appealed to donors on the basis of a solid
economic model that would produce a return dedicated to charitable purposes. The Francke Foundations developed a number of income-generating
businesses, including distribution of pharmaceuticals, publication of Bibles
and other books, and real estate investments, leading Renate Wilson to conclude that the "Francke Foundations merged philanthropic and commercial
interests under the umbrella of an evangelical reform movement that pur-
posely transcended dynastic boundaries."[40]

A parallel evolution of the charitable movement was occurring at the
same time in England. Indeed, the Francke Foundations became a model
for the development of philanthropic institutions throughout Europe, in
particular for the newly developing charity schools in London. The growing body of thought inspired by the search for the natural laws of society
had led many thinkers and political leaders to begin to see philanthropy as
an enlightened means of shaping and regulating the social order. Donna
Andrew traces a clear transition from religious to politically oriented philanthropy in her analysis of the evolution of English philanthropy from

the mid-seventeenth through the eighteenth centuries.[41] Both the types of charitable institutions created and the kinds of appeals made for their support changed dramatically over this period. From the Middle Ages and into the seventeenth century, charity had been seen primarily as a religious duty for the care of one's soul, given without concern for its worldly efficacy or return. As the eighteenth century approached, however, both the understanding of and the motivations for charity began to change. An entirely new philosophy gained wide acceptance, one that emphasized the voluntary nature of charitable giving and its social utility.

Through sermons, annual reports, appeals for donations, and the successes and failures of the charities themselves, Andrew tracks this change of attitude on the part of donors, from a sense of moral obligation to a desire to shape social policy. Different types of organizations flourished at different times during the eighteenth century, corresponding to changing national attitudes toward evolving social needs. Charity schools to educate, workhouses to provide productive work, and hospitals to care for the health of the poor were popular in the first decades of the century, in keeping with the theory that an educated and productive workforce (and one grounded in Christian values, since all institutions also provided spiritual education) was vital to the national interest. By midcentury, however, charitable support had migrated to foundling and maternity hospitals and to institutions such as the Marine Academy that trained poor boys for the navy, in keeping with a new emphasis on population growth and strong armed forces. At the end of the century, yet a third wave of interest moved donors in the direction of programs that supported self-help and aimed to reform the "minds and morals of the laboring poor."[42] The preferred method of support was the "associated charities" system through subscriptions (based on the model of the joint-stock company). Philanthropists were beginning to view themselves as guided by scientific principles. Clearly, Enlightenment philanthropists were inspired by the notion of using private means to address social problems and were convinced of the utility of scientifically harnessing the energies of rational self-interest (both those of donors and those of the needy) to achieve public benefit.

In the many commentaries on the explosive growth of private associations in the eighteenth century, there is a common theme: associations were beginning to display a new character, different from that of the religious and trade-based corporate bodies of the past. Private associations grew out of the scientific, political, and educational interests of their members. In the Enlightenment, Becker reminds us, voluntary associations were

> championed with exceptional fervor. In an increasingly urbanized world, traditional structures were either absent or inappropriate, and it was here that this voluntarism found expression in a wealth of new institutional forms. Patriotic societies, reading clubs, masonic lodges, academies of science and the fine arts are but a sample of the numerous manifestations of these practical social initiatives. In the main they were committed to the general improvement of the individual, his society, and economic life. Geographically, they were located in assembly halls, concert halls, lecture halls, museums, lending libraries, coffee houses, public walks, and theaters. The separation of society and the state enhanced and fortified that public space aptly termed "civil society."[43]

Such associational life was seen by some, especially Ferguson, as a way of combining an older sense of fellowship with new forms of social advancement to create an antidote to the fragmenting, impersonal forces of the modern world.

The three newer themes of the civil society construct—individual rights, toleration, and free expression—are specific products of Enlightenment thought. In Locke's famous articulation of the priority of natural rights in the life of society, the protection of such individual rights becomes foundational for the advancement of human freedom. Locke originally wrote his *Two Treatises on Government*, in which he elaborated the centrality of rights in the framework of government, as a critique of the government of Charles II, but later he published them in order to defend the Glorious Revolution and its potential to protect "the security of civil rights and the liberty and property of all subjects of the nation." Rights, as further elaborated by Kant, Mary Wollstonecraft Shelley, Thomas Paine, Thomas Jefferson, and James Madison, became the signature of Enlightenment thought and a central organizing principle of the experiment that unfolded on the American Continent.[44]

The spirit of toleration that had so notably characterized the culture of the golden-age Dutch Republic gained substantial political strength in England when it was incorporated into the Toleration Act of 1689 by William of Orange after the Glorious Revolution. The passage of the Act seems to have precipitated a tipping point with respect to the idea of toleration in Enlightenment culture. Voltaire expressed the centrality of this idea to his age: "What is tolerance? It is the natural attribute of humanity. We are all formed of weakness and error: let us pardon reciprocally each other's folly. That is the first law of nature."[45] When he marveled that in the commercial societies of Amsterdam and London as well as "Surat or Bassora" the adherents of all faiths, from Jew to Muslim to Chinese Deist to Quaker Christian, could traffic together in peace, he was implicitly admiring the new civil society. Toleration was essential to the peaceful operation of a world consisting of autonomous individuals with fundamentally differing worldviews.

Above all, the Enlightenment is identified with the vast expansion of free expression. The proliferation of pamphlets, books, newspapers, and other print media, along with the dramatic increase in debating clubs and coffeehouse conversations in the eighteenth century, created an entirely new environment for the diffusion of and deliberation over political and social ideas. Habermas describes this as the self-constitution of the public sphere, a new arena of public life operating between domestic life and the state. He points to this arena as the birthplace of the modern idea of "public opinion," which emerges as the result of "critical public debate among private people." However, this public sphere has, in Habermas's view, been eroded over the past two centuries, as private interests have steadily increased control over the vehicles of free expression. In this view, the public sphere has degenerated into a simple aggregation of individualized preferences managed by the publicity industry.[46]

This is the unresolved tension that remains as the Enlightenment's legacy for civil society. The realm of free private interests that creates the space for new forms of thought, expression, and political action also comes to revolve around its own private concerns. The public well-being that is supposed to be achieved through this process remains elusive; the imputed forces of social integration do not ultimately seem adequate to the task. Even Adam Smith expressed misgivings about the functioning of the whole:

> The man of system . . . seems to imagine that he can arrange the different members of a great society with as much ease as the hand arranges the different pieces upon a chess-board; he does not consider that the pieces upon the chess-board have no other principle of motion besides that which the hand impresses upon them; but that, in the great chess-board of human society, every single piece has a principle of motion of its own, altogether different from that which the legislature might choose to impress upon it.

If those two principles coincide and act in the same direction, the game of human society will go on easily and harmoniously, and is very likely to be happy and successful. If they are opposite or different, the game will go on miserably.[47]

How harmoniously or inharmoniously the two principles played out in society in the next two centuries is the story of the most recent chapter in the development of civil society, the American experience.

6 Civil Society in America

The profound influence of the Enlightenment on the development of American political and social thought is well known from the works of the writers and activists who provided the impetus for the American War of Independence and the writing of the Constitution. Among other consequences, this legacy led to the reappearance in American thought of the central question that had occupied the Scottish thinkers: How can society resolve the tension between the pluralistic interests of newly empowered, rights-bearing individuals in civil society and the pursuit of public welfare in the polity as a whole?

In the highly pluralistic and relatively egalitarian society of the American colonies, balancing the claims of individual rights and freedoms against legitimate public authority became an even more urgent political question than it was in Europe. In America, this balancing act became not only the focal point of social commentary but also the central issue in ongoing political power struggles.

Among the Founders, James Madison articulated most clearly the tension between individualistic pluralism and the pursuit of the common good. Madison, who had championed freedom of conscience and the secular state while still a member of the Virginia House of Delegates, was strongly influenced by republican theory and the philosophy of the Scottish Enlightenment, particularly the thought of Francis Hutcheson. That theory, as previously shown, relied heavily on the idea of republican virtue to keep the disintegrative tendencies of a highly pluralistic civil society in check. Madison had championed the idea of republican virtue along with the principles of liberty and diversity in his early writing and political activity. However, as he witnessed the growing self-interested behavior of the squabbling states under the Articles of Confederation, he confessed that the

Articles had been based on a "mistaken confidence" in the ability of political officeholders to pursue the common good.[1]

Madison gradually moved toward acceptance of a strong central government that could act as a neutral arbiter among the necessarily diverse interests of society and as an essential enforcer of unity.[2] In this system, the multiple interests in civil society acted as moderating forces upon one another; thus liberty and pluralism were compatible with a strong central government, as Madison elaborated in the famous *Federalist No. 10*.[3] He thus identified the essential polarities that shaped American civil society from its inception.

Individual Rights and Tolerance in the American Ethos

From the time of the earliest settlements in North America, an individual's right to profess a religious faith in accordance with personal conviction and independent of state control became a central issue in public discourse. Efforts to enforce orthodoxy in particular local jurisdictions were gradually eroded by the increasing religious diversity of settlers within individual colonies and among them. Freedom of conscience was closely tied to the right of free expression, which in turn became identified with individual rights in general. The different paths taken by the colonies of Pennsylvania and Virginia that resulted in proclamations of individual rights illustrate the mutually reinforcing character of the rights of religious belief, free speech, a free press, and free association in the early American experience.[4]

The American inclination to champion the rights of individuals soon revealed its political character in challenges to the increasing intrusion of the English monarchical state into the life of the colonies. The first colonists carried with them a dual heritage that reflected both their allegiance to the European states from which they came and a desire to establish a society that protected private belief and action from state control. Although the colonies were established under general British (or Dutch, in the case of New York) governmental structures, they adopted highly independent social and political systems, in accordance with the varying forms of religious dissent and political belief of their inhabitants. From its Puritan beginnings, Massachusetts understood itself to possess quasi-autonomy from English rule, even as it operated under a direct colonial charter. Indeed, the Massachusetts General Court went so far as to declare in 1678 that "The lawes of England are bounded within the fower seas, and does not reach America."[5]

In the early, Dutch period of its history, New York viewed itself as even more independent than its northern neighbor. While the small outpost of New Amsterdam maintained a nominal colonial status with the Netherlands, it operated relatively independently as a thriving business community. Moreover, the assumption of quasi-autonomy from the parent state carried with it an understanding of the rights of individuals as well, particularly the right of freedom of belief and practice of one's religion. Closely related to this right was an ethic of toleration carried over from the modus vivendi among competing religious constituencies in the Dutch Republic. This unusual quality is highlighted in Russell Shorto's illuminating study of the founding of Manhattan: "As the 'Dutch' emigrated to their New World colony . . . they brought with them not only a ready-made mix of cultures but a tolerance of differences, the prescription for a multicultural society. In its very seeding, Manhattan was a melting pot."[6] Thus, New Amsterdam rather than New England became the leading edge of the growing ethos of tolerance in America.

The Virginia colony underwent an altogether different course of development. Settled primarily by members of the upper and lower classes from the south and west of England, the immigrants brought with them a strong respect for tradition in social relations, religion, and governmental authority. Although this respect meant an initial allegiance to the English Crown, it also entailed a powerful claim to individual rights, as one historian notes in his comment that "the first gentlemen of Virginia possessed an exceptionally strong consciousness of their English liberties."[7] Beginning with Edmund Burke, many have pointed out the bitter irony of the Virginians' overt commitment to individual rights and liberty in a colony that was also defined by the pervasive practice of slavery. Nevertheless, a deep identification with a tradition of rights came to characterize the colony and over time led to an increasing emphasis on autonomy and self-governance. By 1776 the language of this tradition found its way into Thomas Jefferson's draft of the Virginia Declaration of Rights, which in turn became the model for the American Bill of Rights.

The impact of the Glorious Revolution that took place in England on the life of the colonies illustrates the widely shared attachment of Americans to the protection of their liberties from the distant authority of the central state. James II had developed a growing concern about the claims of rights and independent action by the colonies, especially Massachusetts. Therefore in 1686 he had consolidated the colonies of Massachusetts, Maine, New Hampshire, Plymouth, Rhode Island, Connecticut, New Jersey, and New York under a single government with a governor appointed by the crown, abolishing local assemblies and generating great animosity in the colonies.

The arrival on American shores in 1689 of the news of the Glorious Revolution, however, sparked an immediate reassertion of local autonomy, including armed insurrections in Massachusetts, New York, and Maryland, resulting in the disbandment of the consolidated government and the restoration of the separate colonial authorities. This action reinforced an incipient republicanism in American identity—a sense of resistance to absolute royal authority in the name of broader principles of rights and self-government. As a result of this sequence of events, Richard Johnson concludes, "perhaps the most enduring and still potent legacy of 1688–9 within America lay in making the terms 'revolution' and 'constitution' what they had not been before—common watchwords of political discourse and standards (however variously defined) by which to assess the politically proper."[8]

It was but a short step from championing the liberties and rights of self-rule of the colonies to championing the individual rights and freedom of action of the citizens who inhabited them, that is, the rights and freedoms of members of civil society. Thomas Paine's distinctive contribution becomes central to the evolving idea of civil society in America at this juncture. Paine's first widely read work, *Common Sense*, written while he was in the colonies, became a classic American statement of the need to protect the colonists' rights and liberties from the dominating force of the English Crown. In *Common Sense*, Paine drew a sharp distinction between "society" and "government" in a way that became characteristic of American social thought: "Some writers have confounded society with government, as to leave little or no distinction between them; whereas they are not only different but have different origins. Society is produced by our wants, and government by our wickedness; the former promotes our happiness *positively* by uniting our affections, the latter *negatively* by restraining our vices."[9]

The work that followed, *The Rights of Man*, written by Paine on his return to England in 1792, moved to a yet broader level of argument on behalf of civil society's right to defend itself against the state in the name of individual rights and equality. *The Rights of Man* became one of the most influential arguments for the preservation of citizens' rights and their ability to believe, speak, and assemble freely, unrestrained by the overbearing power of the state.[10] For Paine, civil rights proceed from natural rights and governments are creatures of both: "[I]ndividuals, each in his own sovereign and personal right, *entered into a compact with each other* to produce a government; and this is the only mode in which governments have a right to arise."[11]

The vital influence of this tradition of championing the rights of individuals against the state culminated in the American Constitution's Bill of Rights, above all in the First Amendment. Indeed, the First Amendment reads like a proclamation of Enlightenment principles that has been embedded into a charter for civil society in the United States: It declares in one sentence the state's recognition of essential individual rights, including the rights of free expression, religious practice (implicitly including toleration), and association, and presupposes the rule of law as a protector of rights. The First Amendment decisively expresses American civil society's deep rootedness in the private sphere.[12]

The doctrines of rights proclaimed in the First Amendment were of course not unique to America. Indeed, the close identification of the defense of rights with specific freedoms of belief and expression was evident in Spinoza, Milton, and many other thinkers and forcefully articulated by early-eighteenth-century English writers such as Matthew Tindal, who argued for the crucial role of freedom of thought not only in religion but "in all manners of Learning and Knowledge." Tindal's work may have been the first in which freedom of speech and freedom of the press were promoted to the status of natural rights.[13]

Probably the era's most comprehensive and influential writings on freedom of speech and the press were those of John Trenchard and Thomas Gordon, published jointly under the pseudonym "Cato." Their 138 newspaper essays, published in the late 1720s in four volumes under the title of *Cato's Letters*, became the definitive articulation of the central role of free expression in public life: "Without Freedom of Thought there can be no such Thing as Wisdom; and no such Thing as publick Liberty, without Freedom of Speech: Which is the Right of every Man."[14] The *Letters* were widely reprinted in colonial American newspapers, including the *New England Courant*, published by the young Benjamin Franklin during the time his brother was imprisoned by the Massachusetts legislature for printing an article considered offensive to the clergy. Cato's letters on freedom of speech and the press and on libel were republished by John Peter Zenger in his *New York Weekly Journal* in connection with the famous case in 1735 in which Zenger was found innocent of libel by a jury after being accused of publishing seditious articles about Governor William Cosby.

The highly publicized Zenger case reinforced the long-accepted principle in the colonies that individuals in civil society had the right to publish criticism of the government without prior censorship. In subsequent decades the assertion of this right played a central role in fostering the Revolution, and direct efforts by the British Crown to tax and regulate the free press through the Stamp Acts became a precipitating cause. It was natural, therefore, that the First Amendment to the American Constitution would recognize this right as an essential institution of civil society as it unfolded in the new nation of the United States.

The ideal of freedom of the press had in fact been incorporated into ten of the new states' constitutions, with its strongest expression in Pennsylvania: "That the people have a right to freedom of speech, and of writing, and publishing their sentiments; therefore, the freedom of the press ought not to be restrained." Widespread support for this principle led to its inclusion in the federal Bill of Rights and its accepted role as a foundational element of American democracy. These constitutional provisions gave formal recognition to what was fundamentally accepted throughout American society: people had the right to speak and behave freely.[15]

The Growth of Associations

The right to participate in private associational life, a correlate of the rights of free speech and the press, was also incorporated into the First Amendment and came to exercise an equal influence in the development of American civil society. The central importance of private associations to the American experience is symbolized by the career of the quintessential organization man, Benjamin Franklin. In fact, Franklin personified the entire spectrum of characteristics of the early development of American civil society. His career, initially as a printer and later as postmaster of the colonies, promoted a distinctly American system of free expression. While establishing himself as a rising printer and publisher, Franklin founded a host of private associations dedicated to public purposes. Through these associations Franklin championed archetypal civil society ideals—free discussion unrestricted by dogmatic religious beliefs, equal rights to speak and act, the pursuit of public benefit through private initiative, a commitment to philanthropy—and the use of private organizations to accomplish these goals.

The first of his associations, the Junto, has become widely known as a prototype that demonstrated the public benefits of private association. Inspired in part by his experience with printers' guilds and the Freemasons while visiting London, Franklin convened twelve of his artisan friends in 1727 to establish the Junto as a club for, as he described it, "mutual improvement" and the exploration of current questions of intellectual life. The Junto required "that every member, in his turn, should produce one or more queries on any point of Morals, Politics, or Natural Philosophy."[16]

Typical of Franklin's approach, however, was that what began as an association for personal improvement became a vehicle for pursuing a larger vision of the common good. Ideas generated in Junto debates became the basis for the creation of many other voluntary associations, including Junto branches, a subscription lending library, a volunteer fire company, a public hospital, and the University of Pennsylvania. The original Junto eventually became the American Philosophical Society. Associations like the Junto, serving both mutual benefit and political purposes, spread throughout the colonies. All of the associations founded by Franklin embodied the duality of private entities serving public purposes, which he described as pursuing the "Publick Good."

The expansion of such voluntary associations and many other kinds of private bodies was to prove an important factor in the future character of the United States. As Peter Dobkin Hall has thoroughly documented, private associations became the focal point of a subsequent tug-of-war in American political life between those who advocated strong private bodies as a bulwark against the threatening dominance of the state and those who, fearing the growing power of elite private groups, advocated more democratic control.[17] Fears had already been expressed by Madison about the potential divisiveness of particularized interests in the form of "faction." By the end of the eighteenth century, this growing divide manifested itself in the formation of the first American political parties: the Federalists and Jefferson's Democratic Republicans. The two groups differed on many points of ideology and policy, but key among them was whether public purposes were better served through the action of private groups or through democratically controlled government.

The Society of the Cincinnati, founded by George Washington to support the cause of Revolutionary War veterans, became an early rallying point for the Federalists and a target of criticism by the Jeffersonians. The Federalists viewed the Society as a means by which the elite as natural leaders could sustain their dominant role and over time steer the new polity on a course that would maintain the elite's well-being and avoid the perils of democratic leveling, the most ominous form of which appeared in the French Revolution. The Jeffersonians, on the other hand, saw the Cincinnati as a threat, the first step toward the creation of a new aristocracy in the United States. These disputes over the virtues and dangers of private voluntary associations became a central issue in the election of 1800, in which the Jeffersonians prevailed.[18]

The Federalists, however, achieved definitive legal recognition for one of their core principles eighteen years later, when the issue of the rights of private associations and their donors became the centerpiece of a conflict over the control of Dartmouth College. The fundamental opposition between the rights of privately organized bodies and the authority of the state was expressed in the conflicting views of the board of Dartmouth College and of the Jeffersonian leaders of the state of New Hampshire. The question at stake was: Who had the right to exercise control over the governance and operation of the school, the private corporation (Dartmouth's board) or the state? The school's board, represented in the legal case by Daniel Webster, reflected the Federalist position in contending that the college had been the creature of private eleemosynary giving and therefore maintained contractual rights derived from its original charter that empowered it to carry out the functions envisioned by its founders and current overseers. The state, led by the Jeffersonian governor William Plummer, countered that the state legislature, by virtue of its ongoing investment of public funds in the college and the college's performance of a public function (the education of future leaders), had the right to exercise control over the governance and operation of the college.

In a famous decision issued by Chief Justice Marshall, the United States Supreme Court ruled in favor of the college and thus established the right of a private association to maintain its independence from state control. Through its establishment of a sharp separation between private associations and the state's realm of authority, the victory of the Federalist side in the case represented the most important early legal decision that set the direction of American civil society. It led directly to a new generation of private, sectarian colleges and many other privately funded organizations that proliferated in the new atmosphere of freedom from state control.[19]

The tension between the rights of private bodies to pursue their own ends and supervening public authorities remained unresolved and at the heart of public life when Alexis de Tocqueville visited the United States some fifty years after the Revolution. Tocqueville's unusual perceptiveness about the challenge of balancing private interests and the common good led to his much deeper insight into the formation of American civil society that became the central theme of his classic work *Democracy in America*. This was the issue of the protection of society from the state and the growing antagonism between the two. At the same time, Tocqueville was concerned about the potential danger of private interests' engaging in mutually destructive strife or dominating the public interest.

Tocqueville concluded that a significant part of the solution to this new democratic dilemma that he observed in America lay in the development of new social mores, his famous "habits of the heart" that would preserve a delicate balance between the free, unbridled pursuit of individual interests and the beneficial maintenance of public order.[20] Much of *Democracy in America* is devoted to a detailed exploration of this complex relationship and what it portends for the future of the American experiment in democracy. Although it is unknown whether Tocqueville ever read Hegel, Tocqueville's admiration for the independent character of American civil society and his awareness of the need to protect it from the potential oppression of the state read like a response to Hegel's advocacy of the overwhelming dominance of governmental authority.[21]

Tocqueville's further elaboration of the civil society idea thus moved beyond the general concept of a sphere of free individuals expressing and defending their natural rights to more concrete notions of autonomous private citizens acting together in voluntary associations dedicated to public purposes. John Keane notes that Tocqueville observed the rise in importance of private groups who viewed themselves as protectors against state power and that he understood that "forms of civil association such as scientific and literary circles, schools, publishers, inns, manufacturing enterprises, religious organizations, municipal associations, and independent households are crucial barriers against both political despotism and social unfreedom and inequality." This blend of private associational life and public purpose, together with its inherent tensions, was to become both a defining characteristic of the American experiment and a point of ongoing political conflict throughout the subsequent development of institutions in the United States.[22]

The explosive expansion of private associational activity in the first half of the nineteenth century began a new chapter in American public life. Private ventures continued to proliferate throughout the century, exceeding even what Tocqueville might have imagined for the development of a thriving civil society in the new democratic state. Due in part to the vast expansion of religious bodies fostered by the Second Great Awakening (the upwelling of Christian evangelism in the early nineteenth century) and its philanthropic legacy, a growing wave of schools, libraries, scientific organizations, abolitionist groups, hospitals, temperance societies, and other philanthropic organizations, which were dedicated to causes from improved care of the mentally ill to the education of freed slaves, swept across the landscape of the new American civil society.[23]

Acceptance of the central role of private associations both in championing rights and in supplying public goods was reinforced by the broadly held belief that philanthropy was a fundamental civic obligation, understood both in the ancient sense as a moral commitment expressed through volunteer effort and monetary contributions to improve humankind and in the more modern sense as a vehicle of social policy. Kathleen McCarthy stresses this combined theme of moral commitment and policy formation as a powerful force in the development of American civil society, originally fueled by evangelical Protestantism but gradually expanding into the general fabric of social values. She cites the striking example of the language used by the Lowell Female Reform Association, whose members described themselves as "philanthropists and lovers of equal rights" and announced that their purpose was to "kindle the spark of philanthropy in every heart," to "elevate humanity [and] to assert and maintain the rights of a republican people."[24]

In particular, the ascendancy of philanthropy and voluntarism came to be associated with the widespread involvement of women in social movements ranging from support of orphanages to relief of poor widows to abolitionism. The resulting "Benevolent Empire" provided a vital avenue for women, African Americans, and other disenfranchised groups who had been historically excluded from political life to engage in addressing public problems. By championing government action in behalf of important public causes, these private, philanthropically supported associations assumed a newly significant role in shaping public policy.

Yet the very political efficacy of private associations set the stage for a confrontation between groups with quite different visions of the relationship between public and private action in behalf of society: on the one hand, proliferating advocacy groups championing social change, and, on the other hand, a rapidly expanding democratic electorate (limited at the time to white males) seeking to maintain the dominance of the state.[25] Often, the argument was framed in terms of the legitimacy of private groups' acting in the political process. Reformers championed a broad sphere of action for private groups in the pursuit of changes in public policy and in the provision of services, while Jacksonian democrats sought to limit the role of private groups to the fulfillment of basic social welfare needs, reserving to government a dominant role in the setting of social policy.

This conflict came to a head in 1854 with Dorothea Dix's ill-fated campaign regarding federal lands and the construction of insane asylums. An inveterate social reformer with an unprecedented track record in achieving policy change for the mentally ill, Dix had managed to gain support in both houses of Congress to use the proceeds from the sale of ten million acres of federal land to build asylums for the insane. President Pierce, however, representing his Jacksonian constituency, rejected any obligation of the national government to provide large-scale social benefits. His veto message declared that "hospitals and other local establishments for the care and cure of every species of human infirmity" were properly provided through private institutions and that there were no constitutional grounds for making "the Federal Government the great almoner of public charity throughout the United States."[26]

Yet this setback for the participation of private associational players in the public arena lasted for only a brief period in American political life. The social tide was clearly flowing in the direction of increasing involvement by private associations in shaping policy and in meeting important public needs. Their role in the Civil War represented a new, more advanced stage in this trend, exemplified in the dramatic achievements of the U.S. Sanitary Commission. While a multitude of private organizations in the antebellum period had served diverse public functions both independently and in collaboration with local governments, the U.S. Sanitary Commission represented a qualitative advancement of public-private collaboration in serving a vital governmental purpose. The commission, headed by men but staffed mostly by women, served as the clearinghouse for donated money, goods, and services in support of Union troops. It marshaled vast public support both in volunteers and in money (over two hundred million dollars in today's dollars) and became the primary supplier of medical care for the Union army. In blending public and private authority in such an effective way on the national stage, the U.S. Sanitary Commission became a project that demonstrated the power of private associations to serve and shape large public purposes.[27]

The post–Civil War period witnessed another wave of enormous growth in voluntary associations that was to last into the early twentieth century. Two equally important but quite distinct factors lay behind this phenomenon: the well-established tradition of "private power" originating in the Federalist movement and the proliferation of voluntary associations fueled by the huge increase in the immigrant population in the latter half of the nineteenth century. Both charitable organizations and the philanthropy that supported them grew at unprecedented rates during this time, including hospitals, schools, fraternal societies, churches, cultural institutions, settlement houses and other organizations designed to aid immigrants, and a wide range of associations that addressed the needs of disadvantaged populations and that championed myriad public causes.[28]

The massive immigration that flowed into the country between 1850 and 1910 (an estimated 24.4 million people, exceeding the total U.S. population of 1850) led to the creation of a vast number of associations and societies dedicated to meeting the economic and cultural needs of those who had been disconnected from the support networks of their homelands but who were not yet established in their new environment.[29] Many of these associations were mutual aid organizations formed by volunteers to provide assistance to members in need, especially the aged, the infirm, orphans, or other dependent groups. They were modeled on the rapidly expanding mutual benefit societies of Europe. Growing out of the older guild and fraternal societies, these mutual aid organizations provided both social insurance and social cohesion in that they met material and cultural needs together. The associations provided burial services, unemployment insurance, health insurance, and aid to widows, along with comradeship, moral education, and group celebrations of life events.[30]

The Freemasons and Odd Fellows became models for the many fraternal orders that proliferated during the golden age for these organizations in the latter half of the nineteenth century.[31] Such associations illustrated both the merits and deficiencies of private groups: They provided social support and solidarity for people who found great strength in mutual aid, but they also exhibited the parochialism and, frequently, racial exclusivity of those who wished to associate with others like themselves. Faced with economic competition from commercial insurance companies and social competition from a burgeoning service-club movement (for example, the Kiwanis and Rotary clubs), the older fraternal organizations began a long-term decline after the peak of their popularity at the turn from the nineteenth to the twentieth century.[32]

Some private organizations, such as the settlement houses founded by Jane Addams to provide education and cultural enrichment to immigrants, combined the characteristics of philanthropic and mutual aid associations. The intent of the founders of and donors to such enterprises was to care for immigrants and to advance their prospects through philanthropy while speeding their assimilation into the fabric of American culture. At the same time, the aim of most immigrants who joined such organizations was to obtain assistance with jobs, education, and mutual support. Addams herself was acutely aware of the delicate balance between the well-meaning if somewhat paternalistic intentions of sponsors of settlement houses and the self-interested but more democratic motivations of recipients of settlement house services.[33] The blending of public and private purposes, dubbed by one historian as "the Progressive oxymoron—direct democracy with scientific administration," in settlement houses was indicative of a new, dual-purpose configuration of the norms of organizational life that arose at the dawn of the Progressive Era.[34]

Civil Society and the American Media

Specific policy decisions taken in the new American nation furthered the expansion of the media in ways that were unprecedented in Europe. Paul Starr describes these decisions as they relate to the growth of civil society: the development of a postal system that subsidized the proliferation of newspapers through artificially low postage rates, the decision not to impose a tax akin to European stamp taxes on newspapers, and the 1792 act protecting the privacy of letters. A dramatic shift in relations between state and society, in comparison with analogous postal systems of the Old World, followed from such decisions: "The institutions that Americans created in the first decades after Independence reflected a new understanding of the political imperatives for information and communication. Old ideas about who should know what no longer made sense: Popular sovereignty implied a change in the cognitive relationship between the state and the people."[35]

Although postage rates rose during the first decades of the nineteenth century, Congress reduced them again in the 1840s as a conscious social policy intended to increase communication.[36] As Starr notes, this positive subsidization of the flow of information was combined with an intentional policy of government restraint:

> [T]he federal government promoted communications in part by desisting from the use of power. It conducted no surveillance of mail, refrained from using the census to maintain information about individuals, and helped to finance and stimulate development of the common schools at the local level, but did not control what the schools taught.[37]

The result was the creation of a system of public communication that became a historically new force in the shaping of civil society. The mutually reinforcing elements of a low-cost, uncensored postal system, the wide dissemination of newspapers and books, the use of the national census to enhance the democratic process (rather than to supervise and control it, as had been the case in Europe), and the establishment of a broad-based public education system that produced the highest literacy rate in the world created an unprecedented flow of information about public affairs and civic matters, both local and national. In addition, as newspapers became increasingly independent through their growing reliance on advertising dollars rather than public subsidies, they gained even greater freedom from government influence. All of this led to the emergence of a new form of media in America, one that viewed itself as promoting the free flow of information through the public realm and as adopting an autonomous and often critical stance toward the government.

The expansion of this new communications system in America had a particular effect on the growth of voluntary associations. Tocqueville had already noted the close relationship between these two sets of institutions in his observation that there is a "necessary connection between public associations and newspapers; newspapers make associations and associations make newspapers."[38] The first arena in which the enormous impact of print was clearly evident was the use of new printing technologies by religious organizations, particularly evangelical Christians.[39]

The mass dissemination of literature was soon adopted by abolitionists and other movements, and rapidly growing, large-scale associations, like Dix's campaign for the mentally ill, were made possible in large part by the circulation of materials that allowed private groups to coalesce around common purposes and causes. Just as the spread of print culture in the form of newspapers and pamphlets had sparked the formation of many civic-minded associations in seventeenth- and eighteenth-century Europe, the unprecedented expansion of the postal system, ever-increasing newspaper circulation, and the newly created (and privately controlled) telegraph and telephone networks in the nineteenth-century United States allowed widely scattered groups with common interests to form coalitions and to influence broader public opinion.

In addition to expanding public forums for the discussion of political and social issues, the proliferation of all forms of media in the second half of the nineteenth century gave voice to the diverse interests and identities of the American people. Coinciding with the waves of immigration into the United States in the late nineteenth century, foreign-language newspapers and magazines grew rapidly to serve every major ethnic group from Lithuanian to Chinese and reached a combined circulation exceeding two million by 1910. As Starr notes, an oppositional press also flourished in this period in the form of "a multitude of anarchist, socialist, and populist publications; no movement, however small, was complete without a journal to establish its identity, propound its ideals, and communicate with its members."[40] Thus, the new mass media strengthened the development of civil society through the expansion of both the size and pluralistic character of the public sphere.

The emergence of new media structures and the rapid growth of education at the grassroots level in America reinforced the growing role of private groups in setting the public agenda. Wider communication networks also fostered greater interaction among groups separated by geography, culture, and social class, leading to an increased exchange of diverse social and political perspectives. This in turn led to a slow and incremental increase in diverse groups' awareness and eventual toleration of one another's perspectives. It was, however, not a linear or untroubled process. Amid the vast diversity of private groups and associations, there were many that were nativist, insular, racist, and explicitly hostile to other groups' beliefs or even to their right to exist.

The intense debates that took place both within the progressive movement and between the progressives and other groups about how to reconcile the assimilation of newcomers with a respect for immigrants' native cultures reflect the halting but steady growth of a widespread ethic of toleration. As long as there remained an underlying commitment to the American principles of individual liberty and equality, groups of all political stripes gradually came to accept one another. In the early twentieth century, a parallel debate played out over First Amendment rights to free expression between private groups such as the Society for the Suppression of Vice, which was committed to defending conservative moral values, and associations of artists, newspapers, and reformers, which campaigned for the acceptance of free expression in cultural and political life. After early setbacks such as the indictment of Margaret Sanger for publishing a series of essays about birth control, both the courts and the executive branch shifted in the 1920s toward a stronger protection of First Amendment rights, culminating in the 1931 U.S. Supreme Court decision in *Near v. Minnesota*, which prevented the state from shutting down a small newspaper that had a reputation for printing slanderously critical articles on local politicians on the grounds that the press could not be censored through "prior restraint."[41]

The next stage in the intertwined development of the media and civil society took place with the appearance of the newest technological innovation, radio. Following the first experimental public broadcasts in 1920, radio quickly spread in a wild profusion of stations and formats with little direct government involvement or even regulation.[42] In 1927 Congress passed a bill giving the recently formed Federal Radio Commission (FRC) control over frequency allocation, geographical location, and hours of operation for radio stations. Still, in comparison with Europe, the most important resources for the development of radio were in private rather than public hands, with a division of stations between commercial companies (including radio manufacturers, department stores, and broadcasting companies) and private, nonprofit organizations (universities, churches, and other groups).

Thus, unlike John Reith, the first General Manager of the British Broadcasting Company, who promoted radio as a means of advancing the morals and education of the British public, Herbert Hoover, first as U.S. Secretary of Commerce and later as U.S. President, viewed the new broadcasting medium in America as best controlled by private and commercial interests and tastes. Despite the fact that radio, due to the scarcity of frequencies, was necessarily subject to more governmental regulation than were newspapers and was therefore more limited in its capacity to express diversity and dissent, radio broadcasting was to gain a mass appeal and a direct connection to ordinary citizens' lives heretofore unknown in the media.

It was this immediacy and pervasiveness that enabled radio, and, later on, television and other forms of electronic communication, to transform the public conversation. As radio reached into virtually every household, it carried instantaneous coverage of national and world events, the personalities of the figures involved, and the connectedness of the national community. Franklin Delano Roosevelt's famous "fireside chats" exemplified the power of this intimate medium to create a sense of a large public forum. At the same time, the development of radio in America became increasingly steered by large-scale, commercial forces of homogenization at the expense of smaller, more pluralistic, nonprofit voices. In the three years between 1927 and 1930, nonprofit stations declined by two-thirds, from two hundred to sixty-five.[43] This became emblematic of the evolution of American civil society in the twentieth century—a reflection of the growing tug-of-war that became ever more apparent later in the century between nonprofit ideals and commercial forces.

Indeed, broadcasting was to become a microcosm of the development of civil society in the United States during the early twentieth century. The polarity between the pluralistic interests of local and nonprofit stations and the more general public interests reflected by the centralized networks and governmental regulation expresses the classic tension between individual and communal aims in civil society. The federal regulatory commissions, first the FRC and later the Federal Communications Commission (FCC), acted to some degree as referees in this process, establishing the rules of the competition between private and public interests. Radio broadcasting expanded the public forum for the examination of political and social issues and encouraged the growth of a certain measure of toleration.[44] Over the long term, however, this system tended to prioritize commercial interests driven by market forces that exerted a strong influence over the opinions of individual market participants, despite the supposed responsiveness of the system to public preferences. In the expansion and control of radio broadcasting, we can already discern, early in the twentieth century, the tilt in civil society away from forces that championed the common good and toward those that advanced private interests.

The New Philanthropy

The ancient tradition of philanthropy also began to take on a new character in the late-nineteenth-century United States. As previously discussed, the older tradition of charity had already undergone a gradual transformation into the concept of *scientific philanthropy* by the late 1800s. To a degree, this transformation had been underway since the early eighteenth century, when the use of philanthropic funds began to be widely discussed in terms of an improved efficacy in addressing large-scale social problems such as the growing number of orphans and urban poor.[45] Yet the traditional practice of giving aid directly to an institution, a specific cause, or needy individuals was still the prevailing mode of making donations for social purposes. Typically, such donations were solicited by those who were committed to improving a particular social condition or institution; these donations were generated by those working on behalf of a cause rather than by the initiative of a donor.[46]

Several well-known developments signaled a change in this historical pattern of charitable support. Robert Gross has described the direction of this change through which the traditional, guiding value of compassion gradually began to be replaced by philanthropy designed to achieve specific social results.[47] The successful work of the U.S. Sanitary Commission during the Civil War had demonstrated the ability of charitable efforts to address large-scale social issues using huge sums of money and complex organizational structures. By contrast, the rapid spread of competing charities in the final decades of the nineteenth century generated increasing concern about duplication of effort and poor management. Partly in reaction to this concern, there arose a new emphasis on professionalism, ultimately resulting in the redefinition of employees of charitable organizations as "social workers." In the academy, social work began to be studied systematically under the aegis of the developing social sciences in the spirit of the new scientific age. But by far the most influential force for scientific philanthropy in America was the new attitude to the application of wealth to social problems shown by an unprecedentedly wealthy business elite exemplified by John D. Rockefeller and Andrew Carnegie.

Both Rockefeller and Carnegie had started their careers with very modest means and had accumulated vast fortunes through a combination of hard work, persistence, brilliant (and sometimes ruthless) business dealings, and luck. These two men were infused with a deep sense of obligation to use the wealth they had earned for the benefit of society. But both of these individuals, drawing upon their experiences in the rough-and-tumble world of business, were convinced that they should inject their wealth into society by attacking the causes of social problems, and not just by providing relief to those in need. The assumption was that private wealth was the engine of social change and that this change was to be accomplished through technical means, in keeping with the demonstrated success of the applied sciences and the free market. As Kevin Robbins describes this transition, "[T]he paradigm of socially responsible generosity moves toward stringent premeditation and selectivity in giving. Self-assertion increasingly supplants self-denial as a spring for benevolence."[48] These became the precepts of the scientific philanthropy movement.

Andrew Carnegie's famous 1889 manifesto "Wealth" (later dubbed the "Gospel of Wealth" by others) was the precursor of this new movement. In it he enjoins his fellow holders of great wealth to view themselves as stewards of that wealth and to donate their money wisely to charitable causes during their lives. Carnegie's statement begins with a sweeping indictment of those who fail to act in this manner ("the man who dies thus rich dies disgraced") and proceeds to argue that a "man with a genius for affairs," that is, one who has accumulated a great fortune, is better qualified to invest funds for the improvement of society than is the average, rank-and-file citizen: "[T]he man of wealth thus becom[es] the sole agent and trustee for his poorer brethren, bringing to their service his superior wisdom, experience, and ability to administer—doing for them better than they would or could do for themselves."[49] He concludes by listing a set of desired purposes to which philanthropic funds are best directed: universities, libraries, concert halls, and public parks, among others—a set of institutions the overriding purpose of which is to build community and educate the citizenry.

The "Gospel of Wealth" reveals Carnegie to be a transitional figure, one still focused on building institutions and enhancing community spirit in the traditional mode but also expressing the desire of the new breed of entrepreneurs to prevent problems through early intervention and to shape society with private wealth. Soon the full realization of scientific philanthropy arrived with John D. Rockefeller and a small cadre of other early-twentieth-century philanthropists: Olivia Newton Sage, Julius Rosenwald, Edward Harkness (creator of the Commonwealth Fund), and John D. Rockefeller Jr. This group, who established the first large, general-purpose, private foundations in the United States, shared a faith in the application of scientific approaches, both natural and social, to the solution of societal problems. Moreover, they believed in the efficacy of directing at least a portion of their efforts toward formulation of and influence over public policy. These two factors, the use of social science and an involvement in public policy, were linked by the assumption on the part of scientific philanthropists that their foundations, as high-level actors aided by the insights and powers of science, should use those powers and their monetary resources to solve large-scale social problems that the public would not or could not address on its own.[50]

Adding to the sense of scientifically guided leadership was the new phenomenon of professional staffing. Unlike traditional philanthropies, which were typically directed by their donors, the new foundations were headed by professionals drawn from the academy, the ministry, or the law. These professionals included Henry Pritchett, former president of the Massachusetts Institute of Technology, who became the first head of the Carnegie Foundation for the Advancement of Teaching; Frederick Gates, a Baptist minister who became John D. Rockefeller's chief philanthropic adviser; and Robert DeForest, a lawyer who directed the work of the Russell Sage Foundation. The advisers shared a common commitment to a systematic approach to philanthropy, often serving on one another's boards and frequently creating collaborations between the foundations.

These ambitious forays of foundations into the public policy arena in the first three decades of the twentieth century had decidedly mixed results.

The foundations discovered that their initiatives often had unintended consequences, were met with public and political resistance, or produced studies that merely sat on shelves. Among the questions facing the scientific philanthropists, the most difficult to answer was that of political legitimacy: In a democratic society, by what authority were experts empowered by the resources of private wealth justified in determining the direction of public policy? Fiorello La Guardia, then a young congressman from New York, assailed the Russell Sage Foundation's use of "theories and statistics" to intervene in the public arena, described it as the "evil heart of the Charity Trust," and vowed that he would never allow it "to monopolize charity and monopolize welfare work."[51]

There were many other attacks on the work of private philanthropy as anti-democratic. The most spectacular of these occurred in the context of the congressional response to the application of the Rockefeller Foundation for a federal charter (which was denied in 1913) and the hearings of the United States Commission on Industrial Relations, which was authorized by Congress in 1912 to probe the causes of growing strife in developing American industries. In both cases, the primary target was John D. Rockefeller, who symbolized for many the unchecked use of private fortunes to advance the interests of the wealthy.

Nevertheless, the Rockefeller and Carnegie philanthropies, along with a small group of other foundations of like means and purpose, continued to pursue work in the public policy arena, scoring some marked early successes in determining or influencing the direction of governmental programs. Efforts to spur the legislative or executive branches to improve rural vocational education, parenting methods, the provision of mothers' pensions, juvenile courts, sex education, and public recreational opportunities, which were all supported and usually led by a combination of the Rockefeller Foundation, the Russell Sage Foundation, the Commonwealth Fund, and the Rosenwald Foundation, played a significant part in the expansion of the government's role in promoting public health, education, and welfare. Many of these efforts took unexpected twists and turns, but they represented a general trend toward philanthropic involvement in the public arena. This trend continued through the remainder of the twentieth century, bringing into ever-greater focus the delicate balance between the exercise of freedom by private entities in civil society and their aspirations to achieve their particular visions of the common good.

The Web of American Civil Society

In the early American Republic, ancient notions of the well-being of the community and the rule of law became interwoven with new, Enlightenment-era ideas about individual rights, free expression, toleration, private associational life, and philanthropic activism and led to a new stage in the evolution of civil society. Tocqueville captured the distinctive character of this new social structure in his insightful study of American democracy, in which he examined the interplay between the autonomous actors of private associational life and the political authorities of the new democratic state. His oft-quoted observation, cited in chapter 1, about the capacity of Americans to accomplish through self-organization what Europeans sought from the state, highlights the private side of that interaction.

At the same time, Tocqueville's concern about the limitations of the private pursuit of the public good is also present from the very beginning of analysis of the new American democracy. On the twentieth day after his arrival in the new nation on May 29, 1831, Tocqueville penned in his diary an amazingly insightful first impression of the tension that he was beginning to perceive between private interests and the public good in this new country:

> The principle of the republics of antiquity was to sacrifice private interests
> to the general good. In that sense one could say that they were virtuous. The
> principle of this one seems to be to make private interests harmonize with
> the general interest. A sort of refined and intelligent selfishness seems to
> be the pivot on which the whole machine turns. These people here do not
> trouble themselves to find out whether public virtue is good, but they do
> claim to prove that it is useful. If this latter point is true, as I think it is in
> part, this society can pass as enlightened but not virtuous. But up to what
> extent can the two principles of individual well-being and the general good
> in fact be merged? How far can a conscience, which one might say was
> based on reflection and calculation, master those political passions which
> are not yet born, but which certainly will be born? This is something which
> only the future will show.[52]

In this initial impression, Tocqueville displayed his remarkable prescience about the future course of the American polity. As has been seen, the subsequent unfolding of American history was characterized by an increasing tension between the private and public sides of communal life, whether this tension concerned the assertion of rights, the exercise of free expression, the conduct of associations, the control of the media, or the administration of philanthropy. American civil society has always managed to strike a balance between private and public commitments, maintaining a strong grounding in an ethos of individual liberty while facilitating the pursuit of the common good. Major social accomplishments over the course of American history—the expansion of the press and educational institutions in the first half of the nineteenth century, the reform movements of the second half of that century, the gradual strengthening of free expression, the transformative social movements on behalf of disadvantaged constituencies, the relatively unfettered growth of the modern media, and the recent ability of conservative forces to gain broad acceptance of their vision of individual freedom—testify to the resilience of civil society and its ability to balance public and private forces. The question before us today is, how will this balancing act play out in the twenty-first century?

7 Private and Public Goods in the Twenty-first Century

The seven dimensions of civil society that had evolved through the historical developments described in the preceding chapters—institutional structures of philanthropy, the rule of law, private associations, and a system of free expression; norms of the common good, individual rights, and toleration—continued to shape the distinctive development of civil society in the United States during the twentieth century. These elements both contributed to and were reinforced by key legal and policy choices that defined the character of the early American Republic, notably the Maryland Act of Toleration, the First Amendment, the establishment of the Postal Service, and the Dartmouth College case.

The complex interplay between civil society and government throughout this period blended the norms and institutions of private associational life with a variety of public goals. This process was to play a vital role in addressing fundamental domestic and international challenges that ensued from two world wars, an economic depression, and movements that sought to improve the conditions of workers and the poor, to secure civil rights for African Americans and other minorities, to insure equality for women, and to preserve the natural environment. The institutions and norms of civil society enabled the polity to address these challenges by providing a platform for negotiation between parties with competing social and political values.

As argued in this book, civil society's ability to perform this mediating function is rooted in the delicate balancing of the pursuit of individual interests and the common good. Born in opposition to the growing power of the state, civil society was from the outset infused with an aspiration toward individual freedom and a strong commitment to expanding the rights of freedom of belief, expression, and action. Yet in both theory and practice, it presupposed a corresponding commitment to community, a pursuit of public ends for the benefit of society as a whole. In practical terms, what has sustained this balance over time has been a widely accepted but rarely articulated or acknowledged ethos of the common good that has coursed underground, beneath the wild profusion of pluralistic streams in American culture. Throughout the history of the United States, this underlying commitment has been articulated diversely, through a shifting configuration of religious beliefs and social philosophies.

In the second half of the twentieth century, however, new forces began to reshape the character of civil society. Pent-up economic demand that had produced the post–World War II boom led to an unprecedented wave of consumerism. The media, fueled in part by the technological advances of wartime military research and in part by the flourishing economy, expanded into the new arenas of FM radio, television, and the Internet, becoming omnipresent, increasingly subservient to private commercial interests, and profoundly influential on American culture. Nonprofit organizations and philanthropic foundations entered upon a sustained upward trajectory of growth that quadrupled their numbers and their expenditures in real terms between the mid-1970s and the early years of the twenty-first century. Religious organizations experienced a similar surge of growth, in which evangelical churches promoting personal salvation proliferated, while membership in mainstream Protestant churches that traditionally combined social outreach and personal religiosity steadily declined. Cumulatively, the economic and social forces unleashed by the post–World War II era shared a common characteristic: the advancement of private interests and goals, reflected in patterns of economic behavior, spiritual life, media and entertainment, associational activity, and philanthropic expansion.[1]

Many studies of American attitudes during this period have documented this trend and have made similar observations of a major shift in cultural attitudes. One classic commentary is *Habits of the Heart*, in which Robert Bellah and his coauthors argue that, during the latter half of the twentieth century, the growth of individual self-interest gradually undermined the historic place of civic commitment to the public good as the dominant force in American society. What had been an underlying but largely unspoken assumption in American political and social life—that a bond of common concern for the general interest took precedence over the pursuit of fragmented particular interests—began a long period of decline in the postwar era. The new vision of American society was one of autonomous individuals connected through a commitment to the ethos of freedom and a faith in privatized approaches to social problem solving.[2]

Among the analyses providing compelling empirical evidence for a widespread postwar decline in commitment to communal purposes is Robert Putnam's notable *Bowling Alone: The Collapse and Revival of American Community*. Putnam documents an across-the-board fall during this period in civic commitments and in faith in public institutions. One indicator is the long-term decline in membership in local civic organizations—those community organizations that involve face-to-face participation in civic affairs—at the very time when the nonprofit sector as a whole was experiencing unprecedented growth. Although organizations were proliferating, they tended to lack the older sense of civic commitment and engagement. Putnam documents many other indicators of diminishing connection to communal institutions, especially to those that strengthened civic commitment through political, religious, workplace, and informal social connections.[3]

One of the most significant indicators of diminished community affiliation has been the long-term decline in voting in the United States. There has been a steady drop in participation in presidential elections—from 63 percent in 1960 to 51 percent in 2000 (although the 2008 election countered this trend with almost 57 percent participation).[4] Corresponding to this pattern in voting has been a precipitous decline in trust in government and almost all other public institutions. Between 1966 and 2000, the University of Michigan's "trust index," based on survey questions concerning the amount of trust that people placed in the federal government, declined from 61 percent to 36 percent.[5] All of this, in Putnam's view, adds up to a steady reduction in the nation's stock of "social capital," defined as "connections among individuals—social networks and the norms of reciprocity and trustworthiness that arise from them."[6]

In the late 1990s, Putnam's work generated widespread debate in both academic circles and the popular press over the problem of declining social capital and the strains on "its conceptual cousin," community. While the scope of the present work cannot do justice to the complexities of this debate, including suggestions by a number of critics that new forms of social capital such as online communities might be replacing older forms of participation, most commentators agree with the key conclusion of Putnam:

the current era has witnessed a clear trend of weakening commitment on the part of Americans to communal institutions and to a sense of communal purpose.

Putnam attributes part of the decline in social connectedness to the effects of the mass media in the postwar period, in particular to the isolating quality of television and its encouragement of the passive absorption of information. Several decades prior to Putnam's exploration of social capital, Jürgen Habermas critically analyzed the effect on public life of the increasing privatization of the media during the eighteenth through the twentieth centuries. In *The Structural Transformation of the Public Sphere*, Habermas traces the development of what was arguably the first "public sphere" of political and social deliberation during the Enlightenment to exchanges carried on through the means of public expression: newspapers, magazines, salons, coffeehouses, and clubs. Although limited to middle- and upper-class constituencies, this sphere of communication initially constituted a realm of egalitarian dialogue in the form of "critical debate among private people." From this deliberative process emerged the modern notion of public opinion, in which private views on public matters are aired and mutually debated. At its high point in the eighteenth century, this form of deliberation led to the emergence of a kind of "reasoning public" dedicated to the promotion of "legislation based on *ratio*."[7]

While Habermas acknowledges that this portrayal is an idealized vision of eighteenth-century political life, his analysis captures a central feature of early civil society: private voices combining to form a unified public expression intended to guide public policy. However, he notes that, already at the beginning of the eighteenth century, privatizing elements in this opinion-formation process were becoming increasingly dominant and that the next two centuries witnessed the inexorable growth of the influence of private interests over the public sphere through advertising, publicity campaigns, polling, and media ownership. Not limited to the media, this long-term trend toward the privatization of civil society in general became a dominant feature of the norms and institutions of the modern age.

This powerful trend toward privatization is consistent with the overall pattern we have been tracing. Modern civil society was imprinted from its birth with a pattern of opposition between the emerging claims of individual rights and pluralistic beliefs, on the one hand, and the centralized power of the state, on the other. Its challenge from the outset, in both practice and theory, was to preserve the connectedness of a society that was moving at an accelerating pace in the direction of individual autonomy and pluralism. As discussed in chapter 5, the Scottish moral philosophers were among the first to perceive this trend toward fragmentation and to focus on discovering the social glue that would sustain and strengthen the collectivity while respecting the rights and interests of its autonomous members. Although their responses, ranging from the "invisible hand" to the "bonds of empathy," fell short of solving the core problem, the Scottish philosophers identified the central dynamic that was coming to define civil society.

In many respects, modern theorists, particularly those who view themselves as adherents of philosophical liberalism, are still grappling with the same fundamental issue.[8] Isaiah Berlin articulated the dilemma confronted by liberalism in his classic summation of the incommensurability of human values: "[T]he ends of men are many, and not all of them are in principle compatible with one another." This argument has become known as the fundamental principle of "value pluralism." In Berlin's view, as well as in that of most modern liberal theorists, the accurate description of life in society is that of the coexistence of people who hold a vastly diverse range of worldviews, none of which can be subsumed by the others. Thus, the eighteenth-century challenge of seeking coherence among divergent individual interests is even more complex than earlier theorists thought, not only because the interests themselves diverge, but also because the values on which they are based are intrinsically incommensurable and often incompatible.[9]

If we accept Berlin's claim that value pluralism is intrinsic to the human condition, "that some among the great goods cannot live together," there arises a deep challenge at the heart of modern liberalism. For in a society guided by the scattershot effects of individual interests, the pursuit of common goals is frustrated not only by the empirical constraints of collective action, as will be discussed below, but also by disagreement on the *very definition* of the common good. This is the core of the modern liberal dilemma: with the acceptance of a world in which rival value claims about the nature of the good life coexist, there is also a need, in the case of vital collective interests, to transcend those claims and to arrive at generally accepted ends for the benefit of society as a whole. Yet how is this possible in the face of radical disagreement on the most fundamental ends of the good life?

William Galston, a leading contemporary exponent of liberal pluralism, has written extensively about finding an acceptable balance between a pluralism of potentially conflicting values and society's need for common agreement regarding collective purposes. In Galston's view, strong moral and political reasons argue for the primacy of liberal autonomy in the modern democratic state. He holds that any legitimate polity should be organized on the principle of "maximum feasible accommodation" for the pursuit of diverse goods as individuals and their private associations define them, provided that this accommodation also meets minimum standards of human decency: fundamental evils such as tyranny, starvation, genocide, and wanton cruelty are not acceptable in any social scheme.[10]

At the same time, however, Galston remains aware of the dilemma over the consequences of hyperindividualism, including increasing demands on public resources, a focus on present consumption instead of future needs, the spillover effects of market self-interest, the fragmenting tendencies of the pursuit of identity-group interests, and the declining strength of civic associations—in other words, the forces that lead to the destruction of the commons. This leads liberal theorists to stress a renewal of mutualism and civic education as an antidote to the disintegrative effects of exaggerated individualism and accelerating personal consumption in advanced industrial societies. While advocating minimal intrusion by the state into the life of private associations, these theorists encourage using those associations to develop a stronger sense of civic commitment aimed ultimately at achieving communal purposes.[11]

To counter the centrifugal effects of excessive individualism in the modern polity, one might look first to the political process to resolve the tension between private interests and collective needs. But what if the political process itself is dominated by private interests? This problem is one of the primary reasons why Galston and other democratic theorists consider "the status of civil society [to be] clearly one of the central public concerns of liberal democracy in America at the beginning of the twenty-first century." For them, civil society is the first instance in which public and private values must reach an accommodation.[12]

Another group of theorists, the communitarians, begin from a different analytical standpoint but arrive at a similar conclusion concerning the role of civil society. They reframe the problem. Rather than accepting individual voluntarism and private associational rights as appropriate starting points for understanding life in society, they begin with a consideration of the needs of the community as a whole. Ultimately, however, their response to the challenge of growing privatization resembles that of the liberal theorists. Amitai Etzioni, for example, focuses attention on the failures of both private groups and public bodies to address vital collective needs, such as the well-being of children, public health, and environmental protection, and thus champions the pursuit of "a society that is not merely civil but is good."[13] Others, like Michael Sandel, share the critical assessment of hyperindividualism and unrestricted personal choice and argue for a stronger role for local political decision making and greater governmental regulation of economic life. Sandel notes that "the better kind of politics we need is a politics oriented less to the pursuit of individual self-interest and more to the pursuit of the common good."[14]

This problem identified by both the liberal pluralists and the communitarians lies at the heart of contemporary civil society. Since at least the seventeenth century, civil society's solution to public-private tension was to develop a theoretically untidy and always uneasy working balance between a commitment to the autonomous pursuit of private interests, including privately inspired visions of the public good, and a parallel commitment to the well-being of the community that was expressed and implemented in the public arena. In the face of an increasing emphasis on individual autonomy and a decline in the common good as a central cultural norm, however, modern civil society finds itself moving away from this traditional balance. An advancing sphere of private action has steadily encroached upon communal commitment, leaving few resources to restore the traditional balance.

Two Challenges to the Common Good

Before considering the options available to civil society to address this challenge, it is important to understand the dual nature of the problem. The challenge of achieving the common good in contemporary society can be framed in terms of two distinct dilemmas. One is the problem of *value pluralism*—achieving a shared understanding of the common good in the face of radically different concepts of human ends as defined by diverse community members, as, for example, by rival religious groups. The other is the problem of *collective action*—achieving results for the entire community that are superior to those produced by individuals who share a desire to achieve a common end (for example, security or a clean environment) but who are guided by self-interested behavior.

The first dilemma has been discussed above in terms of Isaiah Berlin's analysis of the central problem of liberal pluralism. As William Galston observes, if the diverse values held in society are both heterogeneous and inharmonious, then "both personal and political life regularly confront us with situations in which every option entails a sacrifice of a genuine good."[15] The attempt to resolve this conundrum leads to a further division within liberal pluralist thought: between those who commend toleration among different groups as a way of creating a modus vivendi allowing conflicting views and cultures to coexist and those who place the highest priority on individual autonomy, even if that requires the paradoxical imposition of liberal values on illiberal groups. Both solutions involve a compromise between the acceptance of radical pluralism and the promotion of some basic level of social coherence.[16]

Civil society's primary response to the pluralist dilemma has been expressed through the norm of toleration. This solution allowed individuals and private associations to advance competing cultural and political visions while relying on an overarching sense of communal purpose to maintain social unity. Toleration has also played a central role in modern American law because, as David Fagelson observes, "the concepts of tolerance and law both draw on common characteristics that enable a community to accommodate differences that citizens do not embrace." A series of federal court decisions (most recently the 6th Circuit Court of Appeals decision in *Mozert v. Hawkins County Board of Education*) has demonstrated an underlying commitment to toleration combined with personal autonomy. As a result, the courts have struggled with the same paradoxical consequence of the commitment to liberal pluralism that troubles the philosophers, namely that "in order to create the circumstances in which tolerance will prevail, the state must shape everyone's identity to be tolerant, if only in the public sphere." This facilitates coexistence but does not advance issues of the common good very far.[17]

Indeed, in an era of increased privatization, liberal pluralists of all stripes are hard pressed to find adequate resources of social coherence. They call for expanded civic education; strengthened norms of civic commitment, toleration, and respect; improved mechanisms of collective decision making; and the inculcation of common civic values in individuals and associations. But their solutions tend to be directed toward large-scale public interventions in such arenas as public education, the political process, and the economic system, rather than toward the structures of civil society itself. The need for additional measures is addressed in the next chapter.

The second fundamental challenge to the pursuit of the common good is the generic problem of collective action. Unlike value pluralism, in which the very definition of collective purpose is a matter of dispute and subject to competition between heterogeneous and inharmonious visions of the good life, the problem of collective action concerns individuals who actually pursue a common goal, the achievement of which is paradoxically frustrated by the self-interested behavior of the actors. This dilemma is succinctly captured in Todd Sandler's phrase: "individual rationality is not sufficient for collective rationality."[18]

The classic description of the conundrum of collective action appears in the evocative imagery of Garrett Hardin's "Tragedy of the Commons." In the "Tragedy," herders who share access to a common pasture engage in rational behavior (as seen from their individual perspectives) that defeats collective purposes. Since it is in each herder's individual interest to maximize personal yield, and a herder with one cow can double his or her income by adding one additional cow (and so on), with only marginal detriment to the common pasture, that herder adds more cows. But since all other herders do likewise, the result is destruction of the commons.[19]

Many variations on this problem have been explored by economists and others using game theory in such classic models as the "Prisoner's Dilemma," in which two prisoners, lacking both communication and trust, produce negative sentencing outcomes for both.[20] Game theory demonstrates that the logic of the pursuit of individual self-interest, in the absence of either supervening rules requiring behavior in the interest of the collectivity or a high level of trust and goodwill, leads to results that are suboptimal for the group and thus, paradoxically and ultimately, suboptimal for the individual. An entire field of inquiry has developed over the past several decades that explores the conditions under which collective failure results from individuals' singularly engaging in self-interested behavior.

Economic theories of *public goods* provide insight into the reverse side of the collective action problem. Unlike private goods that are exchanged on a quid pro quo basis, public goods are both "non-rival" and "non-excludable," that is, public goods can be consumed by one person without detracting from consumption by others and the benefits of public goods cannot easily be withheld from anyone who wishes to enjoy them. Some examples are public-radio signals on the open airwaves, fireworks displays, defense systems, clean air, and advances in scientific knowledge. In each case, there are significant costs involved in providing the public good but no easy way to require individuals to pay for the benefits they receive from it. This leads to the free-rider problem, in which many consumers of such goods do not voluntarily contribute to their provision. The flip side of this problem is public "bads"—situations in which individuals can treat the commons as an economic externality without having to pay (at least in the short term) for the consequences of excessive consumption or damaging acts, as in the case of ocean fisheries, air pollution, or Hardin's pasture.[21]

The problem of collective action is illustrated in instances of market failure—cases in which the market is incapable of providing some good that would benefit the entire public (such as clean water) and therefore requires compensating measures. Adam Smith was actually the first to describe the failures of markets to provide public goods, despite his confidence in the ability of the invisible hand to provide productive results in most cases.[22] But the phenomenon of collective action extends far beyond economic markets into the overall aspirations of society to achieve broadly beneficial purposes for the community as a whole, including the provision of such public goods as security, a just legal system, a livable environment, an educated citizenry, a minimum level of public health, a system of free information exchange, and a functioning democratic political process. These are the central elements of the modern commons that are under increasing pressure from the forces of excessive privatization.

Civil Society's Response

Traditionally, the provision of such public goods has been seen primarily as the province of government. But contemporary political and bureaucratic constraints on government, combined with the growing role of private financial power in the political process, limit government's ability to perform this function adequately. This results in "government failure," the term modern analysts use to describe government's inability to provide important public goods, which parallels market failure in the economic realm.[23]

The modern history of civil society has been in part the story of the response by private groups to market and government failure in the provision of public goods. Such groups are often animated by the pursuit of specific public goods, reflecting their particular (and often competing) visions of the common good. In pursuing their goals, civil society organizations have helped establish and have benefited from the normative and institutional foundations for the growth of liberal democracy, including the institutions of a legal system, a system of free expression, and philanthropy. Thus it is a logical next step to look to civil society for solutions to the contemporary problem of public goods. The challenge to civil society is to address simultaneously the tension between private interests and public goods and the problem of competing public goods.

As Michael Edwards and Simon Zadek point out, civil society organizations have to a degree already accepted this challenge in that they "claim to have established a role for themselves in identifying and lobbying for the increased provision of global public goods, a role governments and business have been unable or unwilling to fulfill."[24] There remains the problem, however, of reconciling the diffuse, oppositional nature of private associational efforts with the common good, whether in local, national, or international contexts. In their efforts to pursue public goods, civil society organizations face inevitable issues of legitimacy, representation, and competition.[25]

The history of the development of the law of the commons is instructive here. The earliest legal establishment of protected public resources that were held in common for public use took place by an act of the state ordered by the Eastern Roman emperor Justinian in the *Codex* of AD 529, which claimed "by the law of nature these things are common to mankind—the air, running water, the sea, and consequently the shores of the sea."[26] The resulting legal doctrine presumed that imperial rulers held public lands and waters in trust for the public. In the modern era, this ancient doctrine of public trust emerged as the province of public authority in the democratic state: lands and other resources were held in trust by the state for the use of all the people. Thus, the doctrine can be championed and enforced by individual citizens through the courts, as in cases brought to uphold a right to protect public resources from privatization.

One classic modern case involving principles of the doctrine of public trust was that of *Audubon Society v. the Los Angeles Department of Water and Power*, decided by the California Supreme Court in 1983. In that case, the private Audubon Society, representing the public's interest in preserving the ecosystem of Mono Lake, opposed the City of Los Angeles's desire to increase the water supply for an urban population. The California court, weighing long-term environmental concerns against current consumption needs, ruled in favor of the Audubon Society. In so doing, the court relied upon the "principle of *jus publicum*—that certain resources are of so common a nature they defy private ownership."[27] These are the resources of the commons that both the market and the government fail to protect. It is left to civil society—often, as in this case, the actions of a private association championing a public good through the legal system—to defend the commons against privatization.

Thus one of the most important tasks confronting contemporary civil society is to strengthen its own capacity to achieve the public side of its mission. This is a prerequisite for addressing the modern dilemma of the commons—channeling private efforts to advocate for common public aims that are unattained or common public resources that are threatened. Yet despite periodic successes of civil society in achieving public goods in particular arenas, the fundamental problem of civil society's relationship to the common good remains a challenge in a modern liberal democracy. The dual problems of value pluralism and collective action remain unsolved. In practical terms, they translate into such questions as: Who defines the public interest? Who is empowered to articulate "the common good"? To engage these questions we need to step back and examine what is needed for civil society itself to reconcile its private and public aims and thereby to solve problems of the commons.

Networks and Their Limits

Gaining prominence in the past decade, one approach that aspires in part to restore civil society's ability to balance the oppositional forces of pluralism and the commons is the growing presence of *networks*. Although networks of all types have existed for a very long time, modern network theory builds upon the dramatic growth of the Internet in recent years and embraces this form of electronically mediated communication as a model for developing socially and politically relevant relationships through interactive processes. Network theory maps the patterns of relationships among individuals as they connect through various forms of communication and social environments, exploring the logic and empirical behavior of those interactions. It has become a particular focus for those interested in grassroots, self-organizing communities, such as informal or nonprofit groups that cluster around specific cultural, social, political, or economic interests.

Some writers such as Howard Rheingold and Noortje Marres argue that networks that are created through the Internet and other modern media enable new forms of cooperation and coordinated behavior, including "smart mobs." These ad hoc groups of individuals are separated in time and space but are able to achieve collectively what traditional political or group processes have been unable to do. For instance, vegetarians from Kansas and the Netherlands have worked together to oppose the production of genetically modified foods.[28]

The potential worldwide significance of networking is illustrated in Zixue Tai's comprehensive analysis of the development of the Internet in Chinese society. Tai provides intriguing insight into the complex relationships between evolving new communication networks and civil society. In exploring the explosive growth of the Internet in China and the simultaneous, rapid emergence of a distinctively Chinese mode of civil society, he argues that

> the quick rise of the Internet as a popular tool of public communication in China has essentially turned Chinese cyberspace into an Habermasian public sphere of the twenty-first century, imperfect as it is—important issues are debated and public opinion gets formed.[29]

The sprouting of a multitude of informal groups of concerned citizens loosely organized via the Internet around issues of common concern and their efficacy in achieving changes in policy suggest that networking is indeed aiding in the development of civil society in China. Tai cites a series of grassroots movements expressing grievances over specific governmental abuses. In his analysis, Tai takes the stance of Castells, Ester and Vinken, and others, who conceive of a new form of civil society taking shape on the Internet that opens up new vistas between cyber life and bricks-and-mortar life. This new form of civil society in turn influences the formation of public opinion and public opinion's impact on public policy. Nevertheless, Tai admits that, despite becoming a "hotbed of collective action" for the pursuit of discrete issues in China, the Internet is limited in its ability to develop a full-fledged civil society in the physical world.[30]

Intriguing as such examples of randomly coordinated group activity are in bringing together previously unconnected individuals over topics of common interest, they fall short of addressing the central dilemma of civil society: bridging the gap between individual interests and public goods. The primary limitation of such networked groups or smart mobs is that they are fundamentally demand driven, that is, like consumers in the market, they cluster around the existing interests of all individual participants. This is a traditional function of private associations (albeit prior to the Internet, on a more limited scale). What is missing is the leap to the level of the common good. Cass Sunstein sums up this challenge in his incisive observation that "there is a great difference between the public interest and what interests the public."[31]

A prominent example of the difficulty network-based collectivities face in moving from particularized interests to the larger public interest is exemplified by the history of the development of what is now a large-scale political force, MoveOn.org. During MoveOn.org's early stages of development in the 1990s, the founders of a partner organization named Generation.net aspired to create a new kind of Web-based political forum in which a cross section of the public from a wide range of partisan viewpoints could convene online and collectively (and more or less neutrally) determine the organization's agenda. That agenda, by then representing tens of thousands or even millions of citizens, was to be transmitted to officeholders. What was not clear was the process to be used to formulate or distill the policy choices that would be presented to the participants.

When Generation.net merged with MoveOn.org in the late 1990s (the two organizations were of approximately equal size), it quickly became clear that the combined entity would not be able to play a neutral, facilitating role, but was to become a fairly typical political organization. In this regard, MoveOn.org was similar to traditional political movements but used the newfound power of the Internet to generate financial and endorsement support for predetermined positions. Although MoveOn.org is in many ways a success story about the creative adaptation of modern technology to the political process, the history of the organization also illustrates the difficulty of making the transition from a network-based process of civic involvement to a process of setting social priorities designed to represent and benefit the community as a whole.[32]

The Task Ahead

Civil society organizations, though guided by their particular visions of the common good, must have the capacity to blend a multiplicity of private agendas into coherent public positions if they are to address contemporary problems of the commons. We therefore return to the central question of civil society's essential function of balancing private and public commitments. In order for civil society to perform this function, it must overcome the dilemmas posed by value pluralism and collective action. In the modern era, this means strengthening civil society's historic commitment to the norm of the common good—a commitment that has experienced a significant decline during the past half century. What this means in practice and what resources civil society has available to accomplish this task are the subjects of the final chapter.

8 Philanthropy, Civil Society, and the Commons

Given the enormous challenges involved in reconciling the pursuit of individual interests with the protection of the commons in the twenty-first century, what resources does society have for balancing the two? Our historical review has highlighted civil society's central role in joining private action to public purposes. It has also pointed to philanthropy, with its commitments of both money and time, as the primary resource that frees civil society from purely market-driven or governmentally dominated behavior. Thus, we might anticipate that philanthropy would be a primary source of support for civil society's engagement with problems of the commons.

Philanthropy's Challenge

Indeed, philanthropy's historic blend of individualism, private resources, and concern for community betterment would seem to offer society's most important asset for combining private and public purposes. Practitioners of contemporary philanthropy, particularly those who serve as professionals and board members of large foundations, do view themselves as involved in the creation or preservation of public goods, whether in healthcare, education, the environment, the arts, or myriad other arenas in which public goods are deficient. But key assumptions in contemporary philanthropy, in regard to both operating style and substantive funding choices, limit the ability of foundations to work effectively through civil society on these problems of the commons.

An important insight into this conundrum is provided by moral philosopher David Sidorsky, who describes the problem of value pluralism as posing the same challenge to contemporary philanthropy as it does to civil society as a whole:

The idea of moral pluralism generates a dilemma for the practice of philanthropy. Characteristically, the practice of philanthropy assumes unity, coherence, or convergence among the diverse virtues and moral aims that it pursues. . . . Historically, this reflects the place of a unifying religious vision of the nature of the good or of a secular conception of a public philosophy which recognized the common good. Even etymologically, the love of mankind suggests a single passion that is directed beneficently to the shared values of mankind.

The theory and practice of contemporary philanthropy is necessarily pluralistic, however, and it reflects the range of decisions by individuals with different interests and values in a pluralist, democratic society. The legitimatized and recognized range of philanthropies in modern societies demonstrates divergent and even conflicting perceptions of the common good or the public interest. . . . [T]he tension and possibility of conflict is apparent. It suggests the formal dilemma: if philanthropic plurality is recognized, then the pursuit of some goals which could negate others is appropriate. Hence, the common good will not be served.[1]

The fundamental opposition that Sidorsky describes—between plurality and the common good—manifests itself, as we have seen, in the broad challenges of collective action and value pluralism that face modern civil society. Philanthropy has the potential to address these challenges. But two particular blind spots in the practice of contemporary philanthropy inhibit its ability to do so: an increasingly instrumentalist bias and philanthropy's difficulty in accounting for the problem of "reflexivity."

The Limits of Scientific (and Strategic) Philanthropy

The first of these blind spots is rooted in an epistemological orientation that has shaped modern American philanthropy since the late nineteenth century. The efforts of the great foundations of the early twentieth century—the foundations created by Andrew Carnegie, John D. Rockefeller, John D. Rockefeller Jr., and Margaret Olivia Sage—were generally guided by a set of assumptions that may be described broadly as the epistemology of applied science.[2] As one historian notes, "A buoyantly optimistic faith that major social problems, like ignorance, poverty, and crime, could be solved characterized these foundations."[3] Their large-scale initiatives not only ushered in the age of scientific philanthropy but also blended science and philanthropy in a particular way, on the model of the successful advances of the then newly emerging science of medicine. Applied to social problem solving, this approach pursued the discovery of causal agents behind negative social patterns, agents with a role akin to that of germs in disease, and then sought their eradication through the application of the proper remedies, equivalent to medical antidotes.[4]

The medical model was applied literally to a number of Rockefeller projects, such as the campaign to eradicate hookworm disease, and metaphorically to many other philanthropic interventions. It was the guiding theory behind the development of the new disciplines of the social sciences. These academic disciplines were incubated in part by rapidly growing philanthropic support for and the application of social scientific findings (as they were understood at the time) to the resolution of the problems of society. A prominent example was the work of a group of ambitious young social scientists at the Laura Spelman Rockefeller Memorial in designing a parent education program based on the newly formulated principles of behavioral psychology that were promulgated throughout the United States in the 1920s. The program did not show significant results and was abandoned in 1930. Many other programs in juvenile justice, recreation, vocational education, public welfare, and other realms of social policy were developed in a similar manner by foundations inspired by a belief in the application of scientific knowledge to society.[5]

The fundamental difficulty with this approach lies in its assumption that the epistemology of philanthropy should aspire to the classical notion of *episteme* (certain theoretical knowledge), which is applied to reality through *techne* (technical intervention), as in the methods of natural science, rather than to the use of *mētis* (practical, local knowledge), which emerges from practical experience and involves the exercise of judgment rather than calculation. Given the socially constituted character and complexity of the subject matter of philanthropy, *mētis* fits the requirements of philanthropic engagement and the evaluation of philanthropic results much better than do *episteme* and *techne*. James Scott's insightful analysis of this problem in his *Seeing Like a State* captures the correspondence of *mētis* to the process of understanding and intervening in society, and Scott's discussion of *mētis* applies as much to the practice of philanthropy as it does to his focus on the limits of "scientifically" guided state action: "[*Mētis*] is the mode of reasoning most appropriate to complex material and social tasks where the uncertainties are so daunting that we must trust our (experienced) intuition and feel our way."[6]

The social problems that philanthropy seeks to address are defined by characteristics that run exactly counter to the scientific vision of prediction and control inherent in *episteme* and *techne*: randomness, innumerable variables, the absence of the conditions of controlled experimentation, and indeterminate time horizons are only the most prominent of these. For example, the vast sums expended by both government and philanthropy in recent decades to improve public education, despite the heavy reliance of these efforts on rigorous metrics of standardized testing scores, student retention rates, and so on, have yielded unimpressive results. The reasons? Too many variables and too much randomness in those variables—cultural, political, economic, and environmental—stand between the input of funding and the output of educational quality. Furthermore, what constitutes "educational quality" is itself a matter of highly subjective judgment. There is little evidence to suggest that philanthropists and government officials have learned much more than that which conventional wisdom has long told us: an inspired administrator or teacher trumps almost all other factors in producing educational success. He or she personifies *mētis*. The same can be said of youth development, community organizing, the care of the aging, the arts, policy advocacy, and most other arenas in which philanthropy is active.

The role of randomness is particularly important in this analysis. The hugely influential role of randomness in human affairs undermines almost all attempts to make reliable predictions in conjunction with large-scale (or even small-scale) social planning. This is not to say that it is useless to employ data when seeking to make informed judgments about the direction of social improvement, only that currently unknown "black swans" will inevitably override attempts to calibrate increments of social change according to carefully constructed theories of social causation.[7]

Although the epistemology of science was not the only guiding force in the philanthropy of the early foundations—both Andrew Carnegie's libraries and Julius Rosenwald's broad program of building schools for African Americans exemplified a more open-ended approach to the application of knowledge to community building—the scientific model has left a strong

imprint on the practice of American philanthropy. While later generations of scholars and practitioners began to understand that social problems are enmeshed in a complex web of multidimensional and interactive
relationships and therefore are not straightforwardly solvable through the
direct application of the techniques of laboratory science, the notion of linear causality has exerted a lasting influence on the thinking of American
foundations.

A second powerful influence that has shaped the development of American philanthropy, the drive for the accountability of private wealth employed in the public arena, has political origins. Already present in the
long-standing argument between the Jeffersonians and the Federalists over
the role of private groups in setting social policy, the democratic impulse to
exert public control over the influence of private power surfaced with fresh
force in the Progressive Era. In the first decade of the twentieth century, this
political movement produced growing pressure for greater governmental
oversight of the expanding activity of large foundations.

John D. Rockefeller Sr. became a particular target of attention regarding
the power of private wealth; his companies' predatory business practices
and repressive responses to labor unrest in the early 1900s led to widespread
suspicion of his philanthropic motives and to a congressionally authorized
investigation of his foundation activities. Frank Walsh, a Kansas City trial
attorney who chaired the congressionally mandated U.S. Commission on
Industrial Relations, portrayed the Rockefeller, Carnegie, and other large
philanthropies as vehicles for the anti-democratic and unaccountable expansion of the power of the wealthy. This has been a recurrent theme in
political life throughout the twentieth century. Congressional committees
of diverse political perspectives have expressed similar concerns across the
decades about inadequate public oversight of private philanthropy, ranging
from conservative suspicion of progressively oriented foundations in the
1950s, to concerns expressed by Democrats about tax evasion by wealthy
donors in the 1960s, to criticism by Republicans of lax financial controls in
the 1990s and early 2000s.[8]

These periodic manifestations of governmental pressure for greater accountability in exchange for operational freedom have led to the increasing
attention paid by foundations to issues of procedural responsiveness. Most
observers agree that the resulting measures that foundations have taken to
demonstrate their openness and responsiveness to society—greater trans-

parency, standardized financial practices, and improved governance—have had generally salutary effects on the field.

But a contemporary version of the accountability question has moved in a different and more problematic direction. There is a growing tendency of both governmental oversight bodies and foundations themselves to interpret accountability not only as procedural responsiveness but also as demonstrated substantive impact on society. What originated as a legitimate public interest in avoiding outright fraud or the misdirection of philanthropic resources toward private benefit has become an unrealistic expectation for philanthropy to yield quid pro quo quanta of social benefits (however these are to be measured) equal to or greater than the costs of tax benefits received.

This skewed reinterpretation of the accountability theme stems in part from a third major influence that has shaped the rise of the modern foundation—the effort to apply the commercial success of the business model to philanthropy. This trend originates in the modern tendency to translate the life of society into the language of the market. This language migrates into philanthropy and is expressed in terms of portions of benefit allocated to financial inputs, providing assurance to donors that their "investments" are producing demonstrable results. While it is not unreasonable to expect that contributions will yield some evidence of beneficial results, the exaggerated emphasis on metrics in the form of substantive accountability is becoming a driving force in the field, creating unrealizable expectations and a distortion of organizational priorities.[9]

Guided by a worldview that asserts the primacy of market-oriented relationships, the business model conceives of philanthropic expenditures as investments in social problem solving. In this view, philanthropic investment is the means, and concrete steps toward social problem solving are the product. This approach, with its emphasis on metrics and deliverables (the "huge push toward measurability," as described by Intel founder and philanthropist Gordon Moore), skews the work of nonprofit organizations through its narrow strictures and highly directive requirements of outcome-oriented funding.[10] The early initiatives of Carnegie and Rockefeller had already begun to introduce this perspective into American philanthropy, but it was only in the late twentieth century that the full conceptual framework of the business model began to gain widespread influence in the field.

The psychology of business investing seeks the highest "bang for the buck" in the allocation of philanthropic funds, resulting in the emphasis on bottom-line outcomes for the purpose of accountability. Particularly in its venture philanthropy version, this model increasingly adds other dimensions borrowed from the for-profit world: an emphasis on managerial efficiency and effectiveness, going to "scale," investor control, and exit strategies patterned on the public buyout. With the imposition of the business model on philanthropy, donors become investors or contractors and nonprofit organizations become contractees, a conceptual transference that I have argued elsewhere has important negative consequences for civil society. Commercial markets are very good at accomplishing their intended purpose of efficiently allocating resources in exchange relationships. They are not very good at solving complex social problems.[11]

The cumulative effect of these forces—the epistemology of scientific control, accountability interpreted as accounting for quantitative value delivered, and an economic emphasis on return on investment—creates powerful momentum to move philanthropy in the direction of highly discrete, instrumental objectives geared toward solving specific social problems. In an era when the efficiency and effectiveness of market forces make their presence felt worldwide (though these forces are subject to negative boom-and-bust cycles), this model has wide appeal, especially to those, including many philanthropists, who have experienced substantial success in the business world. But, as has already been argued, the market is fundamentally flawed in its ability to provide public goods, and its conceptual structure is seriously limited in its capacity to address the vastly complex, multivalent, and interactive problems of human society, which do not lend themselves to linear, demand-driven solutions.[12]

The Problem of Reflexivity

Beyond the limits of instrumentalism and the practical problems of randomness, innumerable variables, and indeterminate time horizons, philanthropy also has to confront a yet deeper conceptual issue: the problem of reflexivity. This is a problem that extends beyond the empirical realm of social prediction and control, going to the very heart of what it means to understand human action and social change.

"Reflexivity" in its contemporary use refers to the interactive nature of social knowledge and action—the fact that the thought and action of actor

A in a social situation affects and is affected by the thought and action of actor B. Reflexivity is a concept that has gained contemporary visibility in part through the work of George Soros, who describes the "two-way street" relationship between thinking and social reality. Soros has pointed out the severe limitations of the overly simplistic market model, which have been especially evident in recent times, in understanding and predicting complex social interactions. A significant portion of his critique (he is a writer with deep roots in market economics but also in programs of social change) derives from his insight into the failure of most economic and social analysis to take into account the fact that social intervention is not unidirectional. Social thinkers and actors who do not adequately comprehend the circular mutability of social information—Soros's two-way feedback mechanism—are doomed to misinterpret social reality and misjudge their attempted interventions in it.[13]

The concept of reflexivity is related to a longer epistemological tradition that has to do with the description and explanation of human action. Beyond human beings' responses to one another's expectations as illustrated in chapter 7 with respect to game theory and the Prisoner's Dilemma, there is a deeper challenge in creating mutual comprehension through the process of intersubjective understanding. A centerpiece of philosophical thought in a wide range of traditions, this exploration has focused recently on an analysis of the way language structures social reality and on critiques of reductionist modes of describing human action that fail to take into account reflexivity or the hermeneutics of describing intentional behavior. For example, the English "ordinary language" philosopher Gilbert Ryle's notion of a "category mistake" critiques the misguided attempt to impose one conceptual framework, such as economic cost-benefit analysis, onto another, such as human action conceived in moral terms. For Ryle, this represents a fundamental conceptual error and thus an error in understanding the world. From a very different Continental tradition, Jürgen Habermas arrives at a similar conclusion in his critique of the distortion of the multivalent and diversely interpreted nature of social reality into the well-managed world of prediction and control, a process that he describes as "colonization of the life-world."[14]

Understanding the reflexive nature of human knowledge as a means of taking into account the intentions and actions of other human beings also has an important democratic dimension. Treating the subject of one's knowledge and action as an equal participant in defining a problem and shaping its potential solution is fundamental to democracy. The democratic process requires not only the right to vote on a given policy choice but also the ability to participate in conceptualizing and shaping what that choice is. Thus, in a democratic polity, taking reflexivity into account is crucial to all attempts to intervene in the public arena, such as in the creation and protection of public goods.[15]

The tendency of philanthropic foundations to place ever more emphasis on narrowly defined funding targets and quantitative assessments propels philanthropy toward the imposition of a conceptual model (the input-output paradigm of market transactions) that fails to do justice to the fundamental complexity of life in society. The market model flows from the requirements of the economic sphere, in which there is a single purpose and a simple, one-dimensional test of success: does it make money or not? There is no equivalent unitary test in the broader social world. To seek to impose one in order to justify dollars invested in solving social problems distorts the very nature of civil society.

What misleads here is the attempt to impose the notion of financial investment expressed in monetary terms on the judgment of social objectives expressed in a range of actions, beliefs, and behaviors. We might imagine two parallel flowcharts, one depicting an increment of dollars as an input (as in a financial investment), followed by a range of mechanisms such as technology, marketing, and production, with an output of a larger increment of dollars earned (as in a profitable business venture). The other flowchart would similarly depict an increment of dollars as an input (as in a philanthropic grant), followed by a range of activities conducted by a nonprofit organization, such as training, services provided, and fund-raising, leading to multiple outputs: youth development, strengthened community, and potential changes in values or policy, among many others.

In business investments, both inputs and outputs are measured in dollars. In nonprofit "investments," the input is also measured in dollars (together with volunteer time and in-kind contributions), but the outcomes include a much wider range of subjectively understood actions, behaviors, and values that are differentially judged by donors, providers, recipients, and the public. Of course, philanthropists can legitimately turn to the market itself in pursuit of social goals, as illustrated by several recent cases of foundation alliances with commercial enterprises, for instance, ThinkMTV

.com, the Clinton Foundation, and the Omidyar Network. But the goals remain plural and complexly subjective. Moreover, it is precisely because market-based, commercial transactions fail to produce or even adequately account for public goods that civil society has developed as an alternative mode of satisfying public needs.

Thus philanthropy finds itself in a conundrum. The most pervasive problems facing society today—deficient provision of such public goods as education, public health, environmental protection, intercultural under-standing, and global security—are problems of the commons which philan-thropy should be most able to engage. Philanthropy can play a special role here, because neither the political process nor the market deals well with the complexity, uncertainty, or long time horizons of such public goods problems. Yet modern philanthropy finds itself limited in its ability to ad-dress just those problems.

The reason lies in the trend noted above: the increasing tendency in phi-lanthropy to pursue narrowly focused, self-directed programs that promise market-like results (increments of measurable outcomes that can be corre-lated with increments of investment) rather than use of a different category of judgment, exemplified by *mētis*, which conceives of social success and failure in terms more appropriate to the complexity and multidimensional-ity of the problems of civil society. If philanthropy can better understand its role in a world characterized by the problems of collective action, value plu-ralism, instrumentalism, and reflexivity, it will have a much better chance of engaging problems of the commons.[16]

I am suggesting that, by approaching their work as *mētis*-guided en-gagement with other players in the social arena rather than as a managed process with product outcomes, foundations will have a better prospect of beginning to resolve the value-laden, reflexive problems of the commons. This holds true for approaches to the full range of social issues addressed by philanthropy—from education to climate change—but it is especially ap-plicable to the basic problem explored in this book: the weakened public dimensions of civil society itself. To this we now turn.

Philanthropy's Role in Strengthening Civil Society

Although they seek to address a very wide range of problems faced by societ-ies throughout the world, philanthropic organizations tend to overlook the more fundamental weaknesses of civil society that can determine the abilities of communities to engage those problems. Simply put, philanthropic foundations pursue solutions to deficiencies in the commons while failing to address the underlying weakness of the civil framework in which problems of the commons might be resolved. Since civil society is the domain in which citizens potentially connect their private interests with a larger sense of public commitment and collective action, this represents a fundamental failure in the practice of philanthropy.

This shortcoming is highlighted by William Galston's catalogue of basic public goods problems that are related to the diminished strength of civil society. In his view, these public goods problems are shared by almost all Western democracies:

> an emerging imbalance between the social promises of the welfare state and the resources that governments can mobilize to meet those promises, an increasing orientation toward present consumption at the expense of investments for future needs; increasing tension between the requirements of national unity and the centrifugal tugs of subnational identity groups based on region, ethnicity or religion; an escalating citizen mistrust of government and established institutions in general; and a weakening of the voluntary associations of civil society that should discharge many of the functions that governments do not.[17]

Galston is in effect indicting the diminished ability of Western civil society itself to perform its vital role of constituting citizens—citizens who are able to overcome the gap between the pursuit of their individual interests and the achievement of public goods.

Such a task—strengthening civil society so that it may address vital public goods problems—deserves a central position on the philanthropic agenda. Admittedly an ambitious undertaking, it is a prerequisite for the achievement of most other philanthropic goals. The preceding analysis of the historical development of and the contemporary challenges to civil society suggests that sustaining the vitality of the seven constitutive elements—philanthropy, the rule of law, private associations, a system of free expression, the common good, individual rights, and tolerance—is essential to maintaining the overall well-being of civil society. Since the elements are mutually reinforcing, a significant weakness in one or more can adversely affect the vitality of civil society as a whole. In accordance with the particular political and cultural environment in which a civil society emerges, this can mean the direction of philanthropic resources to any one or more of these elements in need of targeted support.

In the contemporary United States, recent decades have witnessed the steady erosion of two of the elements of civil society in particular: the normative commitment to the common good and the institutional system of free expression. Although rarely on philanthropy's radar screen, these are appropriate targets for philanthropic focus. In addition to strengthening these constitutive elements, if foundations were seriously to engage this agenda, two further efforts would lend themselves to the overall advancement of civil society: the expansion of civic engagement and the strengthening of the organizational infrastructure of civil society.

Commitment to the common good

The essential balancing norm in the age of the ascendancy of individualism has been, as argued in the description of the rise of civil society, a commitment to a sense of the common good. This vital normative pillar of civil society is under significant stress from the economic and cultural forces of the modern world. It is, of course, easy to become nostalgic about the historical importance of this cultural value in the American experience, which has always competed with the long-standing pursuit of individual interests, as illustrated by Tocqueville's observation in his diary entry noted at the end of chapter 6. From the early emphasis on individual liberty to the modern political rhetoric about freedom as the central defining American value, individualism has been the most prominent theme.

Yet, since the arrival of the earliest settlers, broad agreement on the common good as an aspirational goal has also been a continuing thread in American history. The classic statement of this commitment appeared in John Winthrop's "City upon a Hill" declaration on board the *Arbella* as it approached the Massachusetts Bay Colony in 1630. The sense of community and the goal of solidarity conveyed in Winthrop's words defined the character of the societies established by the earliest American colonists. The ethos of the common good radiated from the common spiritual and practical bonds of the settlers; it was sustained and cultivated in the subsequent course of development of the colonies and the early United States.

This ancient norm of civil society has experienced waves of increasing and decreasing emphasis throughout the course of American history, but a broad pattern of declining commitment to the ethos of the common good has developed since the mid-twentieth century. Robert Putnam's portrayal of a dramatic drop in civic participation and social trust has been the most prominent among many analysts' descriptions of a steadily diminishing set of core values related to communal commitment, civic-mindedness, and concern for the well-being of the commons, accompanied by a corresponding increase in the pursuit of individual ends and competition. This story of a progressively diminishing sense of communal attachment in the post–World War II era in the United States is reinforced by many studies and is supplemented by more recent analysis of the contemporary cultural ethos that leads to the erosion of civic commitment, particularly through the corrosive power of unrestrained markets.[18]

Although analysts differ in their reading of the degree of decline, the fact of a decline in a shared sense of commitment to the common good— "a steady attenuation of everyday cooperation and civic friendship"—is acknowledged by a wide spectrum of social observers.[19] Because of its central role as a defining norm of civil society, the ethos of the common good should thus be a major concern of philanthropy that seeks to build the capacity for collective action. But, as noted above, this concern appears almost nowhere on the radar screen of contemporary philanthropy. If foundations were to begin to pay attention to strengthening social commitment to the common good, how might this effort be translated into action?

A growing body of research on social capital and the provision of public goods suggests that a healthy civil society with a high level of civic commitment is a prerequisite for addressing the kind of "wicked problems" that inhibit the provision of public goods.[20] One avenue for strengthening civic commitment would be to follow the recommendations of Putnam and others for supporting work that builds social capital. Putnam and his colleagues have developed a series of recommendations, described in the Better Together report of the Saguaro Seminar, as steps to help generate new forms of social capital in the United States. These include encouraging businesses to create flexible work hours and to allow civic groups to use their facilities for meetings; establishing incentives for community service; changing educational goals and curricula to mandate service learning, sponsor after-school activities, and encourage the participation of students on public boards and agencies; strengthening religious organizations through funding and partnerships; increasing opportunities for participation in community-based arts activities; and reforming the political system to increase the public's access to civic spaces, expand civic uses of the Internet, and encourage greater consideration of the impact of public policies on family and community connections.[21]

Among these recommendations, one in particular stands out as widely endorsed by scholars and public commentators across the political spectrum: strengthening civic education.[22] William Galston, surveying the most recent research on the relationship between civic education and civic commitment, concludes that there is solid evidence that civic education based on substantive and experiential learning leads to enhanced support for democratic values, tolerance, civic participation, and social trust: "The more knowledge we have of civic affairs, the less we have a sort of generalized mistrust and fear of public life. Ignorance is the father of fear, and knowledge is the mother of trust."[23] This relationship appears to be true whether civic education is provided through schools, voluntary associations, or other modes of adult learning. In all circumstances, the important characteristics of effective civic education appear to be an emphasis on ideals and principles combined with learning in real-life situations that have direct relevance and consequences for the participants.[24] While a few foundations have sponsored research and education projects in this arena, notably the Carnegie Corporation, the Rockefeller Brothers Fund, and The Pew Charitable Trusts, enormous opportunities exist for greater foundation support for civic education.

The civic function of media

The declining quality of media, particularly the deteriorating conditions of communication about news, public affairs, and civic concerns, has been exhaustively described and analyzed.[25] Jürgen Habermas and many others have examined how the forces of privatization continue to erode the public sphere in Western democracies, inhibiting the ability of citizens to communicate with each other about issues affecting the central concerns of the commons. In the increasingly privatized world of the media, segments of the public "mindshare" are bought and sold, and those who control major political and economic resources seek to manage public opinion through polling and advertising. The result is a civic process increasingly controlled by market forces and political strategy.

This development has particularly detrimental consequences for civil society, since civic communication is both a formative influence on citizens' attitudes about public affairs and the primary vehicle for the expression of their preferences. A healthy system of free expression is a vital constitutive element of civil society and one which has been intimately connected to civil society's historical development. A fundamental operating assumption in modern democracies is that citizens arrive freely at opinions in the public forum through open deliberation and determine public policy though periodic elections based on those opinions. With the increasing marketization of the public sphere, elections tend to become "one-day sales." Political managers employ polling, focus groups, and mass-advertising techniques in order to market their candidates and issues, while the vital processes of civil society's interactive communication recede into the background.[26]

Nor is the accelerating trend toward managed communication through the buying and selling of public opinion limited to the commercial marketplace. Governments also place increasing emphasis on using their own agents of spin to influence the public to support desired policy positions. These communications techniques have now been developed and refined to a high level and are spreading worldwide, as illustrated by recent studies of government strategies for shaping public opinion in countries as disparate as China and Germany.[27]

The declining civic role of media worldwide presents foundations with a unique challenge and opportunity. How information is generated, deliberated over, and acted upon in the public arena is vitally important to the health of civil society and the consequent ability of societies to find solutions to problems of public goods. Foundations should allocate significantly greater resources to the improvement of information development and dissemination, transparency, deliberative processes, and central structures of the media throughout the world. Because they stand outside the marketplace and government, philanthropic donors are in fact the only entities with the ability to devote substantial financial resources to these purposes from the perspective of the common good. But the philanthropic world pays dramatically insufficient attention to this cardinal problem of civil society.

Some of the arenas in need of greater philanthropic support are strengthening the practice of professional journalism, transparency of public institutions, analysis and presentation of information about public policy issues, deliberative polling, policy work on the structure of the media, and exploration of new communications vehicles for advancing the knowledge of issues and public deliberation. Several foundations have been notable exceptions to the broader pattern of neglect: the Charles F. Kettering Foundation's support of deliberative processes for communities, the Florence and John Schuman Foundation's work on transparency, the John S. and James L. Knight Foundation's programs to improve journalism, The Pew Charitable Trusts' long-standing support for objective polling on policy issues (although Pew has ended its earlier funding of public journalism), the Benton Foundation's media policy initiatives, the Wallace Alexander Gerbode Foundation's continuing support for documentary film production, and the William and Flora Hewlett Foundation's initiative on international media. In 2009, the Hellman Family Foundation announced a grant of five million dollars for the creation of a hybrid venture involving a university school of journalism, a public television station, and one or more major newspapers to provide regional news coverage and to feed stories to media partners. Yet the total amount of foundation support for this important component of strengthening civil society remains quite modest.[28]

The contemporary challenge facing major newspapers is a particularly stark example of the precarious state of the civic media and of the need for philanthropic intervention. Newspapers not only serve as vital conduits for the dissemination of information about public issues but also foster the journalism that builds a base of knowledge about public policy. Their continued decline poses a dramatic threat to the health of civil society. Many of these major news sources are disappearing or are currently on the verge of bankruptcy. Since the commercial marketplace appears no longer able to sustain newspapers and government sponsorship is inappropriate for obvious reasons, philanthropy would seem the logical source of continued support. Although some proposals have emerged for exploring this option, no significant steps have yet been taken.[29]

The potential and limits of the new media (the Internet, cell phones, iPods, and other means of electronic communication) for building and sustaining civil society are still unclear. If the aspirations of new media optimists begin to be realized, the prospect of the growth of civic communication through the Internet is great not only in the United States but worldwide. A modest investment by foundations in the exploration of the relationship between civil society and the Internet—both the possibilities and the limitations—could create great leverage in the future development of mass communications with a civic purpose.[30]

Civic engagement

Beyond attending to specific constitutive elements of civil society, the field of civic engagement is a third important domain in which both the values and the institutions of civil society can be strengthened. "Civic engagement" is the term commonly used to describe a broad range of phenomena including community involvement, voting, advocacy, voluntarism, and active discussion of public affairs. A healthy democracy both permits and relies on active civic engagement. Its enemies are apathy or even open hostility to involvement in the public arena. As in the case of the weakening commitment to the value of the common good, declining civic engagement is a many-faceted phenomenon that is difficult to identify with precision or to address in a way that yields clearly demonstrable results. Yet this decline poses a major threat to a functioning civil society.

The skills and mores of civic engagement are learned in community service, associational activity, civic education, political campaigning, and other modes of involvement in the civic and political life of society. Putnam, Bellah, Galston, and many others have suggested that the elements of civic engagement, civic education, and social trust can move in either virtuous or vicious circles: In the positive mode, they create mutual reinforcement. In the negative mode, they generate a destructive cycle that undermines civil society. In fact, the decline in civic participation over the past half century is highly correlated with with similar declines in civic education and social trust. Although there is continuing scholarly debate about the nature of and the causal relationships between the trends documented by Putnam and others under the rubric of social capital, steadily declining levels of both political participation and social trust over the last decades of the twentieth century are indisputable.

Many theorists draw a distinction between *political* and *communal* forms of civic engagement, the former having to do with activity specifically related to the state and the political process, and the latter with all other types of civic and community participation. Putnam's concept of social capital suggests that a high level of involvement in communal associations tends to lead to productive political involvement and the development of social trust, along with an ethos of "generalized reciprocity" that is associated with the pursuit of the common good.[31] Others, such as Matthew Crenson and Benjamin Ginsberg, worry that intensive participation in civic organizations and community service may actually become a substitute for political engagement and represent a change in the conception of citizenship, away from organizing for collective action and toward performing individualized public service.[32] Similarly, E. J. Dionne expresses concern about the effects of this trend on the young and worries that it may contain a crucial paradox:

> [T]here exists a powerful impulse, especially among the young, toward service to others and engagement in civic life. But this impulse is accompanied by a profound mistrust of the nation's political institutions and a national ethic that . . . pushes individuals (particularly the young) toward individual achievement, often at the expense of community engagement.[33]

A 2004 study of all forms of engagement across the generations indicates that such concerns about a shift of the young away from political involvement may be well founded. The authors found that, while the "DotNet" (ages 15–28) and "GenX" (ages 29–40) generations tend to show communal involvement at levels at least equivalent to those of older groups of Americans, their *political* involvement is drastically lower. This holds true even when the younger groups are compared with the past behavior of older groups when the latter were in their younger years. The authors conclude that "we may be witnessing a subtle but important shift in citizenship, away from a focus on government and elections as the mechanisms for determining the public good and toward alternative avenues such as the private sector and the nongovernmental public sector," and they warn that "the implications of this shift . . . are ominous."[34]

Some analysts see a possible counter to this trend in the rapidly rising participation, especially by young people, in virtual communities, many of which involve discussion of and action on civic topics. MoveOn.org is a prime example of this form of civic involvement; the hugely popular practices of blogging and the civic use of social media are others. Internet-mediated communication shows great promise as a new form of civic engagement for the millennial generation.[35] However, a number of researchers who have looked carefully at the relationship between electronically mediated communication and political participation are less sanguine about prospects for the future. Norman Nie and D. Sunshine Hillygus, for example, have found that time spent on the Internet tends to displace social activities.[36] Whether such decreased face-to-face socializing also leads to decreased political involvement remains an open question, but the trends of declining participation in elections and other forms of overt political activity by youth do not give strong grounds for optimism.

For Crenson and Ginsberg, the trend toward the privatization of the public sphere in the latter half of the twentieth century has gradually transformed the idea of the citizen from that of an active political participant to that of a consumer. The political consumer makes individual, market-like judgments about the delivery of governmental services but decreasingly sees his or her role as joining with others to shape or change government policy.[37]

Active citizenship in a democracy requires active civic engagement, which in turn requires access to information about public affairs, the right to join in collective action, and a commitment to achieving one's interpretation of the common good. What is called for, according to Cliff Zukin and his colleagues, is a "conscious, collective, and systematic effort to provide young Americans with the motivation, skills, and opportunities to participate in politics [to avoid] a slow but steady exodus from this realm of the public sphere."[38] Foundations can support the expansion of civic engagement in many ways: directly, through programs that draw people into public decision-making processes such as deliberative polling, public forums, community organizing, volunteerism, and community service; and indirectly, through support of improved media and civic education.[39]

Organizational infrastructure of civil society

One generic dimension of activity in the field of civil society is commonly overlooked even by those philanthropic foundations that are interested in the general health of the nonprofit sector: organizational work that supports and promotes the essential processes and structures of civil society itself. This the work carried out by the membership, research, and advocacy institutions that create the knowledge base for understanding civil society and champion its development worldwide.

The recent dramatic growth in the size and importance of civil society throughout the world has not been accompanied by a corresponding expansion of organizations dedicated to generating knowledge and support for civil society as a field of inquiry and action.[40] Compared to the support structures focused on the business and government sectors, organizational activity dedicated to analyzing and building civil society remains quite limited. Yet, absent a similar support base to those that exist for business and government, civil society organizations have a vital need for such information and advocacy.

Among the most prominent organizations that represent civil society are Independent Sector in the United States and CIVICUS internationally. Both have a history of sponsoring research to generate essential information about the field and of creating a broad base of cooperative action among the diverse organizations that populate civil society. Along with similar organizations in many countries, these two entities perform an essential role in increasing public awareness of civil society, advancing the development of its legal structure, generating financial support, and promoting supportive public policy.

The importance of the work of civil society support organizations is illustrated by the CIVICUS *Global Survey of the State of Civil Society* (Volume 2), released in 2008. As the most comprehensive cross-national study yet undertaken of the state of civil society, the Survey uses CIVICUS's Civil Society Index (CSI) to report on the status of civil society in fifty-four nations in the period 2003–2006. Based on consultations with more than seven thousand stakeholders and interviews with twenty-four thousand respondents, the *Survey* assesses the strengths and weaknesses of civil society in major regions of the world, analyzes key factors that affect the well-being of civil society, and recommends steps that private donors and governments can take to improve the health of civil society worldwide.[41]

The study concludes that among the most important factors bearing on the strength of civil society are the vitality of a civil society's institutional infrastructure and the level of social trust. Both are consistent with the themes developed here—that strengthening the constitutive elements of civil society, particularly those related to the development of common civic commitment and robust public communication, as well as the infrastructure of civil society, are critically important in determining how well civil society can perform its vital function of generating civic collaboration in the pursuit of public goods.

Funders interested in the well-being of civil society, either nationally or internationally, thus ought to consider supporting civil society infrastructure organizations—membership organizations, research and policy institutes, and publications (print and electronic)—that direct their efforts toward strengthening civil society in specific geographic areas or around the globe. A comprehensive approach is recommended in a report issued by the Organization for Economic Cooperation and Development:

> Special funds could be set up for strengthening civil society as a whole rather than individual organisations. These (possibly multi-donor) funds would be managed within host countries by representatives of civil society, designated by several associations together. Insights may be drawn from experience of the UNDP and bilaterals (e.g., a Danish fund for democratisation in Albania whose board includes representatives of NGOs and government, and independent personalities; an EC-supported fund for NGO empowerment in various East European countries; and CIDAs funds managed in association with governments and civil society).[42]

Conclusion

This book had three tasks: to clarify the concept of civil society in a liberal democracy, to trace the particular course of civil society's historical development in the West, and to examine civil society's role in addressing a primary challenge to the modern world—how to reconcile the vast pluralism of individual interests and aspirations, which exists in all societies, with the pursuit of solutions to problems of public goods, which are vital to the future of humankind.

Clearly, the ultimate vehicle for the attainment of public goods in a democracy is the democratic process itself. But as argued here, modern liberal democracy rests on a platform of civil society. And civil society incorporates elements that both contain the tension between the private and the public and represent the possibility of balancing those polar forces in the search for solutions to public goods problems. Born in the defense of individual agency against the advancing power of the state, civil society has the capacity to create the common ground necessary for connecting individual interests with public needs.

Yet because of powerful contemporary trends toward individualization and marketization, societies throughout the world, particularly those in the West, face increasing challenges in attempting to address large-scale public problems. The result is the drastically inadequate provision of public goods and its converse, the proliferation of global public "bads." Among the many examples of the former are serious global deficiencies of education, food distribution, security, and healthcare.[43] A premier example of the latter is global climate change resulting from the cumulative effect of individual consumption patterns throughout the world. These problems are hugely challenging to current generations and will be even more so to the next, facts that only add to their complexity and encourage free riding on others' efforts to address problems that will have the greatest impact on future generations.[44]

To the degree that nations can establish regulatory frameworks to provide enforceable rules mandating the provision of public goods and limiting free riding, tragedies of the commons can be avoided. But contemporary democratic governments have difficulty achieving this goal, because the modern electoral process operates to some degree like a specialized market. This is central to Crenson and Ginsberg's observation that "Policies of private choice promote responsiveness, but not responsibility. The primary responsibility lies with the customers who are expected to make intelligent choices consistent with their preferences." But as Crenson and Ginsberg also observe, the collective results of such self-interested choices may prove inimical to the larger public interest.[45]

If modern electoral politics is incapable of adequately addressing vital problems of public goods, where else is there to turn? The argument here has been that civil society is the logical vehicle for this task because it represents both sides of the equation—the freedom and creativity of individual action and the conscience of public responsibility. However, to the degree that civil society becomes dominated by models of individual choice and market processes, it increasingly replicates the behavior of the for-profit market, with a consequent reduction in its ability to achieve public goods. To the degree, on the other hand, that it is able to reinvigorate its defining tradition of championing the common good, it will provide an essential means of balancing individual interests in the pursuit of critical public goods.

In the largest sense of their mission, philanthropic donors, both individuals and foundations, should understand that one of their overarching tasks is to address these issues of the commons and that, to do so, they need to dedicate resources to strengthening the fundamental structures of civil society. In the current climate in the United States, this means a renewed emphasis on the agenda that enhances civil society's commitment to the common good and that strengthens the media's ability to serve its public function. The unanswered question is whether such an aspirational goal is in fact achievable in an era when so many social forces are moving in the opposite direction. That remains unclear, but one thing is certain: with so much at stake, the fate of the commons depends on civil society's ability to take on this task.

Notes

Introduction

1. Ludwig Wittgenstein, *Philosophical Investigations: 50th Anniversary Edition*, trans. G. E. M. Anscombe (Oxford: Blackwell Publishing, 2001), sec. 67.
2. Simone Chamber and Will Kymlicka, eds., *Alternative Conceptions of Civil Society* (Princeton, NJ: Princeton University Press, 2002); Sudipta Kaviraj and Sunil Khilnani, *Civil Society: History and Possibilities* (Cambridge: Cambridge University Press, 2001).
3. William Galston, *The Practice of Liberal Pluralism* (Cambridge: Cambridge University Press, 2005), 145.
4. For an insightful analysis of this transformation of politics, see Matthew A. Crenson and Benjamin Ginsberg, *Downsizing Democracy: How America Sidelined Its Citizens and Privatized Its Public* (Baltimore: Johns Hopkins University Press, 2004). George Soros elucidates the sharp distinction between "market values" and "social values" in his advocacy of separating roles: "As market participants, people ought to pursue their individual self interests; as participants in the political process, they ought to be guided by the public interest." *Open Society: Reforming Global Capitalism* (New York: Public Affairs, 2000), 152. Michael Sandel's 2009 Reith Lectures highlight the same theme; he calls for "a politics of the common good [that] invites us to think of ourselves less as consumers, and more as citizens." Michael Sandel, "A New Politics of the Common Good," *The Reith Lectures*, BBC, http://www.bbc.co.uk/programmes/bookt7rg.
5. Robert D. Putnam, *Bowling Alone: The Collapse and Revival of American Community* (New York: Simon and Schuster, 2000), xx.

Chapter 1: The Concept of Civil Society

1. Michael Walzer, *Thick and Thin: Moral Argument at Home and Abroad* (Notre Dame, IN: University of Notre Dame Press, 1994). I explore the interconnectedness of these meanings of "civil society" later in this chapter. Part of the appeal of the term is its generality of meaning—what Michael Walzer describes as the broad resonance of a "thin" concept, the wide attractiveness of which is due to its abstractness and corresponding lack of "thick" reference to concrete circumstances. Despite the variability of the interpretation of its "thick" meanings, however, "civil society" is used with increasing consistency worldwide. A

prominent example of this is its use for designating the broad field encompassing nonprofit and nongovernmental organizations by CIVICUS, the international body representing this sector.

2. Roger Lohmann, *The Commons: New Perspectives on Nonprofit Organizations and Voluntary Action* (San Francisco: Jossey-Bass, 1992). Lohmann advances the notion of subsuming the entire sphere of what is referred to here as civil society, including the nonprofit sector and philanthropy, under the rubric of "the commons." While such an application of the term has interesting theoretical implications (as well as roots in Aristotelian political writings) and relates to my emphasis on the common good as a defining element of civil society, it tends to blur the important distinction I make here between the composite character of civil society, as defined in the following text, and the standard notion of the commons as shared social resources. My argument is that, while civil society is essential to solving the problems of the commons, it is important to distinguish between the two concepts.

3. Charlotte Hess and Elinor Ostrom, "Introduction: An Overview of the Knowledge Commons," in *Understanding Knowledge as a Commons*, ed. Charlotte Hess and Elinor Ostrom (Cambridge, MA: MIT Press, 2007), 3.

4. Garrett Hardin, "The Tragedy of the Commons," *Science* 162 (1968): 1244; Mancur Olson, *The Logic of Collective Action: Public Goods and the Theory of Groups* (New York: Schocken, 1965). There is now an international research association devoted to the study of the commons: http://www.iascp.org.

5. Robert Payton, *Philanthropy: Voluntary Action for the Public Good* (New York: Macmillan, 1988); Kathleen McCarthy, *American Creed: Philanthropy and the Rise of Civil Society, 1700–1865* (Chicago: University of Chicago Press, 2005). See also Robert Payton and Michael Moody, *Understanding Philanthropy: Its Meaning and Mission* (Bloomington: Indiana University Press, 2008); and Peter Halfpenny, "Trust, Charity, and Civil Society," in *Trust and Civil Society*, ed. Fran Tonkiss, Andrew Passey, Natalie Fenton, and Leslie Hems (New York: St. Martin's Press, 2000), 132–50.

6. CIVICUS is an international alliance of organizations "dedicated to strengthening citizen action and civil society throughout the world." (www.civicus. org). Helmut Anheier, "The CIVICUS Civil Society Index: Proposals for Future Directions," in *CIVICUS Global Survey of the State of Civil Society, Volume 2, Comparative Perspectives*, ed. V. Finn Heinrich and Lorenzo Fioramonti (Bloomfield, CT: Kumarian, 2008); Michael Walzer, "The Idea of Civil Society: A Path to Social Reconstruction," *Dissent* 38 (Spring 1991): 293–304; Charles Taylor, "Modes of Civil Society," *Public Culture* 3, no. 1 (1990): 95–118; Amitai Etzioni, "The Capabilities and Limits of Global Civil Society," *Millennium—Journal of International Studies* 33 (2004): 341–53; and Amitai Etzioni, "Law in Civil Society, Good Society, and the Prescriptive State," *Chicago-Kent Law Review* 75 (1999): 355–78.

7. Ralf Dahrendorf, "Threats to Civil Society East and West," *Harper's Magazine* (July 1990): 24–26; and Ralf Dahrendorf, *Reflections on the Revolution in Europe* (New York: Transaction, 2004). See also Adam Seligman's discussion of

the origins of the concept of civil society in natural law theory in Adam Seligman, *The Idea of Civil Society* (Princeton, NJ: Princeton University Press, 1992), 10. See also Gordon A. Christenson, "World Civil Society and the International Rule of Law," *Human Rights Quarterly* 19 (1997): 724–37; and Edward Shils, *The Virtue of Civility: Selected Essays on Liberalism, Tradition, and Civil Society*, ed. Steven Grosby (Indianapolis, IN: Liberty Fund, 1997).

8. Gerhard Luf, "Zivilgesellschaft und staatliches Rechtsmonopol," in *Das Rechtssystem zwischen Staat und Zivilgesellschaft: Zur Rolle gesellschaftlicher Selbstregulierung und vorstaatlicher Schlichtung*, ed. Jürgen Nautz, Emil Brix, and Gerhard Luf (Vienna: Passagen Verlag, 2001), 6062.

9. Lester Salamon and Helmut Anheier, eds., *Global Civil Society: Dimensions of the Nonprofit Sector* (Johns Hopkins University Press, 1999); Michael O'Neill, *Nonprofit Nation: A New Look at the Third America* (San Francisco: Jossey-Bass, 2002); and Brian O'Connell, *Civil Society: The Underpinnings of American Democracy* (Hanover, NH: University Press of New England, 1999).

10. Seligman, *Idea of Civil Society*, 202. See also John Keane, "Despotism and Democracy: The Origins and Development of the Distinction between Civil Society and the State 1750–1850," in *Civil Society and the State*, ed. John Keane (New York: Verso, 1988), 35–71; Ernest Gellner, *Conditions of Liberty: Civil Society and Its Rivals* (London: Hamish Hamilton, 1994); and Ernest Gellner, "The Civil and the Sacred," in *The Tanner Lectures on Human Values* 12 (1991), ed. Grethe B. Peterson (Salt Lake City: University of Utah Press, 1991), 301–49.

11. Jürgen Habermas, T*he Structural Transformation of the Public Sphere: An Inquiry into a Category of Bourgeois Society* (1962), trans. Thomas Burger (Cambridge, MA: MIT Press, 1991); Charles Taylor, "Modes of Civil Society," *Public Culture* 3, no. 1 (1990): 95–118; John Keane, *Civil Society: Old Images, New Visions* (Stanford, CA: Stanford University Press, 1998); and Michael Edwards, *Civil Society* 2nd ed. (Cambridge: Polity Press, 2009).

12. Dominique Colas, *Civil Society and Fanaticism: Conjoined Histories*, trans. Amy Jacobs (Stanford, CA: Stanford University Press, 1997), xxiii; John A. Hall, "In Search of Civil Society," in *Civil Society: Theory, History, Comparison*, ed. John A. Hall (Cambridge, MA: Polity Press, 1995), 1–31; Ernest Gellner, "The Importance of Being Modular," in *Civil Society: Theory, History, Comparison*, 32–55; and Shils, *Virtue of Civility*, 320–55.

13. Edwards, *Civil Society*. This book exemplifies a body of recent work that incorporates a range of conceptual approaches to the study of civil society. Edwards analyzes the concept from three competing theoretical perspectives: civil society as associational life, as normatively conceived "good" society, and as a public sphere in which the public is constituted through deliberation and action. He treats the three perspectives as alternative but potentially complementary views and concludes by suggesting that they might be fused into a set of integrated but still contesting analytical stances to provide multiple perspectives on the core phenomenon of civil society.

14. Anheier, "CIVICUS Civil Society Index," 30. A comprehensive definition that encompasses most of the strands that will be elaborated here is that of Jürgen

Kocka who describes the core of the civil society concept as the "space of societal self-organization existing between the state, market, and private sphere, a realm of associations, circles, networks, and non-governmental organizations (NGOs) that assume and expect it to be a space of public discussion, conflict, and understanding, a sphere of independence of individuals and groups, a realm of dynamic change and innovation and a place for the pursuit of the common good, however differently that may be understood in a pluralistic society" (my translation). "Zivilgesellschaft als historisches Problem und Versprechen," in *Europäische Zivilgesellschaft in Ost und West: Begriff, Geschichte, Chancen*, ed. Manfred Hildermeier, Jürgen Kocka, and Cristoph Conrad (Frankfurt: Campus Verlag, 2000), 21.

15. Compare the description by Fran Tonkiss and Andrew Passey of the role of private associations in civil society that invokes the concepts of "*trust* . . . contract, confidence, law, loyalty, and rights" in "Trust, Voluntary Association and Civil Society," in *Trust and Civil Society*, 32.

16. Robert C. Post and Nancy L. Rosenblum, "Introduction," in *Civil Society and Government*, ed. Nancy L. Rosenblum and Robert C. Post (Princeton, NJ: Princeton University Press, 2002), 16. Philip Nord succinctly states, "An autonomous civil society is judged the sine qua non of democratic government." Philip Nord, "Introduction," in *Civil Society Before Democracy: Lessons from Nineteenth-Century Europe*, ed. Nancy Bermeo and Philip Nord (New York: Rowman and Littlefield, 2000), xiv.

17. James Harrington, "The Commonwealth of Oceana" (1656), in *The Commonwealth of Oceana* and *A System of Politics*, ed. J. G. A. Pocock (Cambridge: Cambridge University Press, 1992), 8.

18. John Locke, "The Second Treatise: An Essay Concerning the True Original, Extent, and End of Civil Government (1679–81)" in *Two Treatises of Government and A Letter Concerning Toleration*, ed. Ian Shapiro (New Haven, CT: Yale University Press, 2003).

19. Fred D. Miller Jr., "Natural Law, Civil Society, and Government," in *Civil Society and Government*, 195.

20. William Galston, *The Practice of Liberal Pluralism* (Cambridge: Cambridge University Press, 2005), 1–2.

21. Ibid.; 4, 122. Galston emphasizes the conditions required for liberal democracy to provide the maximum level of protection for individual expression from "totalizing state power" while maintaining the public's ability to pursue common purposes.

22. Many scholars who write about the constitutive elements of civil society also connect those elements to the effective functioning of liberal democracy. For example, regarding the development of the liberal democratic state, see Galston, *Practice*, on the interaction among the normative elements of individual rights, tolerance, and the common good; Habermas, *Structural Transformation*, on the coevolution of the sphere of free expression with modern democracy; Dahrendorf, *Reflections*, on the importance of the rule of law; Edwards, *Civil Society*, on the nature of private, voluntary associations; and Michael Walzer,

"Socialism and the Gift Relationship," *Dissent* 29, no. 4 (Fall 1982): 431–41, on the role of philanthropy.

23. Galston, *Practice*, 123. Seligman is even more pessimistic in his assessment that "The assumed synthesis of public and private, individual and social concerns and desiderata, upon which the idea of civil society rests, no longer holds." Seligman, *Idea of Civil Society*, 206. Beyond hyperindividualism, other commentators suggest that civil society can be defined in a way that is inimical to the practice of liberal democracy in the sense that it would include "hate groups," that is, those who promote hate, bigotry, or racism and who deny other citizens the status of moral agents deserving of civility. See Simone Chambers and Jeffrey Kopstein, "Bad Civil Society," in *Political Theory* 29, no. 6 (December 2001): 837–65. In the definition offered here, such groups would not be included, because they fail to uphold the defining norm of tolerance.

24. George Soros, *Open Society: Reforming Global Capitalism* (New York: Public Affairs, 2000), xiii.

Chapter 2: Institutional Structures

1. See for example A. R. Hands, *Charities and Social Aid in Greece and Rome* (Ithaca, NY: Cornell University Press, 1968); Kevin C. Robbins, "The Nonprofit Sector in Historical Perspective: Traditions of Philanthropy in the West," in *The Nonprofit Sector: A Research Handbook*, 2nd ed., ed. Walter W. Powell and Richard Steinberg (New Haven, CT: Yale University Press, 2006), 13–31; Richard M. Titmuss, *The Gift Relationship: From Human Blood to Social Policy* (New York: Vintage Books, 1971); and Lewis Hyde, *The Gift: Imagination and the Erotic Life of Property* (New York: Vintage Books, 1979).

2. For a description of the various strategies employed by Greek and Roman donors, often using public bodies as recipients, see Hands, *Charities and Social Aid*, 17–25.

3. Scott Davis, "Philanthropy as a Virtue," in *Giving: Western Ideas of Philanthropy*, ed. J. B. Schneewind (Bloomington: Indiana University Press, 1996), 11–12. John Henderson, *Piety and Charity in Late Medieval Florence* (Chicago: University of Chicago Press, 1994), 241.

4. Timothy Miller describes hospitals as "agents of charity where pilgrims, poor persons, the aged, and those who suffered from disease or accident could find food, shelter, and care" in his *The Birth of the Hospital in the Byzantine Empire* (Baltimore: Johns Hopkins University Press, 1997); 5, 30–49. See also Sheila Sweetinburgh, *The Role of the Hospital in Medieval England: Gift-Giving and the Spiritual Economy* (Dublin: Four Courts Press, 2004), 27; and Guenter B. Risse, *Mending Bodies, Saving Souls: A History of Hospitals* (Oxford: Oxford University Press, 1999).

5. For descriptions of this expansion of philanthropy and of institutions supported by charity, see James Allen Smith and Karsten Borgmann, "Foundations in Europe: The Historical Context," in *Foundations in Europe*, ed. Andreas Schulter (Gütersloh, Germany: Bertelsmann Stiftung, 2001), 3–11; and

Bronislaw Geremek, *Poverty: A History*, trans. Agnieszka Kolakowska (Cambridge, MA: Blackwell Publishers, Inc., 1994), 23–25.

6. For an overview of this process of increasingly secular control of charities, see Smith and Borgmann, "Foundations in Europe," 3–11; and Miri Rubin, *Charity and Community in Medieval Cambridge* (Cambridge: Cambridge University Press, 1987); 96–97, 123–25.

7. John Henderson describes this gradual process of commingling the authority and the funding for aid to the destitute in Florence in *Piety and Charity*, 297–442. See also Suzanne Roberts, "Contexts of Charity in the Middle Ages," in *Giving* (see note 3), 40–42.

8. Frank Rexroth, "Stiftungen und die Frühgeschichte von Policey in spätmittelalterlichen Städten," in *Stiftungen und Stiftungswirklichkeiten: Vom Mittelalter bis zur Gegenwart*, ed. Michael Borgolte (Berlin: Akademie Verlag, 2000), 111–31.

9. Benjamin Scheller, "Der Streit um den Stiftungsvollzug der Vöhlinschen Prädikatur bei St. Martin in Memmingen nach der Reformation (1526–1543)," in *Stiftungen und Stiftungswirklichkeiten*, 258.

10. See Brian Pullan, "Good Government and Christian Charity in Early Modern Italy," in *With Us Always: A History of Private Charity and Public Welfare*, ed. Donald T. Critchlow and Charles H. Parker (Oxford: Rowman and Littlefield, 1998), 77–98.

11. For a detailed description of this philanthropic behavior, see Christine Göttler, "Religiöse Stiftungen als Dissimulation? Die Kapellen der portugiesischen Kaufleute in Antwerpen," in *Stiftungen und Stiftungswirklichkeiten*, 279–305.

12. Rubin, *Charity and Community*, 295.

13. See for example Geremek's discussion of Charles V's Edict of 1531 prescribing specific regulations for the administration of charitable resources in the Netherlands, which he describes as "a clearly articulated programme of secularization of social aid which nevertheless takes care to provide the clergy with a well-defined role in the reforms. . . ." Geremek, *Poverty*, 146.

14. For a description of how August Francke created the Halle Orphanage on the Dutch model, see Jo Spaans, "Early Modern Orphanages between Civic Pride and Social Discipline: Francke's Use of Dutch Models," in *Waisenhäuser in der Frühen Neuzeit*, Halleschen Forschungen 10, ed. Udo Sträter and Josef N. Neumann (Tübingen: Max Niemeyer Verlag, 2003), 183–96.

15. The 1601 Statute was actually the end product of a developmental process that unfolded through the previous century, when earlier statutes were passed relating to care of the poor and charitable endowments. For a description of this transformation, see W. K. Jordan, *Philanthropy in England 1489–1660: A Study in the Changing Pattern of English Social Aspirations* (New York: Russell Sage Foundation, 1959), 114–22.

16. Jordan notes that the charitable impulse was still encouraged and articulated largely through religious sources but that it became directed primarily to social causes, especially the problem of poverty: "Quietly, steadily, and irresistibly a profoundly important metamorphosis in men's aspirations had occurred

which led them to devote their energies and their substance to the creation of new institutions having as their concern the fate of men in this world." Ibid., 297.

17. Most of Jordan's work is dedicated to documenting "the immensity of the achievement which had been wrought in England by private charity" and the process of private charity's secularization. Ibid.; 119, 240.

18. Edward Harris, *Law and Society in Ancient Athens* (Cambridge: Cambridge University Press, 2006). See also Michael Gagarin, *Early Greek Law* (Berkeley: University of California Press, 1989).

19. Brian Tierney, *Religion, Law, and the Growth of Constitutional Thought 1150–1650* (Cambridge: Cambridge University Press, 1982), 11.

20. Francis Sejersted, "Democracy and the Rule of Law: Some Historical Experiences of Contradictions in the Striving for Good Government," in *Constitutionalism and Democracy*, ed. Jon Elster and Rune Slagstad (Cambridge: Cambridge University Press, 1988), 135.

21. Tierney, *Religion, Law, and the Growth*, 106–8.

22. Theorists ranging from Roscoe Pound to Richard Tuck agree on the seminal influence of Grotius in shaping the new legal tradition. See Roscoe Pound, "Grotius in the Science of Law," *American Journal of International Law* 19 (1925): 685–88. Richard Tuck notes: "For Grotius . . . it was as if cultures were Venn diagrams which happened to overlap at a particular, minimal spot . . . it was simply that there were some human needs which were so universal that all societies would have to recognise them in some fashion, and others which were not." "Rights and Pluralism," in *Philosophy in an Age of Pluralism: The Philosophy of Charles Taylor in Question*, ed. James Tully (Cambridge: Cambridge University Press, 1994); 165, see also 159–70. Ross Harrison makes a parallel argument in his *Hobbes, Locke, and Confusion's Masterpiece: An Examination of Seventeenth Century Political Philosophy* (Cambridge: Cambridge University Press, 2003), 136–44.

23. Norberto Bobbio explores Hobbes's complex ideas about the relationships among sovereignty, natural law, and civil law in his *Thomas Hobbes and the Natural Law Tradition*, trans. Daniela Gobetti (Chicago: University of Chicago Press, 1993). See also Johann Sommerville, *Thomas Hobbes: Political Ideas in Historical Context* (New York: St Martin's Press, 1992).

24. The long, evolving contest between Hobbesian notions of law as the product of sovereign edicts and the common law tradition actually began with Hobbes himself, in his debate with the famous common law exponent Sir Edward Coke, in Thomas Hobbes, *A Dialogue between a Philosopher and a Student of the Common Laws of England*, ed. Joseph Cropsey (Chicago: University of Chicago Press, 1971). For a discussion of this debate, see M. M. Goldsmith, "Hobbes on Law," in *The Cambridge Companion to Hobbes*, ed. Tom Sorell (Cambridge: Cambridge University Press, 1996), 289–98.

25. Francis Sejersted, "Democracy and the Rule of Law," 133.

26. The German expressions are *Genossenschaften* and *Gemeinwesen*, respectively. Otto von Gierke, *Community in Historical Perspective*, ed. Antony Black, trans.

Mary Fischer (Cambridge: Cambridge University Press, 1990), originally published as *Das deutsche Genossenschaftsrecht* (1868), vol. 1.

27. Antony Black, *Guild and State: European Political Thought from the Twelfth Century to the Present*, rev. ed. (New Brunswick, NJ: Transaction, 2003), 4.

28. Ibid., 8.

29. Ibid., 27.

30. Johannes Althusius, *Systematic Analysis of Politics* (1603), introduction by C. J. Friedrich (Cambridge, MA: Harvard University Press, 1932).

31. Black, *Guild and State*, 132.

32. Margaret C. Jacob, *The Origins of Freemasonry: Facts and Fictions* (Philadelphia: University of Pennsylvania Press, 2006), 47.

33. Roy Porter, *The Creation of the Modern World: The Untold Story of the British Enlightenment* (New York: Norton, 2000), 37.

34. Alexis de Tocqueville, *Democracy in America* (1840), vol. 2, Book 2, chap. 5, ed. Alan Ryan, trans. Francis Bowen (New York: Alfred A. Knopf, Everyman's Library, 1972), 106–7.

35. Ibid., 111.

36. Paul Starr, *The Creation of the Media: Political Origins of Modern Communications* (New York: Basic Books, 2004), 23–46.

37. Craig Harline, *Pamphlets, Printing, and Political Culture in the Early Dutch Republic* (Dordrecht, Netherlands: Martinus Nijhoff, 1987), 22–33.

38. Ahasver Fritsch in *Die ältesten Schriften für und wieder die Zeitung*, ed. K. Kurth (Munich: Brünn, 1944), 117.

39. Brendan Dooley uses this phrase in his "Introduction," in *The Politics of Information in Early Modern Europe*, ed. Brendan Dooley and Sabrina A. Baron, (London: Routledge, 2001), 1. Dooley observes that "by the end of the seventeenth century, newspapers had become the method *par excellence* for conveying political information." "Introduction," 9.

40. For descriptions of the birth of newspapers in European nations in the seventeenth century, see Dooley and Baron, eds., *Politics of Information*.

41. Jürgen Habermas, *The Structural Transformation of the Public Sphere: An Inquiry into a Category of Bourgeois Society*, trans. Thomas Burger (Cambridge, MA: MIT Press, 1991), (originally published in 1962), 12.

Chapter 3: Normative Traditions

1. Guido O. Kirner, "Polis und Gemeinwohl: Zum Gemeinwohlbegriff in Athen vom 6. bis 4. Jahrhundert v. Chr.," in *Gemeinwohl und Gemeinsinn: Historische Semantiken politischer Leitbegriffe*, vol. 1, ed. Herfried Münkler and Harald Bluhm (Berlin: Akademie Verlag, 2001), 31.

2. See the discussion of the early history of this concept in Herfried Münkler and Harald Bluhm, "Einleitung: Gemeinwohl und Gemeinsinn als politisch-soziale Leitbegriffe," in *Gemeinwohl und Gemeinsinn*, vol. 1, 9–30.

3. Ibid., 60.

4. Aristotle, *Politics*, Book 2, chap. 6, in *The Pocket Aristotle*, ed. Justin Kaplan

and W. D. Ross, trans. Benjamin Jowett (New York: Washington Square Press, 1961), 306.

5. For further explication of Aristotle's view of the common good, see Ernst-Wolfgang Böckenförde, "Gemeinwohlvorstellungen bei Klassikern der Rechts- und Staatsphilosophie," in *Gemeinwohl und Gemeinsinn im Recht: Konkretisierung und Realisierung öffentlicher Interessen*, vol. 3, ed. Herfried Münkler and Karsten Fischer (Berlin: Akademie Verlag, 2002), 48–49. I draw upon Böckenförde's interpretation of Cicero and Thomas Aquinas in the following paragraph as well.

6. Antony Black, *Guild and State: European Political Thought from the Twelfth Century to the Present*, rev. ed. (New Brunswick, NJ: Transaction, 2003).

7. Otto Gerhard Oexle, "Konflikt und Konsens: Über gemeinschaftsrelevantes Handeln in der vormodernen Gesellschaft," in *Gemeinwohl und Gemeinsinn*, vol. 1, 71.

8. Walter Ullmann, *Medieval Political Thought* (New York: Peregrine Books, 1976). See also John B. Morrall, *Political Thought in Medieval Times* (New York: Harper, 1962).

9. W. M. Spellman, *European Political Thought 1600–1700* (New York: St. Martin's Press, 1998), 2–3. Spellman, describing the emergence of the modern idea of the state, reminds us that the use of the term "state" in conjunction with organized political authority did not actually occur until Machiavelli.

10. M. S. Kempshall, *The Common Good in Late Medieval Political Thought* (Oxford: Clarendon Press, 1999), 26–27.

11. Francis Oakley, "Christian Obedience and Authority, 1520–1550," in *The Cambridge History of Political Thought 1450–1700*, ed. J. H. Burns (Cambridge: Cambridge University Press, 1991), 172.

12. David Wootton, "Introduction," in *Republicanism, Liberty, and Commercial Society: 1649–1776*, ed. David Wootton (Stanford, CA: Stanford University Press, 1994), 5–19. John Dunn describes a similar duality in the lineage of republican ideas in "The Identity of the Bourgeois Liberal Republic," in *The Invention of the Modern Republic*, ed. Biancamaria Fontana (Cambridge: Cambridge University Press, 1994), 213–15.

13. In fact, the word for both "right" and "law" (for example, the French *droit* and the German *Recht*) grew out of a single common root, the Latin *ius*. Law grounds and justifies the rights claimed by individuals or governments concerning obligations to or protections from other individuals or governments. Law as "right" also incorporates a moral dimension, along with its regulative function, which later becomes the core of the distinct notion of individual rights. Stephen McGrade credits William of Ockham as an originator of the notion of subjective right in "Ockham and the Birth of Individual Rights," in *Authority and Power: Studies on Medieval Law and Government Presented to Walter Ullmann on His Seventieth Birthday*, ed. Brian Tierney and Peter Linehan (Cambridge: Cambridge University Press, 1980), 149–66. See also J. Finnis, *Natural Law and Natural Rights* (Oxford: Oxford University Press, 1980).

14. Annabel S. Brett, *Liberty, Right, and Nature: Individual Rights in Later Scho-

lastic Thought (Cambridge: Cambridge University Press, 2003), 3. Fernando Vázquez de Menchaca, *De successionibus et ultimis voluntatibus*, translated and quoted in Brett, *Liberty, Right, and Nature*, 182.

15. Richard Dagger, "Rights," in *Political Innovation and Conceptual Change*, ed. Terence Ball, James Farr, and Russell L. Hanson (Cambridge: Cambridge University Press, 1989), 298. After commenting upon the dispute between two schools of thought (represented by John Finnis, Michel Villey, and Brian Tierney on the one hand, and Alan Gewirth on the other) about the ultimate origins of the concept of "rights," Dagger sides with the former group in locating the fundamental shift in the fourteenth through sixteenth centuries.

16. Richard Tuck analyzes the construction of this theory in *Philosophy and Government: 1572–1651* (Cambridge: Cambridge University Press, 1993), 154–69.

17. Hugo Grotius, *De iure praedae commentarius I* (1604–08), trans. Gwladys Williams (New York: Oceana, 1964), 21.

18. John Locke, *The Second Treatise: An Essay Concerning the True Original, Extent, and End of Civil Government*, in *Two Treatises of Government and A Letter Concerning Toleration*, ed. Ian Shapiro (1679–81), chap. 8, sec. 95 (New Haven, CT: Yale University Press, 2003), 141–42.

19. Dominique Colas, *Civil Society and Fanaticism: Conjoined Histories*, trans. Amy Jacobs (Stanford, CA: Stanford University Press, 1997), 20–31.

20. Ibid., 110–33; see also 133–34: "Melanchthon could be all the more direct in his critique of Anabaptism and its goal of destroying the Earthly City because unlike Luther, who denied that human beings could play any role in their own salvation, Melanchthon accorded a certain efficacy to human works. Civil society was for him, as for Aristotle, the place where humanity might seek its own good—not the ultimate good, to be sure, but one eminently worthy of respect .... Melanchthon may well be thought of as a sort of synthesis of Erasmus and Luther: though he sought to purify Christianity, he was also a humanist whose regard for the Greek and Latin heritage was inseparable from his defense of the polity and made all fanaticism hateful to him."

21. Michael Walzer, *On Toleration* (New Haven, CT: Yale University Press, 1997); xi–xii, 94. Of course, this very acceptance of coexisting but sometimes clashing worldviews does require the universal acceptance of the underlying norm of toleration itself, which may be anathema to those who believe in a single transcendent theological or other overriding value system. This leads to the conundrum of liberalism discussed in chapter 7.

Chapter 4: The Emergence of Civil Society in the Dutch Republic

1. Although the application of the term "civil society" to this construct did not occur until later in the philosophical and political literature (see chapter 5 for a discussion of the evolution of the modern use of the term), its conceptual structure was already present in the seventeenth-century Dutch Republic.

2. These principles were articulated, for example, in William of Orange's *Apology*, written in 1581 in response to the edict of Philip II of Spain banning William.

See Martin Van Gelderen, *The Political Thought of the Dutch Revolt 1555–1590* (Cambridge: Cambridge University Press, 1992) for a complete discussion of the contractual foundation of the Dutch Republic.

3. For a description of the complex relationships of the stadtholders with the state assemblies and the States General, see ibid.; 20–22, 60.

4. E. H. Kossmann, "Freedom in Seventeenth-Century Dutch Thought and Practice," in *The Anglo-Dutch Moment: Essays on the Glorious Revolution and Its World Impact*, ed. Jonathan I. Israel (Cambridge: Cambridge University Press, 1991), 282–83.

5. Jonathan Israel, "The Intellectual Debate about Toleration in the Dutch Republic," in *The Emergence of Tolerance in the Dutch Republic*, ed. C. Berkvens-Stevelick, Jonathan I. Israel, and G. H. M. Posthumus Meyjes (Leiden, Netherlands: Brill, 1997), 24–25.

6. Marnix van St. Aldegonde announced a specific right to conscience in his *Advice concerning the Dispute in the Dutch Church of London in England*: "Each specific member of the community [had] the freedom to judge the doctrine which is expounded to him." Cited in Van Gelderen, *Political Thought*, 100. Van Gelderen's summary of this position is that "No institution, ecclesiastical or governmental, should attempt to force man's conscience." Ibid.

7. Kossmann, "Freedom in Dutch Thought," 295. Some, like Kossmann, describe the emergence of Dutch toleration as a balance of power between opposing religious groups; others ascribe it to commercial forces and the historical need for coexisting groups to cooperate in common defense of a small country in a vulnerable corner of Europe.

8. J. L. Price, *Culture and Society in the Dutch Republic during the Seventeenth Century* (New York: Charles Scribner's Sons, 1974), 171.

9. Lucien Febvre and Henri-Jean Martin, *The Coming of the Book: The Impact of Printing 1450–1800*, trans. David Gerard (London: Verso, 1990), 196–97.

10. Margaret Spufford, "Literacy, Trade, and Religion in the Commercial Centres of Europe," in *A Miracle Mirrored: The Dutch Republic in European Perspective*, ed. Karel Davids and Jan Lucassen (Cambridge: Cambridge University Press, 1995), 248–63.

11. Israel, "Intellectual Debate about Toleration," in *Emergence of Tolerance*, 563.

12. Craig Harline, *Pamphlets, Printing, and Political Culture in the Early Dutch Republic* (The Hague: Martinus Nijhoff, 1987), 231. Harline also observes that "the very phenomenon of pamphleteering depended on the interrelated conditions of technological capability, the establishment of a book trade to wield that capability efficiently, a general demand for reading materials, and the nature of the Republic's political structure." Ibid., 227.

13. Ibid.; 10, 22.

14. See also Jeremy D. Popkin, "Print Culture in the Netherlands on the Eve of the Revolution," in *The Dutch Republic in the Eighteenth Century: Decline, Enlightenment, and Revolution*, ed. Margaret C. Jacob and Wijnand W. Mijnhardt (Ithaca, NY: Cornell University Press, 1992), 273–91.

15. Israel emphasizes the large extent to which religious differences were enmeshed

in political life: "Church allegiance and confessional rivalry were inextricably entwined in early modern times with political life and statecraft. Religion was such a powerful force in society, culture, and education that it was literally impossible for any political or ideological grouping to remain aloof from the world of confessional strife. In a variety of ways, the Dutch political factions in the Golden Age were linked with confessional streams, and theological tendencies, and it was impossible that it should be otherwise whether in Dutch or any society of the time." Jonathan I. Israel, *The Dutch Republic: Its Rise, Greatness, and Fall 1477–1806* (Oxford: Oxford University Press, 1998), 390.

16. W. M. Spellman provides an extensive analysis of this historical evolution in *European Political Thought 1600–1700* (New York: Palgrave Macmillan, 1999).

17. Biancamaria Fontana, "Introduction: The Invention of the Modern Republic," in *The Invention of the Modern Republic*, ed. Biancamaria Fontana (Cambridge: Cambridge University Press, 1994), 2.

18. J. L. Price, *The Dutch Republic in the Seventeenth Century* (New York: St. Martin's Press, 1998), 62.

19. Hugo Grotius, *The Law of War and Peace*, trans. Francis Willey Kelsey (New York: Oceana, 1964), 1.4.2, originally published as *De Jure Belli ac Pacis, Libri Tres* (1625). Grotius's argument concerning the foundation of natural law is thoroughly explicated by Ross Harrison in *Hobbes, Locke, and Confusion's Masterpiece: An Examination of Seventeenth Century Political Philosophy* (Cambridge: Cambridge University Press, 2003), 151.

20. Uytenhage de Mist, *Apologie*, 58, cited in Israel, *Dutch Republic*, 764.

21. Antony Black, *Guild and State: European Political Thought from the Twelfth Century to the Present*, rev. ed. (New Brunswick, NJ: Transaction, 2003), 137. Black views Althusius's theory as a key link in the transition from medieval to modern political thought.

22. Jo Spaans, "Early Modern Orphanages between Civic Pride and Social Discipline: Francke's Use of Dutch Models," in *Waisenhäuser in der Frühen Neuzeit, Halleschen Forschungen 10*, ed. Udo Sträter and Josef N. Neumann (Tübingen: Max Niemeyer Verlag, 2003), 187.

23. See Anne E. C. McCants, *Civic Charity in a Golden Age: Orphan Care in Early Modern Amsterdam* (Champaign, IL: University of Illinois Press, 1998).

24. Quoted in Van Gelderen, *Political Thought*, 181. See also John Sellars, "Justus Lipsius (1547–1606)," sec. 3, in *Internet Encyclopedia of Philosophy*, http://www.iep.utm.edu/lipsius/.

25. Gerhard Oestreich describes Lipsius's criteria for the ideal conduct of an individual: "The ideal of the individual in the political world, in Lipsius's view, is the citizen who is governed by reason, has an inner sense of responsibility, restrains his feelings, and avoids conflict" (my translation). Gerhard Oestreich, *Strukturprobleme der frühen Neuzeit* (Berlin: Duncker und Humblot, 1980), 315. A community of such individuals could aspire to the realization of a natural community of spirit. Franz Borkenau describes this neostoic philosophy of Lipsius as the first belief system to embrace the spirit of capitalism in *Der*

Übergang vom feudalen zum bürgerlichen Weltbild: Studien zur Geschichte der Philosophie der Manufakturperiode (Paris: Felix Alcan, 1934).

26. Stuart Hampshire, *Spinoza and Spinozism* (Oxford: Oxford University Press, 2005), 197. Hampshire also stresses the centrality of individualism in Spinoza's thought with his observation that "Spinoza anticipates the liberals and radicals of the following centuries in the supreme value which he attaches to individual liberty, and to freedom of thought and religious toleration." Ibid., 148.

27. Benedict de Spinoza, *Ethics*, Part 2, Proposition 36, in *A Spinoza Reader*, ed. and trans. Edwin Curley (Princeton, NJ: Princeton University Press, 1994), 217.

28. Benedict de Spinoza, *Theologico-Political Treatise*, chap. 5, paragraph 2, cited in Etienne Balibar, *Spinoza and Politics* (London: Verso, 1998), 66. Balibar emphasizes Spinoza's innovation in political thought, namely, Spinoza's linking of the well-being of the state to the protection of individual liberty.

29. Ian Hunter, *Rival Enlightenments: Civil and Metaphysical Philosophy in Early Modern Germany* (Cambridge: Cambridge University Press, 2001); 62–66, 156–60.

30. Israel, *Dutch Republic*, 353–54.

31. Ibid., 354–60.

32. Ibid., 354. Almost everywhere else in Europe at that time, welfare functioned under the auspices of a single church, whether Catholic or Protestant. But in the Dutch context, the town governments not only took overall charge of the system and funded many charitable institutions but also decided to what extent and in what ways the public Church and also the other tolerated Churches were to participate. In some towns, the city's almoners, poor chest, and boards of charitable foundations exercised overall control.

33. For a description of the diverse ways in which these conflicting authorities engaged in power struggles in three Dutch cities during the late sixteenth century, see Charles Parker, "Poor Relief and Community in the Early Dutch Republic," in *With Us Always: A History of Private Charity and Public Welfare*, ed. Donald Critchlow and Charles Parker (Oxford: Rowman and Littlefield, 1998), 12–33. Parker contrasts the Dutch situation with other European states: "While most other Protestant states in Europe were trying to standardize the new poor relief program, the cities of Holland were attempting to reconcile the overlapping demands of civic welfare and Protestant charity at the end of the sixteenth century." Ibid., 25.

34. Sir William Temple, *Observations of the United Provinces of the Netherlands* (1673), ed. G. Clark (Oxford: Oxford University Press, 1972), cited in Davids and Lucassen, "Introduction," in *Miracle Mirrored* (see note 10), 1. Davids and Lucassen describe the Dutch as being "both normal and ahead of their time" in their social, secular, religious, and political arrangements.

35. Willem Witteveen, "Inhabiting Legality: How the Dutch Keep Reconstructing Their 'Rechtstaat,'" in *Understanding Dutch Law*, ed. Sanne Taekema (Den Haag: Boom Juridische uitgevers, 2004), 81.

36. James Tracy, "The Acceptance of Religious Disunity in the Body Politic," in *Emergence of Tolerance*, 60.

37. Israel, *Dutch Republic*, 354. Parker, "Poor Relief and Community," 15.

38. A similar point about the distinctiveness of the Dutch Republic is made by Davids and Lucassen in their concluding essay from *A Miracle Mirrored*: "The Dutch Republic thus outstripped its predecessors not merely in the scale and scope of the different developments in the political, cultural and economic spheres examined in this volume, but in the range of combination between these developments as well." Davids and Lucassen, "Conclusion," in *Miracle Mirrored* (see note 10), 441.

39. Israel, *Dutch Republic*, 23. The broad sweep of changes brought about by the Glorious Revolution in Scotland, Ireland, the American colonies, and other countries is chronicled in Israel, ed., *Anglo-Dutch Moment* (see note 4).

40. For extensive analysis of Spinoza's role in articulating the founding principles of liberalism, see Lewis Feuer, *Spinoza and the Rise of Liberalism*, rev. ed. (New York: Transaction, 1987) and Steven Smith, *Spinoza, Liberalism, and the Question of Jewish Identity* (New Haven, CT: Yale University Press, 1998).

Chapter 5: The Enlightenment Legacy

1. Ian Hunter, *Rival Enlightenments: Civil and Metaphysical Philosophy in Early Modern Germany* (Cambridge: Cambridge University Press, 2001), 153. This "uncoupling of political sovereignty from moral truth" stressed the conditions for free expression and social harmony, representing the "civil" side of the Enlightenment.

2. Ibid., 376.

3. Immanuel Kant, "An Answer to the Question: What is Enlightenment?" in *What Is Enlightenment?: Eighteenth-Century Answers and Twentieth-Century Questions*, ed. and trans. James Schmidt (Berkeley: University of California Press, 1996), 58–64. Originally published as "Beantwortung an der Frage: Was ist Aufklärung?" in *Berlinerische Monatschrift* 4 (1784): 481–94. Elisabeth Ellis emphasizes the distinctive character of Kant's formulation of the concept of civil society: "Kant's essay offers an important new conception of the role of civil society and its relationship to the state . . . [it provides] a preliminary solution to the old problem via a new conception of the civil society-state relationship, in which authoritative political judgment is located in the public sphere." "Immanuel Kant's Two Theories of Civil Society," in *Paradoxes in Civil Society: New Perspectives on Modern German and British History*, ed. Frank Trentmann (New York: Berghahn Books, 2003), 123. Modern writers have frequently criticized this rationalist side of the Enlightenment as a futile search for ideal unitary truths in society. For example, Isaiah Berlin characterizes Enlightenment thinking as based on the presumption of "the perfect society in which all true human ends are reconciled." *The Crooked Timber of Humanity: Chapters in the History of Ideas* (New York: Vintage, 1992), 81. Berlin conceives of the Enlightenment as essentially an epistemological undertaking that presupposed

"one single, harmonious body of knowledge," driven by the assumption that "all the sciences and all the faiths, the most fanatical superstitions and the most savage customs, when 'cleansed' of their irrational elements by the advance of civilization, can be harmonized in the final true philosophy which could solve all theoretical and practical problems for all men everywhere for all time." Isaiah Berlin, *The Age of Enlightenment: The Eighteenth Century Philosophers* (New York: Mentor Books, 1956), 28.

4. See Hunter's contrast between the "privatization of salvation or moral regeneration" of the civic Enlightenment and the rationalists' "moral renovation of political governance through the figure of the rational community," Hunter, *Rival Enlightenments*; 161, 376). Charles Taylor points to this conceptual division in early thinking about civil society in his insightful analysis of the divergence between the theoretical positions of Locke and Montesquieu. Taylor highlights this difference as one between the "L-stream," which features individual economic and social members of civil society acting independently of state authority, and the "M-stream," which views members of civil society as acting in a symbiotic relationship with the state, shaping public authority much in the way that Kant understood public opinion to influence state policy. See Charles Taylor, "Modes of Civil Society," *Public Culture* 3, no. 1 (Fall 1990): 95–118.

5. Jonathan Israel, *Radical Enlightenment: Philosophy and the Making of Modernity 1650–1750* (Oxford: Oxford University Press, 2001), 15.

6. Roy Porter, *The Creation of the Modern World: The Untold Story of the British Enlightenment* (New York: Norton, 2000), 48.

7. Jürgen Habermas, *The Structural Transformation of the Public Sphere: An Inquiry into a Category of Bourgeois Society* (1962), trans. Thomas Burger (Cambridge, MA: MIT Press, 1991), 53.

8. Marvin B. Becker, *The Emergence of Civil Society in the Eighteenth Century: A Privileged Moment in the History of England, Scotland, and France* (Bloomington: Indiana University Press, 1994), 69.

9. This theoretical structure is described by many writers as the Enlightenment's contribution to the creation of civil society. See, for example, Becker, *Emergence of Civil Society* and John Keane, ed., *Civil Society and the State* (London: Verso, 1988).

10. Becker, *Emergence of Civil Society*, 27–32.

11. For a description of Shaftsbury's relationship to Locke on this point, see ibid., 42–46.

12. Interestingly, another foil for Mandeville was the theory propounded by Pieter de la Court (noted above in chapter 4) as part of the civic republican tradition in the Dutch Republic. De la Court had used the example of the beehive (in which bees pursue their own pleasure) as a negative contrast to human social behavior. Mandeville turned this example on its head by arguing that the bees' productive social behavior paralleled human action.

13. E. J. Hundert, *The Enlightenment's Fable: Bernard Mandeville and the Discovery of Society* (Cambridge: Cambridge University Press, 1994), 13.

14. Cited by E. J. Hundert in his "Introduction," in *Bernard Mandeville, The Fable of the Bees and Other Writings*, ed. E. J. Hundert (Indianapolis: Hackett Publishing, 1997), xv.

15. Cited in Hundert, *Enlightenment's Fable*, 8.

16. Bernard Mandeville, "An Essay on Charity and Charity Schools" (1723), reprinted in ibid., 109–30.

17. James Buchan, *Crowded with Genius: The Scottish Enlightenment: Edinburgh's Moment of the Mind* (New York: HarperCollins Publishers, 2003), 1. Sir Walter Scott's assessment of the change that occurred in this period appears in his novel *Waverly*: "There is no European nation which, within the course of a half century, or little more, has undergone such a complete change as this kingdom of Scotland." He was particularly referring to the transition from traditional to commercial values. Cited in Becker, *Emergence of Civil Society*, 97.

18. Buchan, *Crowded with Genius*, 1.

19. T. D. Campbell, "Francis Hutcheson: 'Father' of the Scottish Enlightenment," in *The Origins and Nature of the Scottish Enlightenment*, ed. R. H. Campbell and A. S. Skinner (Edinburgh: J. Donald Publishers, 1982), 167–85.

20. For an insightful discussion of Smith's empirical orientation, see Milton L. Myers, *The Soul of Modern Economic Man* (Chicago: University of Chicago Press, 1983), 95–97.

21. Dugwald Stewart, "Account of the Life and Writings of Adam Smith," in *Adam Smith, Essays on Philosophical Subjects*, ed. W. D. Wightman and J. Bryce (Oxford: Oxford University Press, 1980), 314.

22. Norbert Waszek, *The Scottish Enlightenment and Hegel's Account of Civil Society* (Dordrecht, Netherlands: Kluwer Academic Publishers, 1988), 35.

23. David Hume, *A Treatise on Human Nature: Being an Attempt to Introduce the Experimental Method of Reasoning into Moral Subjects* (1739), Part 2, sec. 2, excerpted in David Hume, *Hume's Ethical Writings*, ed. Alasdair MacIntyre (New York: Collier Books, 1965), 217.

24. David Hume, *Political Essays* (1752), ed. K. Haakonssen (Cambridge: Cambridge University Press, 1994), 107.

25. Adam Ferguson, *An Essay on the History of Civil Society* (1767), ed. Fanny Oz-Salzberger (Cambridge: Cambridge University Press, 1995), 117.

26. Ibid., 118.

27. John Locke, *The Second Treatise: An Essay Concerning the True Original, Extent, and End of Civil Government* (1679–81), chap. 7 in *Two Treatises of Government and A Letter Concerning Toleration*, ed. Ian Shapiro (New Haven, CT: Yale University Press, 2003), 133–41.

28. Ferguson, *History of Civil Society*, 218.

29. There is a significant body of literature about the thriving world of associational life in Scotland. Increasingly, during the eighteenth century, Marvin Becker notes, "Voluntary forms of associative life served as a bridge to join professional men, middling tradesmen, and skilled artisans with their social superiors. Again we might refer to the experiences of Scottish cities such as Edinburgh to underline the extent to which clubs, lodges, fraternities, and

academies permitted literate and affluent Scots to confront rapid change in economic and political life with a substantial degree of confidence. . . . The proliferation of associations and institutions hospitable to a civil culture was an indispensable ingredient of the Scottish Enlightenment." Becker, *Emergence of Civil Society*, 75–76.

30. John Keane, "Despotism and Democracy: The Origins and Development of the Distinction between Civil Society and the State 1750–1850," in *Civil Society and the State*, ed. John Keane (New York: Verso, 1988), 44.

31. Waszek, *Scottish Enlightenment*.

32. Ellis, "Immanuel Kant's Two Theories," in *Paradoxes in Civil Society* (see note 3), 111.

33. Cited in Becker, *Emergence of Civil Society*, 103.

34. James Schmidt, "A Paideia for the 'Bürger als Bourgeois': The Concept of 'Civil Society' in Hegel's Political Thought," in *History of Political Thought* 2, no. 3 (Winter 1981): 478. Schmidt traces the development of this theme in Hegel's thought, noting that Hegel broke with convention and invented new uses of the terms "civil society" (*bürgerliche Gesellschaft*) and "citizen" (*Bürger*) in the German sense.

35. Hundert, "Introduction," in Mandeville, *Fable of the Bees* (see note 14), xxviii.

36. See J. B. Schneewind, "Philosophical Ideas of Charity," in *Giving: Western Ideas of Philanthropy*, ed. J. B. Schneewind (Bloomington: Indiana University Press, 1996), 70–72.

37. Waszek, *Scottish Enlightenment*, 146.

38. Waszek repeats Hegel's emphasis of this point, noting that for Hegel this "advanced type of *Rechtspflege* ('administration of justice') that is achieved in civil society [derives from the fact that] for the first time in history, 'a man counts as a man in virtue of his manhood alone, not because he is a Jew, Catholic, Protestant, German, Italian, etc.'" Ibid., 168, citing Georg Wilhelm Friedrich Hegel, *The Philosophy of Right*, sec. 209, in *Hegel's Philosophy of Right*, ed. T. M. Knox (Oxford: Oxford University Press, 1976), 134.

39. William Godwin, *An Enquiry concerning Political Justice* (1793), Book 8 (*Of Property*), chap. 1, in *Godwin's "Political Justice,"* ed. H. S. Salt (London: Swan Sonnenschein, 1890), 46.

40. Renate Wilson, "Philanthropy in Eighteenth-Century Central Europe: Evangelical Reform and Commerce," *Voluntas: International Journal of Voluntary and Nonprofit Organizations* 9, no. 1 (1998): 89. Wilson describes Francke's leadership role in the movement "that transformed traditional church and local charity during the eighteenth century."

41. Donna Andrew, *Philanthropy and Police: London Charity in the Eighteenth Century* (Princeton, NJ: Princeton University Press, 1989).

42. Ibid., 201. Andrew adds that "Charity had ceased being a hobby and became a serious, scientific avocation."

43. Becker, *Emergence of Civil Society*, 59.

44. See in particular Michael Zuckert, *The Natural Rights Republic: Studies in the Foundation of the American Political Tradition* (South Bend, IN: University

of Notre Dame Press, 1996) for a comprehensive discussion of the definitive stamp of the individual rights tradition on the early American polity.

45. Voltaire, *Philosophical Dictionary* (1821), trans. H. I. Woolf, in *The Portable Voltaire*, ed. Ben Ray Redman (New York: Penguin, 1968), 212.

46. Habermas, *Structural Transformation*, 53. See also Luke Goode, *Jürgen Habermas: Democracy and the Public Sphere* (London: Pluto Press, 2005), 24–25.

47. Adam Smith, *The Theory of Moral Sentiments*, 6th ed. (1790), part 6, sec. 2, chap. 2 (Mineola, NY: Dover, 2006), 235.

Chapter 6: Civil Society in America

1. James Madison, "Vices of the Political System of the United States," in *The Writings of James Madison*, ed. Gaillard Hunt (New York: G. Putnam, 1900), 2:364.

2. Madison wrote George Washington advocating that government in a republican polity serve as a "disinterested and dispassionate umpire in disputes between different passions and interests in the states." James Madison, "Letter to George Washington, April 16, 1787," in *Writings of James Madison* (see note 1), 2:346.

3. James Coniff's excellent analysis of Madison's intellectual odyssey details this evolution in his thought. James Coniff, "The Enlightenment and American Political Thought: A Study of the Origins of Madison's Federalist Number 10," *Political Theory* 8, no.3 (August 1980): 381–402.

4. The close identification made between theories of individual rights and the broad underlying ethos of the American colonies is highlighted in Bernard Bailyn's classic *The Ideological Origins of the American Revolution* (Cambridge, MA: Harvard University Press, 1967): "The rights that constitutions existed to protect were understood in the early years of the [pre-revolutionary] period, as we have seen, to be at once the inalienable, indefeasible rights inherent in all people by virtue of their humanity, and the concrete provisions of English law as expressed in statutes, charters, and court decisions; it was assumed that the 'constitution' in its normal workings would specify and protect the inalienable rights of man." Ibid., 184–85.

5. Cited in Richard Johnson, "The Revolution of 1688–9 in the American Colonies," in *The Anglo-Dutch Moment: Essays on the Glorious Revolution and Its World Impact*, ed. Jonathan I. Israel (Cambridge: Cambridge University Press, 1991), 219.

6. Russell Shorto, *The Island at the Center of the World: The Epic Story of Dutch Manhattan and the Forgotten Colony That Shaped America* (New York: Doubleday, 2004), 125. A second colony that became known for its acceptance of religious pluralism and toleration was Maryland. It was Maryland that passed the first official statute sanctioning this principle, the Maryland Act of Toleration of 1649.

7. David Hackett Fischer, *Albion's Seed: Four British Folkways in America* (Oxford: Oxford University Press, 1989), 410.

8. Johnson, "Revolution of 1688–9," in *Anglo-Dutch Moment* (see note 5), 236.

9. Thomas Paine, *Common Sense*, in *The Thomas Paine Reader*, ed. Michael Foot and Isaac Kramnick (London: Penguin, 1987), 66. John Keane emphasizes Paine's importance to this evolution of the civil society idea in "Despotism and Democracy: The Origins and Development of the Distinction between Civil Society and the State 1750–1850," in *Civil Society and the State*, ed. John Keane (New York: Verso, 1988), 44–50. As noted in chapter 5, other figures who delineated the framework of civil society for Keane include Ferguson, Hegel, and Tocqueville.

10. John Keane distills Paine's central message as follows: "The state is deemed a necessary evil and civil society an unqualified good." Ibid., 45. Although the defense of a domain of free action at the intersection of private and public realms was an especially strong theme in American thought, Keane points out that it also began to be widely expressed in European writings, from the French Declaration of the Rights of Man to Thomas Spence's *The Restorer of Society to Its Natural State in a Series of Letters to a Fellow Citizen*.

11. Thomas Paine, *The Rights of Man*, in *Thomas Paine Reader* (see note 9), 220.

12. The long tradition of the theory of rights that culminates in the Bill of Rights is described in chapter 3. For insightful analysis of a specific precursor of it in the English Declaration of Rights of 1689, see Pauline Maier, *American Scripture: Making the Declaration of Independence* (New York: Alfred A. Knopf, 1997).

13. Matthew Tindal, *Reasons Against Restraining the Press* (1704), cited in Leonard Levy, *Emergence of a Free Press* (Oxford: Oxford University Press, 1985), 102. Levy suggests that Tindal may have been the first to claim free speech as a natural right. See also Stephen Lalor, *Matthew Tindal, Freethinker: An Eighteenth-Century Assault on Religion* (London: Continuum, 2006).

14. John Trenchard and Thomas Gordon, "Letter No. 15: Of Freedom of Speech," in *Cato's Letters: Or, Essays on Liberty, Civil and Religious*, 6th ed. (1755), facsimile reprint ed. Leonard Levy (New York: De Capo Press, 1971), 96.

15. Section 25, Pennsylvania Constitution of 1776, in *The Federal and State Constitutions, Colonial Charters, and Other Organic Laws*, ed. Francis Newton Thorpe (Washington, D.C.: Government Printing Office, 1909), 5:3083. Compare Leonard Levy's observation that "Constitutional guarantees did not set people free; they were already free and behaved and spoke accordingly." Levy, *Emergence of a Free Press*, 188.

16. Benjamin Franklin, *Autobiography of Benjamin Franklin*, ed. Frank Woodworth Pine (Middlesex, England: Echo Library, 2007), 115.

17. Peter Dobkin Hall, "An Historical Overview of Philanthropy, Voluntary Associations, and Nonprofit Organizations in the United States, 1600–2000," in *The Nonprofit Sector: A Research Handbook*, 2nd ed., ed. Walter W. Powell and Richard Steinberg (New Haven, CT: Yale University Press, 2006), 35–42.

18. The Federalist-Jeffersonian conflict remained a strong force in American politics through the first quarter of the nineteenth century, playing out in many areas of public life. For example, a major early test pitting the Federalists against the Jeffersonians occurred over the right to free speech guaranteed under the

First Amendment. The passage of the Sedition Act in 1789 and its blatantly political application by the Federalists in attempts to suppress the Republican press led to a series of lawsuits in which the two sides squared off over the right to criticize the government. The issue was only resolved in favor of free speech with Jefferson's presidential election victory, leading to his de facto nullification of the Act. Jefferson was reflecting overwhelming, popular sentiment in favor of free speech. See Paul Starr, *The Creation of the Media: Political Origins of Modern Communications* (New York: Basic Books, 2004), 77–82.

19. For a perceptive analysis of the background and implications of the *Dartmouth College* case, see Mark D. McGarvie, "*The Dartmouth College Case* and the Legal Design of Civil Society," in *Charity, Philanthropy, and Civility in American History*, ed. Lawrence J. Friedman and Mark D. McGarvie (Cambridge: Cambridge University Press, 2003), 91–106.

20. Alexis de Tocqueville, *Democracy in America*, trans. Francis Bowen (New York: Alfred A. Knopf, Everyman's Library, 1972); vol. 1 (1835), chap. 17, 316–23; vol. 2 (1840), Book 4, chap. 1, 287–88. For an insightful discussion of Tocqueville's understanding of the role of social mores in regulating the relationship between the state and free associations, see Henk E. S. Woldring, "State and Civil Society in the Political Philosophy of Alexis de Tocqueville," in *Voluntas: International Journal of Voluntary and Nonprofit Organizations* 9, no. 4 (December 1998): 363–73. See also Sheldon Wolin, *Tocqueville between Two Worlds: The Making of a Political and Theoretical Life* (Princeton, NJ: Princeton University Press, 2001), 192–201.

21. See John Keane's discussion of Tocqueville's and Hegel's views on civil society in Keane, "Despotism and Democracy," 50–66.

22. Ibid.; 61, 65–66. Henk E. S. Woldring analyzes Tocqueville's attempt to balance the essential freedom of associational life against the state's need to preserve public order in "Political Philosophy of Alexis de Tocqueville," 363–73.

23. See Robert H. Bremner, *American Philanthropy*, 2nd ed. (Chicago: University of Chicago Press, 1988).

24. Kathleen McCarthy, *American Creed: Philanthropy and the Rise of American Civil Society* (Chicago: University of Chicago Press, 2005), 184.

25. McCarthy describes this as a conflict between "two very different notions of governance, philanthropy, and political culture," represented most clearly by the opposition between Jacksonian democrats and the increasingly inclusive social movements populated by women, African Americans, and political minorities. McCarthy, *American Creed*, 142.

26. Franklin Pierce, "Veto Message, May 3, 1854," in *A Compilation of the Messages and Papers of the Presidents of the United States, 1789–1897*, ed. J. D. Richardson (Washington, D.C.: United States Congress, 1898), 5:247–56.

27. The role of the U.S. Sanitary Commission is described in depth in McCarthy, *American Creed*, 193–97; Robert Bremner, *The Public Good: Philanthropy and Welfare in the Civil War Era* (New York: Alfred A. Knopf, 1980); Judith Ann Giesberg, *Civil War Sisterhood: The U.S. Sanitary Commission and Women's*

Politics in Transition (Boston: Northeastern University Press, 2000); and Charles J. Stillé, *History of the United States Sanitary Commission: Being the General Report of Its Work During the War of Rebellion* (New York: Hurd and Houghton, 1868).

28. For example, in his discussion of Harvard President Charles Eliot's defense of private institutions, Peter Dobkin Hall states that "northern advocates of private power combined older notions of private responsibility for the public good with social Darwinism to forge a justification of the role of elites and the private institutions they supported." Peter Dobkin Hall, "Historical Perspectives on Nonprofit Organizations in the United States," in *Jossey-Bass Handbook of Nonprofit Leadership and Management*, ed. Robert D. Herman and Associates (San Francisco: Jossey-Bass, 1994), 13. Hall cites Eliot's defense of the university's tax exemption as a precedent-setting legal argument with regard to Eliot's analysis of the benefits that private charitable institutions provide to the public.

29. Michael O'Neill describes the strong relationship between the huge increase in immigrants to the United States in this period and the rapid growth of private associations in his *The Third America: The Emergence of the Nonprofit Sector in the United States* (San Francisco: Jossey-Bass, 1989).

30. A comprehensive view of the growth of such organizations worldwide in the nineteenth and twentieth centuries is provided in Marcel van der Linden, ed., *Social Security Mutualism: The Comparative History of Mutual Benefit Societies* (Bern, Switzerland: Peter Lang AG, 1996).

31. Simon Cordery, "Fraternal Orders in the United States," in *Mutual Benefit Societies* (see note 30), 89.

32. See Mary Ann Clawson, *Constructing Brotherhood: Class, Gender, and Fraternalism* (Princeton, NJ: Princeton University Press, 1989).

33. This complicated relationship is insightfully analyzed by Rivka Shpak Lissak in *Pluralism and Progressives: Hull House and the New Immigrants 1890–1919* (Chicago: University of Chicago Press, 1989). Lissak concludes that the difference in aims between benefactors and immigrants led to a divide between the settlement houses and immigrant community centers that "demonstrated the different goals pursued by them, in both their ethnic composition and cultural orientation. The ultimate objective of the Hull House club policy was the dissolution of the ethnic group through the integration of individuals into the cosmopolitan or ethnically mixed general community; while the ultimate objective of the club policy of immigrant community centers and immigrant settlements was the preservation of ethnicity through the social, ethical segregation of newcomers." Ibid., 131. See also Jean Bethke Elshtain, *Democracy on Trial* (New York: Basic Books, 1995).

34. James Morone, *The Democratic Wish: Popular Participation and the Limits of American Government* (New York: Basic Books, 1990), 126. Many writers of the era captured the ambiguity of the often well-intentioned but controlling acts of private philanthropists and the desire by many of those whom they wished to help to be able to determine the direction of their own lives. For ex-

ample, there is the injunction by Margaret Schlegel in E. M. Forster's *Howard's End* to "Give them a chance. Give them money. Don't dole them out poetry-books and railway-tickets like babies. Give them the wherewithal to buy these things. . . . Money: give Mr. Bast money, and don't bother about his ideals. He'll pick up those for himself." E. M. Forster, *Howard's End* (1921) (New York: Penguin, 1992), 101. George Bernard Shaw's *Major Barbara* strikes a similar note by implicitly endorsing the superiority of a munitions company that provides a living wage and good working conditions over the paternalistic benevolence of private charity administered by the Salvation Army.

35. Starr, *Creation of the Media*; 83, 86, 90. Starr points out that between 1790 and 1835, while the population of the United States increased about fourfold, the number of newpapers increased elevenfold. He also notes that by 1832 newspapers accounted for 95 percent of the weight of postal communications.

36. Jane Kennedy, "Development of Postal Rates: 1845–1955," *Journal of Land Economics* 33, no. 2 (May 1957): 93–112.

37. Starr, *Creation of the Media*, 110.

38. Tocqueville, *Democracy in America*, 2:517–18.

39. David Paul Nord, "The Evangelical Origins of Mass Media in America, 1815–1835," *Journalism Monographs*, no. 88 (1984).

40. Starr, *Creation of the Media*, 264.

41. *Near v. Minnesota*, 283 U.S. 697 (1931).

42. By the mid-1920s, the number of receivers in the U.S. had grown to 2.75 million, thought to be approximately 80 percent of all those in the world, and the U.S. had five times as many broadcast stations as the rest of the world combined. See Louise M. Benjamin, *Freedom of the Air and the Public Interest: First Amendment Rights in Broadcasting to 1935* (Carbondale: University of Illinois Press, 2001), 73–74.

43. Starr, *Creation of the Media*, 352. This sharp decline was the combined result of the lack of a strong financial base of support and of decisions by the Federal Radio Commission to award licenses for the high-power, clear-channel stations to commercial broadcasters and to give low-power licenses to the nonprofit broadcasters.

44. After initial resistance (abetted by the newspapers, who feared competition) to the coverage of public affairs, broadcasting flooded into the arena of public affairs in the early 1930s to such a degree that by 1938 three times as many Americans said they preferred radio news for following the growing European crisis as those who said they preferred newspapers. Although broadcasting countenanced a far more limited range of political and social views than what was expressed in newspapers, American radio featured a much wider spectrum of views than did the European broadcasting systems. One of the best examples of the use of radio to expand the toleration of differences was the series sponsored in the New Deal era by the U.S. Office of Education "Americans All—Immigrants All," which encouraged all Americans to increase their understanding and acceptance of diverse ethnic groups. See Starr, *Creation of the Media*, 363–84.

45. See chapter 5. There was also growing criticism of traditional philanthropy as wasteful (Thoreau's "foolish philanthropists") and narcissistic, as noted by Kevin Robbins in his description of the charge by a number of English parliamentarians that many charitable contributions operated under "pretenses drawn from piety, charity, and a compassion for the poor . . . that only . . . cloak the vanity, pride, and ambition of private men who have got into, or expect to get into the management of what they call a charitable foundation." Quoted in Kevin C. Robbins, "The Nonprofit Sector in Historical Perspective: Traditions of Philanthropy in the West," in *The Nonprofit Sector: A Research Handbook*, 2nd ed. (see note 17), 27.

46. The classic overview of this trend in early American philanthropy is provided by Robert Bremner in *American Philanthropy* (Chicago: University of Chicago Press, 1988). There were of course important exceptions to this pattern, such as the large donation given by James Smithson to establish the Smithsonian Institution and other gifts to individual institutions and causes.

47. Robert A. Gross, "Giving in America: From Charity to Philanthropy," in *Charity, Philanthropy, and Civility* (see note 19), 29–48.

48. Robbins, "Nonprofit Sector in Historical Perspective," 28.

49. Andrew Carnegie, *The "Gospel of Wealth": Essays and Other Writings* (1889), ed. David Nasaw (New York: Penguin, 2006), 10.

50. The definitive analysis of this period of philanthropic evolution is that provided by Judith Sealander, *Private Wealth and Public Life: Foundation Philanthropy and the Reshaping of American Social Policy from the Progressive Era to the New Deal* (Baltimore: Johns Hopkins University Press, 1997). Sealander describes the assumption shared by the new philanthropies: "A buoyantly optimistic faith that major social problems, like ignorance, poverty, and crime, could be solved characterized these foundations. So did a belief that private foundations could play a role in stimulating better decisions in a public arena." Ibid., 15.

51. Cited in ibid., 125.

52. Alexis de Tocqueville, notebook entry, May 29, 1831, cited in *The Tocqueville Reader: A Life in Letters and Politics*, ed. Oliver Zuna and Alan S. Kahan (Oxford: Blackwell Publishers, 2002), 51.

Chapter 7: Private and Public Goods in the Twenty-first Century

1. The gross domestic product of the United States doubled in real terms between 1945 and the early 1960s and more than quintupled by the end of the century (http://www.data360.org), with corresponding increases in consumer spending. For discussion of the structural changes in the media, see Paul Starr, *The Creation of the Media: Political Origins of Modern Communications* (New York: Basic Books, 2004), 385–402; Maxwell E. McCombs and Chaim H. Eyal, "Spending on Mass Media," *Journal of Communication* 30, no. 1 (2006): 153–58; and Lawrence W. Lichty, "Television in America: Success Story," *The Wilson Quarterly* 5, no. 1 (Winter 1981): 53–65. Overviews of the explosive growth of

the nonprofit sector are provided by Lester M. Salamon, *America's Nonprofit Sector: A Primer*, 2nd ed. (New York: The Foundation Center, 1999) and Kennard T. Wing, Thomas H. Pollak, and Amy Blackwood, *The Nonprofit Almanac 2008* (Washington, D.C.: The Urban Institute Press, 2008).

2. Robert N. Bellah, Richard Madsen, William M. Sullivan, Ann Swidler, and Steven M. Tipton, *Habits of the Heart: Individualism and Commitment in American Life*, 3rd ed. (Berkeley: University of California Press, 2007). Other classic analyses of this trend include David Riesman, Nathan Glazer, and Reuel Denney, *The Lonely Crowd: A Study of the Changing American Character*, rev. ed. (New Haven, CT: Yale University Press, 2001); Christopher Lasch, *The Culture of Narcissism: American Life in an Age of Diminishing Expectations*, rev. ed. (New York: Norton, 2001); Richard Sennett, *The Fall of Public Man* (New York: Norton, 1992); Neil Postman, *Amusing Ourselves to Death: Public Discourse in the Age of Show Business*, 20th anniversary ed. (New York: Penguin, 2005); and Garrett Hardin, *Exploring New Ethics for Survival: Voyage of the Spaceship Beagle* (Baltimore: Penguin, 1972). A recent critical analysis of the disintegrative forces of the market is Ben Barber, *Consumed: How Markets Corrupt Children, Infantilize Adults, and Swallow Citizens Whole* (New York: Norton, 2008).

3. See Robert D. Putnam, *Bowling Alone: The Collapse and Revival of American Community* (New York: Simon and Schuster, 2000); 48–64, 65–79, and 437–44.

4. Source: Federal Election Commission, available on the Web site: http://www.infoplease.com/ipa/A0781453.html.

5. Cited in R. Andrew Holbrook, "Trust in Government," in *Public Opinion and Polling around the World: A Historical Encyclopedia*, ed. John Gray Geer (New York: ABC-CLIO, 2004), 1:360.

6. Putnam, *Bowling Alone*, 19.

7. Jürgen Habermas, *The Structural Transformation of the Public Sphere: An Inquiry into a Category of Bourgeois Society* (1962), trans. Thomas Burger (Cambridge, MA: MIT Press, 1991), 53.

8. "Liberal" as used here does not refer to the popular notion of a "liberal" versus a "conservative" slant in American politics, but rather to the much broader concept in political theory which understands political life as based on individual rights and autonomy as opposed to a philosophical approach that prioritizes community, often described under the rubric of "communitarianism." (See note 20 below.) Leading contemporary theorists of liberalism include John Rawls, William Galston, George Crowder, Ronald Dworkin, and Richard Flathman.

9. Isaiah Berlin, "Two Concepts of Liberty," a lecture delivered at Oxford in 1958 and published in *Four Essays on Liberty* (Oxford: Oxford University Press, 1969), 169. Berlin develops this same argument in many other essays, including *The Roots of Romanticism* (Princeton, NJ: Princeton University Press, 1999). Although some theorists argue that value pluralism is not a necessary precondition of liberal theory—for example, John Gray, *Enlightenment's Wake* (Lon-

don: Routledge, 2005)—most view the two as fundamentally connected. See for example Mark Lilla, Ronald Dworkin, and Robert Silvers, eds., *The Legacy of Isaiah Berlin* (New York: New York Review of Books, 2001).

10. William Galston, *The Practice of Liberal Pluralism* (Cambridge: Cambridge University Press, 2005), 117.

11. Writing from the perspective of both a social theorist and a former active participant in the political process (as White House Advisor to President Clinton), Galston notes that "individualism is a central value, and society is seen as the expression of choice that is consistent with self-interest. At the same time, mutualism insists that individuals are linked through a dense network of natural duties and that societies exist in part to give force to these duties." Ibid., 167.

12. Ibid., 123.

13. Amitai Etzioni, *The Third Way to a Good Society* (London: Demos, 2000), 11. See also Amitai Etzioni, "Communitarianism and the Moral Dimension," in *The Essential Civil Society Reader*, ed. Don E. Eberly (Lanham, MD: Rowman and Littlefield, 2000), 123–39.

14. Michael Sandel, "Markets and Morals," June 9, 2009, the first of four Reith Lectures in a series entitled *A New Citizenship*, http://www.bbc.co.uk/programmes/b00kt7rg. Etzioni's description of the core tenets of communitarianism appeared in each issue of *The Responsive Community*, a journal oriented to the communitarian viewpoint, which ceased publication in 2004. In addition to Etzioni and Sandel, those whose views align generally with communitarian perspectives (although not necessarily or fully self-identifying as "communitarian theorists") include Michael Walzer and Charles Taylor. Daniel Bell notes that "Communitarians begin by positing a need to experience our lives as bound up with the good of the communities out of which our identity has been constituted." Daniel Bell, "Communitarianism," (first published October 4, 2001; substantive revision December 28, 2004), in *The Stanford Encyclopedia of Philosophy*, ed. Edward N. Zalta (Stanford, CA: Stanford University Center for the Study of Language and Information, Fall 2008 Edition) http://plato.stanford.edu/archives/fall2008/entries/communitarianism/. Accessed September 26, 2009.

15. Galston, *Practice*, 16.

16. William Galston exemplifies the first and George Crowder the second. See George Crowder, "Two Concepts of Liberal Pluralism," in *Political Theory* 35, no. 2 (April 2007): 121–46.

17. David Fagelson, "Perfectionist Liberalism, Tolerance, and American Law," *Res Publica* 8 (2002): 41, 69. See *Mozert v. Hawkins County Board of Education*, 827 F.2d. 1058 (6th Cir. 1987).

18. Todd Sandler, *Collective Action: Theory and Applications* (Ann Arbor: University of Michigan Press, 1992), 3. Other classic works on this topic are Mancur Olsen, *The Logic of Collective Action: Public Goods and the Theory of Groups* (Cambridge, MA: Harvard University Press, 1971) and Garrett Hardin, "The Tragedy of the Commons," *Science* 162 (1968) 1243–48.

19. Garrett Hardin, "The Tragedy of the Commons," 1244–46.

20. See for example the description of the Prisoner's Dilemma in Sandler, *Collective Action*; 4–5, 20–22.

21. Public goods are thus "goods in the public domain: available for all to consume and so potentially affecting all people." Inge Kaul, Pedro Conceição, Katell Le Goulven, and Ronald U. Mendoza, "Why Do Global Public Goods Matter Today?" in *Providing Global Public Goods: Managing Globalization*, ed. Inge Kaul and others (Oxford: Oxford University Press, 2003), 3.

22. Smith observed that some products, "though they may be in the highest degree advantageous to a great society, are, however, of such a nature that the profits could never repay the expenses to any individual or small number of individuals, and which it therefore cannot be expected that any individual or small number of individuals should erect." Adam Smith, *An Inquiry into the Nature and Causes of the Wealth of Nations*, vol. 2 (1776), ed. Edwin R. A. Seligman (New York: E. P. Dutton, 1910), 210–11.

23. Burton Weisbrod, *The Voluntary Sector* (Lexington, MA: Lexington Books, 1977). This work provided the initial formulation of the government failure concept; a recent comprehensive discussion of the "three failures theory" appears in Richard Steinberg, "Economic Theories of Nonprofit Organizations," in *The Nonprofit Sector: A Research Handbook*, 2nd ed., ed. Walter W. Powell and Richard Steinberg (New Haven, CT: Yale University Press, 2006), 119–23.

24. Michael Edwards and Simon Zadek, "Governing the Provision of Global Public Goods," in *Providing Global Public Goods* (see note 21), 203.

25. Edwards and Zadek, for example, warn of the need to "guard against the potentially distorting effects of those who shout loudest. The huge number and diversity of nonstate actors, and the inequalities of voice and resources among them, make rules, standards, and protocols essential." Ibid., 214–15.

26. *Codex Justinianus*, Book II, in *Internet Medieval Sourcebook*, ed. Paul Halsall (New York: Fordham University Center for Medieval Studies, last update December 22, 2006), http://www.fordham.edu/halsall/sbook.html.

27. Mark Dowie, "In Law We Trust: Can Environmental Legislation Protect the Commons Now?" *Orion Magazine* 22, no. 4 (July/August 2003), 22–23. Dowie provides an insightful analysis of the evolution of the public trust doctrine from antiquity to the present, including the complexities of its modern application.

28. Howard Rheingold, *Smart Mobs: The Next Social Revolution* (Cambridge, MA: Basic Books, 2002) and Noortje Marres, "Net-Work is Format Work," in *Reformatting Politics: Information Technology and Global Civil Society*, ed. Jodi Dean, Jon W. Anderson, and Geert Lovink (New York: Routledge, 2006), 3–17. Dean, Anderson, and Lovink go a step further in arguing that contemporary networks actually transform the political process, moving a newly expanded civil society into a more prominent role in setting political agendas and encouraging action: "The hybridity, reflexivity, mobility and performativity characteristic of networked society and networked community exceed the capacities of previously conceived notions of democracy." Jodi Dean, Jon W. Anderson, and Geert Lovink, "Introduction: The Postdemocratic Governmentality of Networked Societies," in ibid., xx.

29. Zixue Tai, *The Internet in China: Cyberspace and Civil Society* (Oxford: Routledge, 2006), 206.

30. Tai, *Internet in China*, 191–207. He concludes that although "one should not expect the Internet alone to be the sole agent of change; it is the use of the Internet by real people and civil society groups, such as the Tiananmen Mothers and the Falun Gong activists, that can bring the hope of change. However, I believe the biggest potential does not merely lie in one or a limited few social movements; rather it rests with the Internet being ingrained in the everyday life of the ordinary citizens so that it becomes a way of life. That will be the most revolutionizing effect of the Internet on Chinese civil society—which has not fully occurred yet, but there are cumulative signs that things are going in that direction." Ibid., 207. See also Manuel Castells, *The Rise of the Network Society* (Cambridge, MA: Blackwell, 1996); Zaheer Baber, "Engendering or Endangering Democracy? The Internet, Civil Society, and the Public Sphere," in *Asian Journal of Social Science* 39, no. 2 (2002): 287–303; Peter Ester and Henk Vinken, "Debating Civil Society: On the Fear for Civic Decline and Hope for the Internet Alternative," *International Sociology* 28, no. 4 (2003): 659–80; and James Gomez, "Think Center: The Internet and Politics in the New Economy," *Asian Journal of Social Science* 30, no. 2 (2002): 304–18.

31. Cass Sunstein, "Das Fernsehen und die Öffentlichkeit," in *Die Öffentlichkeit der Vernunft und die Vernunft der Öffentlichkeit: Festschrift für Jürgen Habermas*, ed. Lutz Wingert and Klaus Günther (Frankfurt: Suhrkamp, 2001), 678 (my translation).

32. These observations are based on personal discussions of the author with leaders of Generation.net in the late 1990s concerning philanthropic support for the initiative.

Chapter 8: Philanthropy, Civil Society, and the Commons

1. David Sidorsky, "Moral Pluralism and Philanthropy," *Social Philosophy and Policy* 4, no. 2 (Spring 1987): 93–94.

2. For detailed discussions of the science-guided approaches of the early foundations, see Judith Sealander, *Private Wealth and Public Life: Foundation Philanthropy and the Reshaping of American Social Policy from the Progressive Era to the New Deal* (Baltimore: Johns Hopkins University Press, 1997) and Ellen Condliffe Lagemann, *The Politics of Applied Knowledge: The Carnegie Corporation, Philanthropy, and Public Policy* (Middletown, CT: Wesleyan University Press, 1989).

3. Sealander, *Private Wealth and Public Life*, 15.

4. See James Allen Smith, "The Evolving Role of American Foundations," in *Philanthropy and the Nonprofit Sector in a Changing America*, ed. Charles T. Clotfelter and Thomas Ehrlich (Bloomington: Indiana University Press, 1999), 34–51.

5. Sealander emphasizes the strong aspiration of the early foundations to link social scientific research to changes in public policy, in the "belief that carefully

and scientifically collected information was a key to good social policy-making." Sealander, *Private Wealth and Public Life*, 240. The Russell Sage Foundation, with its strong emphasis on survey research and the use of social science to guide policy, was a leader in this work.

6. James Scott, *Seeing Like a State: How Certain Schemes to Improve the Human Condition Have Failed* (New Haven, CT: Yale University Press, 1998), 327. My description of the relationship between *mētis*, *episteme*, and *techne* and the self-defeating nature of overly rationalized schemes of social change is grounded in Scott's definitive treatment of the subject. He defines *mētis* as follows: "Mētis is typically translated into English as 'cunning' or 'cunning intelligence.' While not wrong, this translation fails to do justice to the range of knowledge and skills represented by *mētis*. Broadly understood, *mētis* represents a wide range of practical skills and acquired intelligence in responding to a constantly changing natural and human environment." Ibid., 313.

7. Among the writers who have compellingly argued for the dominant impact of randomness on human affairs are Nassim Nicholas Taleb in *The Black Swan: The Impact of the Highly Improbable* (New York: Random House, 2007) and in *Fooled by Randomness: The Hidden Role of Chance in the Markets and in Life* (New York: TEXERE, 2001); and Leonard Mladinow, *The Drunkard's Walk* (New York: Pantheon Books, 2008).

8. The most important of these congressional investigations were the hearings conducted by the U.S. Commission on Industrial Relations headed by Walsh in 1915 (in which Walsh described foundations as a "menace to the welfare of society"); the Reece and Cox Committees in the period 1952–54, which accused foundations of left-wing subversion; the hearings in the late 1960s led by Wright Patman, which resulted in the 1969 Tax Act; and, most recently, the Senate Finance Committee hearings chaired by Senator Charles Grassley in the first decade of the twenty-first century, which examined whether foundations and nonprofits were abusing their tax privileges. Kenneth Prewitt, Mattei Dogan, Steven Heydemann, and Stefan Toepler describe the long-standing tension between government and private philanthropy in *The Legitimacy of Philanthropic Foundations: United States and European Perspectives* (New York: Russell Sage Foundation, 2006) and Mark Dowie provides a related historical overview in *American Foundations: An Investigative History* (Cambridge, MA: MIT Press, 2002).

9. Many writers concerned with evaluation in philanthropy describe the negative effects of applying overly simplistic metrics to the field. See for example Patricia Patrizi and Edward Pauly, "Field Based Evaluation as a Path to Foundation Effectiveness," in *Foundations and Evaluation: Contexts and Practices for Effective Philanthropy*, ed. Marc T. Braverman, Norman A. Constantine, and Jana Kay Slater (San Francisco: Jossey-Bass, 2004), 185–200; Gary Walker and Jean Grossman, "Philanthropy and Outcomes: Dilemmas in the Quest for Accountability," in *Philanthropy and the Nonprofit Sector* (see note 4), 449–60; and Peter Frumkin, *Strategic Giving: The Art and Science of Philanthropy* (Chicago: University of Chicago Press, 2006).

10. Quoted in John Hechinger and Daniel Golden, "The Great Giveaway," *The Wall Street Journal*, July 8, 2006.

11. I have written on this issue elsewhere; see Bruce Sievers, "If Pigs Had Wings," *Foundation News and Commentary* 38, no. 6 (November/December 1997): 44–46; "Philanthropy's Blindspots," in *Just Money: A Critique of Contemporary American Philanthropy*, ed. H. Peter Karoff (Boston: TPI Editions, 2004), 129–50; and "A Tale of Three Cities," in *Linkages: The Newsletter of Rockefeller Philanthropy Advisors* (Spring 2006): 1–6. In the large body of literature analyzing the limits of market mechanisms, three works are especially insightful about the social deficiencies of those mechanisms: Charles Lindblom, *The Market System: What It Is, How It Works, and What to Make of It* (New Haven, CT: Yale University Press, 2002); Albert Hirschman, *Rival Views of Market Society* (Cambridge, MA: Harvard University Press, 1992); and Michael Sandel, "Markets and Morals," June 9, 2009, the first of four Reith Lectures (in a series entitled *A New Citizenship*, http://www.bbc.co.uk/programmes/b00kt7rg). Sandel provides a particularly incisive critique of the negative effects of "market triumphalism," with its single-minded focus on bottom-line results.

12. Lindblom's description of the limitations of the market remains one of the most succinct: "Market systems, as we have seen, do not make place for collectively imposed compulsions. Claims about market freedom tie individual choices to the market system but fall silent on collective free choices. They simply fail to confront the difference between a society of free people and a free collectivity." Lindblom, *Market System*, 191. A yet more comprehensive critique of the "reductive and dehumanizing" assumptions behind what he calls the ideology of the Market Ideal is that of Michael Taylor: "It is an ideology of disconnection, of disintegration, because it assumes and idealizes a world in which a person's acts are disconnected from his or her life and people's lives are disconnected from cultural practices. It is a world without coherent lives and without coherent communities and cultures. . . . The world of the Market Ideal is a world in which everything of value is a privately owned and enjoyed, separable good or service whose value is fully fungible, a world of universal commodification, of perfect mobility. It is the antithesis of relation, attachment, community, and coherence." Michael Taylor, *Rationality and the Ideology of Disconnection* (Cambridge: Cambridge University Press, 2006), 87–88. The problem of reflexivity, discussed later, adds yet another dimension to the differentiation between social and commercial problem solving.

13. George Soros, *Open Society: Reforming Global Capitalism* (New York: Public Affairs, 2000); xxii–xxiii, 6–9, 38–45. See also George Soros, *The Age of Fallibility: Consequences of the War on Terror* (New York: Public Affairs, 2007) and Karl Popper, *The Poverty of Historicism* (New York: Harper and Row, 1957), 12–14.

14. Jürgen Habermas, "A Reply to My Critics," in *Habermas: Critical Debates*, ed. John B. Thompson and David Held (Cambridge, MA: MIT Press, 1982), 280–81. In his early work, Habermas elaborated on the contrast between "mono-

logic" and "dialogic" approaches to knowledge and understanding, the former referring to the imposition of categories upon the subject matter of nature, and the latter to the development of intersubjective understanding between conscious agents. The meaning of the dialogic mode is close to the sense of reflexivity used here. Another classic explication of the reflexive character of social problems is to be found in Donald Schon, *Beyond the Stable State: Public and Private Learning in a Changing Society* (London: Maurice Temple Smith, 1971).

15. An especially interesting analysis of the challenge of solving reflexive problems is Frank Fischer's concept of "wicked problems" in "From Theory to Practice: Confronting 'Wicked Problems,'" in *Policy Sciences* 26 (1993): 172–81. David Mathews, President of the Kettering Foundation, has highlighted the importance of understanding the interactive nature of public problem solving in his writings on facilitating public dialogue in the policy-making process. See in particular his *Politics for People: Finding a Responsible Public Voice* (Champaign, IL: University of Illinois Press, 1999); *For Communities to Work* (Dayton, OH: Kettering Foundation Press, 2002); and *Reclaiming Public Education by Reclaiming Our Democracy* (Dayton, OH: Kettering Foundation Press, 2006).

16. In place of the approach of the social engineer, foundations need to adopt the stance of the civic participant, and their modes of judgment should resemble more those of the jurist, coach, or other evaluator of human activity than that of a cost-per-unit analyst in a commercial enterprise.

17. William Galston, *The Practice of Liberal Pluralism* (Cambridge: Cambridge University Press, 2005), 120–21.

18. See Robert N. Bellah, Richard Madsen, William M. Sullivan, Ann Swidler, and Steven M. Tipton, *Habits of the Heart: Individualism and Commitment in American Life*, 3rd ed. (Berkeley: University of California Press, 2007) and Ben Barber, *Consumed: How Markets Corrupt Children, Infantilize Adults, and Swallow Citizens Whole* (New York: Norton, 2008).

19. Michael Walzer, "A Better Vision: The Idea of Civil Society," *Dissent* (Spring 1991): 297.

20. Per Frank Fischer's definition of "wicked problems" noted above, these are intractable problems that involve indeterminate elements, both normative and empirical. Because both the definition of the problem and possible solutions are social constructs, "Wicked problems are those in which we not only don't know the solution but are not even sure what the problem is." Frank Fischer, *Citizens, Experts, and the Environment: The Politics of Local Knowledge*, 2nd ed. (Durham, NC: Duke University Press, 2000), 128.

21. The report is available online at http://www.bettertogether.org/thereport.htm or in printed form from the Saguaro Seminar on *Civic Engagement in America* at Harvard University's Kennedy School of Government.

22. See for example Diane Ravitch and Joseph Viteritti, eds., *Making Good Citizens: Education and Civil Society* (New Haven, CT: Yale University Press, 2001) for a variety of recommendations on improving civic education.

23. William Galston, "Civic Education and Political Participation," *PS: Political Science and Politics* 37, no.2 (April 2004): 263–66. Galston notes the critical debate that has taken place since the 1970s over the efficacy of civic education, but he points to the conclusive evidence from studies in the past decade and a half that civic education can have quite successful results if undertaken from an approach that includes several key elements: a strong focus on concrete civic outcomes such as voting, engagement with relevant "real world" issues without a particular partisan stance, and a supportive school culture that promotes civic engagement by all students.

24. See "The Civic Mission of Schools," a report by the Carnegie Corporation and CIRCLE: The Center for Information and Research on Civic Learning and Engagement (New York and Washington, D.C.: Carnegie Corporation of New York, 2003). Available at civicyouth.org.

25. A range of studies have documented the deteriorating quality of the mass media's coverage of public affairs, including Jeremy Tunstall, *The Media Were American: U.S. Mass Media in Decline* (Oxford: Oxford University Press, 2007); Mark Hertzgaard, *On Bended Knee* (New York: Farrar, Straus and Giroux, 1988); Robert W. McChesney, *Rich Media, Poor Democracy: Communication Politics in Dubious Times* (Champaign: University of Illinois Press, 1999); and James Fallows, *Breaking the News: How the Media Undermine American Democracy* (New York: Vintage Books, 1997).

26. Tony Schwartz, *The Responsive Chord* (New York: Doubleday, 1974), 91.

27. See Simon Shen, *Redefining Nationalism in Modern China: Sino-American Relations and the Emergence of Chinese Public Opinion in the 21st Century* (New York: Palgrave Macmillan, 2007); Wenfang Tang, *Public Opinion and Political Change in China* (Stanford, CA: Stanford University Press, 2005); and Carlos Wing Hung Lo and Sai Wing Leung, "Environmental Agency and Public Opinion in Guangzhou: The Limits of a Popular Approach to Environmental Governance," *The China Quarterly*, no. 163 (September 2000): 677–704. A recent study of the effects of polling in Germany is Thorsten Faas, Christian Mackenrodt, and Rüdiger Schmidt-Beck, "Polls That Mattered: Effects of Media Polls on Voters' Coalition Expectations and Party Preferences in the 2005 German Parliamentary Elections," *International Journal of Public Opinion Research* 20, no. 3 (2008): 299–325.

28. A welcome expansion of these efforts by a small number of foundations that have explicit funding programs related to public information and deliberation was the joint announcement in 2008 by the Carnegie Corporation and the Knight Foundation of significantly increased support for journalism education.

29. For example, David Swenson and Michael Schmidt proposed a specific plan to endow newspapers in "News You Can Endow," *New York Times*, January 27, 2009, national edition. In May 2009, Senator John Kerry chaired a hearing of the Senate Commerce Committee on "The Future of Journalism," in which a range of ideas for sustaining newspapers were explored, including a bill introduced on March 24, 2009, by U.S. Senator Benjamin Cardin, The Newspaper

Revitalization Act (S. 673), to facilitate the conversion of newspapers into non-profit organizations, if they chose to do so.

30. See Jodi Dean, Jon W. Anderson, and Geert Lovink, eds., *Reformatting Politics: Information Technology and Global Civil Society* (New York: Routledge, 2006) and Zixue Tai, *The Internet in China: Cyberspace and Civil Society* (New York: Routledge, 2006).

31. Putnam elaborates on the strong relationship between associational involvement and generalized reciprocity in Robert D. Putnam, *Bowling Alone: The Collapse and Revival of American Community* (New York: Simon and Schuster, 2000), 20–21 and in Robert D. Putnam, ed., *Democracies in Flux: The Evolution of Social Capital in Contemporary Society* (Oxford: Oxford University Press, 2004), 7.

32. Matthew Crenson and Benjamin Ginsberg, *Downsizing Democracy: How America Sidelined Its Citizens and Privatized Its Public* (Baltimore: Johns Hopkins University Press, 2004), 8.

33. E. J. Dionne, "Service, Citizenship, and the New Generation," a talk delivered to the Grantmaker Forum on Community and National Service (June 2000).

34. Cliff Zukin and others, *A New Engagement? Political Participation, Civic Life, and the Changing American Citizen* (Oxford: Oxford University Press, 2006), 86–87.

35. Morley Winograd and Michael Hais, *Millennial Makeover: MySpace, YouTube and the Future of American Politics* (Piscataway, NJ: Rutgers University Press, 2008).

36. Norman Nie and D. Sunshine Hillygus, "The Impact of Internet Use on Sociability: Time-Diary Findings," *ITT and Society* 1, no.1 (Summer 2002): 1–20.

37. Crenson and Ginsberg observe that "The transformation of citizens into customers is significant. Citizens were thought to own government. Customers, by contrast, are merely expected to receive pleasant service from it. Citizens, moreover, are members of a political community with a collective existence created for public purposes. Customers are individual purchasers seeking to meet their private needs in a market. What is missing from the experience of customers is collective mobilization to achieve collective interests." Crenson and Ginsberg, *Downsizing Democracy*, x.

38. Zukin and others, *A New Engagement?* 204. For suggestions of specific strategies that can be adopted to increase the level of civic engagement, see John Gastil and Peter Levine, eds., *The Deliberative Democracy Handbook: Strategies for Effective Civic Engagement in the Twenty-first Century* (San Francisco: Jossey-Bass, 2005).

39. Only a tiny fraction of foundation support is currently directed toward civic engagement purposes. Exceptions are specific initiatives of the Kettering, Ford, Kellogg, Soros, and Hewlett foundations, along with programs of a handful of other private and community foundations. A number of the supported programs have yielded important results: Oregon Health Decisions, leading to a state policy for prioritizing health benefits and services; the 21st Century Town Meeting sponsored by AmericaSpeaks; the Shaping America's Youth Project

on childhood obesity; interactive polling projects sponsored by the Center for Deliberative Polling at Stanford University; and Common Sense California, a project that engages a wide spectrum of California citizens in shaping major state policies for the future.

40. This explosion in growth has been widely documented, most prominently in Lester M. Salamon, "The Rise of the Nonprofit Sector: A Global 'Associational Revolution,'" *Foreign Affairs* 74, no.3 (July/August 1994): 109–24. Helmut Anheier and Lester Salamon have documented that civil society organizations account for an average of approximately 4.5 percent of total employment in the thirty-five countries studied and that the organizations represent the fastest-growing force for social problem solving. Helmut Anheier and Lester Salamon, "The Nonprofit Sector in Comparative Perspective," in *The Nonprofit Sector: A Research Handbook*, 2nd ed., ed. Walter W. Powell and Richard Steinberg (New Haven, CT: Yale University Press, 2006), 100.

41. V. Finn Heinrich and Lorenzo Fioramonti, eds., *CIVICUS Global Survey of the State of Civil Society*, vol. 2, Comparative Perspectives (Bloomfield, CT: Kumarian Press, Inc., 2008).

42. Amanda Bernard, Henny Helmich, and Percy B. Lehning, *Civil Society and International Development* (Paris: OECD, 1998), 142. These organizations include but go well beyond the nonprofit management support organizations that exist in many countries. In addition to CIVICUS and Independent Sector, the list includes the participating institutions in the CIVICUS Survey, university-based and independent research institutes, scholarly associations such as the Association for Research on Nonprofit Organizations and Voluntary Action (ARNOVA) and the International Society for Third-Sector Research (ISTR), and publications such as the *Journal of Civil Society*.

43. Inge Kaul, Isabelle Grunberg, and Marc A. Stern, eds., *Global Public Goods: International Cooperation in the 21st Century* (Oxford: Oxford University Press, 1999), xxi.

44. Todd Sandler, "Intergenerational Public Goods: Strategies, Efficiency and Institutions," in *Global Public Goods* (see note 43), 38.

45. Crenson and Ginsberg, *Downsizing Democracy*, 220.

Bibliography

Althusius, Johannes. *Systematic Analysis of Politics*. 1603. Introduction by C. J. Friedrich. Cambridge, MA: Harvard University Press, 1932.

Andrew, Donna. *Philanthropy and Police: London Charity in the Eighteenth Century*. Princeton, NJ: Princeton University Press, 1989.

Anheier, Helmut. "The CIVICUS Civil Society Index: Proposals for Future Directions." In *CIVICUS Global Survey of the State of Civil Society*, edited by V. Finn Heinrich and Lorenzo Fioramonti. Vol. 2, *Comparative Perspectives*, 27–35. Bloomfield, CT: Kumarian, 2008.

Anheier, Helmut, and Lester Salamon. "The Nonprofit Sector in Comparative Perspective." In *The Nonprofit Sector: A Research Handbook*, 2nd ed., edited by Walter Powell and Richard Steinberg, 89–114. New Haven, CT: Yale University Press, 2006.

Aristotle. *Politics*. Book 2, chapter 6. Edited by Justin Kaplan and W. D. Ross, translated by Benjamin Jowett. New York: Washington Square Press, 1961.

Baber, Zaheer. "Engendering or Endangering Democracy? The Internet, Civil Society, and the Public Sphere." *Asian Journal of Social Science* 39, no. 2 (2002): 287–303.

Bailyn, Bernard. *The Ideological Origins of the American Revolution*. Cambridge, MA: Harvard University Press, 1967.

Balibar, Etienne. *Spinoza and Politics*. London: Verso, 1998.

Barber, Benjamin. *Consumed: How Markets Corrupt Children, Infantilize Adults, and Swallow Citizens Whole*. New York: W. W. Norton, 2008.

Becker, Marvin B. *The Emergence of Civil Society in the Eighteenth Century: A Privileged Moment in the History of England, Scotland, and France*. Bloomington: Indiana University Press, 1994.

Bell, Daniel. "Communitarianism." In *The Stanford Encyclopedia of Philosophy* (Fall 2008 Edition), edited by Edward N. Zalta. First published October 4, 2001; substantive revision December 28, 2004 (Stanford, CA: Stanford University Center for the Study of Language and Information. http://plato.stanford.edu/archives/fall2008/entries/communitarianism/ (Accessed July 18, 2009.)

Bellah, Robert N., Richard Madsen, William M. Sullivan, Ann Swidler, and Steven M. Tipton. *Habits of the Heart: Individualism and Commitment in American Life*. 3rd ed. Berkeley: University of California Press, 2007.

Benjamin, Louise M. *Freedom of the Air and the Public Interest: First Amendment Rights in Broadcasting to 1935.* Carbondale: University of Illinois Press, 2001.

Berlin, Isaiah. *The Age of Enlightenment: The Eighteenth Century Philosophers.* New York: Mentor Books, 1956.

———. *The Crooked Timber of Humanity: Chapters in the History of Ideas.* New York: Vintage, 1992.

———. *The Roots of Romanticism.* Princeton, NJ: Princeton University Press, 1999.

———. "Two Concepts of Liberty." A lecture delivered at Oxford University in 1958. Published in *Four Essays on Liberty.* Oxford: Oxford University Press, 1969.

Bernard, Amanda, Henny Helmich, and Percy B. Lehning. *Civil Society and International Development.* Paris: OECD, 1998.

Black, Antony. *Guild and State: European Political Thought from the Twelfth Century to the Present.* London: Transaction, 2003.

Bobbio, Norberto. *Thomas Hobbes and the Natural Law Tradition.* Translated by Daniela Gobetti. Chicago: University of Chicago Press, 1993.

Böckenförde, Ernst-Wolfgang. "Gemeinwohlvorstellungen bei Klassikern der Rechts- und Staatsphilosophie." In *Gemeinwohl und Gemeinsinn im Recht: Konkretisierung und Realisierung öffentlicher Interessen.* Vol. 3, edited by Herfried Münkler and Karsten Fischer, 43–65. Berlin: Akademie Verlag, 2002.

Borkenau, Franz. *Der Übergang vom feudalen zum bürgerlichen Weltbild: Studien zur Geschichte der Philosophie der Manufakturperiode.* Paris: Felix Alcan, 1934.

Bremner, Robert H. *American Philanthropy.* 2nd ed. Chicago: University of Chicago Press, 1988.

———. *The Public Good: Philanthropy and Welfare in the Civil War Era.* New York: Alfred A. Knopf, 1980.

Brett, Annabel. *Liberty, Right, and Nature: Individual Rights in Later Scholastic Thought.* Cambridge: Cambridge University Press, 2003.

Buchan, James. *Crowded with Genius: The Scottish Enlightenment; Edinburgh's Moment of the Mind.* New York: HarperCollins Publishers, 2003.

Burns, J. H., ed. *The Cambridge History of Medieval Political Thought c. 350–c. 1450.* Cambridge: Cambridge University Press, 1988.

Campbell, T. D. "Francis Hutcheson: 'Father' of the Scottish Enlightenment." In *The Origins and Nature of the Scottish Enlightenment,* edited by R. H. Campbell and A. S. Skinner. Edinburgh: J. Donald Publishers, 1982.

Carnegie, Andrew. *The "Gospel of Wealth": Essays and Other Writings* (1889). Edited by David Nasaw. New York: Penguin, 2006.

Carnegie Corporation and CIRCLE: The Center for Information and Research on Civic Learning and Engagement. "The Civic Mission of Schools." New York and Washington, DC: Carnegie Corporation of New York, 2003. Available at www.civicyouth.org (Accessed August 5, 2009).

Castells, Manuel. *The Rise of the Network Society.* Cambridge, MA: Blackwell, 1996.

Chambers, Simone, and Jeffrey Kopstein. "Bad Civil Society." *Political Theory* 29, no. 6 (December 2001): 837–65.

Chambers, Simone, and Will Kymlicka, eds. *Alternative Conceptions of Civil Society*. Princeton, NJ: Princeton University Press, 2002.

Christenson, Gordon A. "World Civil Society and the International Rule of Law." *Human Rights Quarterly* 19 (1997): 724–37.

Clawson, Mary Ann. *Constructing Brotherhood: Class, Gender, and Fraternalism*. Princeton, NJ: Princeton University Press, 1989.

Colas, Dominique. *Civil Society and Fanaticism: Conjoined Histories*. Translated by Amy Jacobs. Stanford, CA: Stanford University Press, 1997.

Coniff, James. "The Enlightenment and American Political Thought: A Study of the Origins of Madison's Federalist Number 10." *Political Theory* 8, no.3 (August 1980): 381–402.

Crenson, Matthew A., and Benjamin Ginsberg. *Downsizing Democracy: How America Sidelined Its Citizens and Privatized Its Public*. Baltimore: Johns Hopkins University Press, 2004.

Crowder, George. "Two Concepts of Liberal Pluralism." *Political Theory* 35, no. 2 (April 2007): 121–46.

Dagger, Richard. "Rights." In *Political Innovation and Conceptual Change*, edited by Terence Ball, James Farr, and Russell L. Hanson, 292–308. Cambridge: Cambridge University Press, 1989.

Dahrendorf, Ralf. *Reflections on the Revolution in Europe*. New York: Transaction, 2004.

———. "Threats to Civil Society East and West." In *Harper's Magazine* (July 1990): 24–26.

Davids, Karel, and Jan Lucassen, eds. *A Miracle Mirrored: The Dutch Republic in European Perspective*. Cambridge: Cambridge University Press, 1995.

Davis, Scott. "Philanthropy as a Virtue." In *Giving: Western Ideas of Philanthropy*, edited by J. B. Schneewind, 1–23. Bloomington: Indiana University Press, 1996.

Dean, Jodi, Jon W. Anderson, and Geert Lovink, eds. *Reformatting Politics: Information Technology and Global Civil Society*. New York: Routledge, 2006.

Dionne, E. J. "Service, Citizenship, and the New Generation." Address to the Grantmaker Forum on Community and National Service (June 2000).

Dooley, Brendan, and Sabrina A. Baron, eds. *The Politics of Information in Early Modern Europe*. London: Routledge, 2001.

Dowie, Mark. *American Foundations: An Investigative History*. Cambridge, MA: MIT Press, 2002.

———. "In Law We Trust: Can Environmental Legislation Protect the Commons Now?" *Orion Magazine* 22, no. 4 (July/August 2003): 19–25.

Dunn, John. "The Identity of the Bourgeois Liberal Republic." In *The Invention of the Modern Republic*, edited by Biancamaria Fontana, 206–25. Cambridge: Cambridge University Press, 1994.

Edwards, Michael. *Civil Society*. 2nd ed. Cambridge: Polity Press, 2009.

Edwards, Michael, and Simon Zadek. "Governing the Provision of Global Public Goods." In *Providing Global Public Goods: Managing Globalization*, edited by Inge Kaul, Pedro Conceição, Katell Le Goulven, and Ronald U. Mendoza, 200–24. Oxford: Oxford University Press, 2003.

Ellis, Elisabeth. "Immanuel Kant's Two Theories of Civil Society." In *Paradoxes in Civil Society: New Perspectives on Modern German and British History*, edited by Frank Trentmann, 105–31. New York: Berghahn Books, 2003.

Elshtain, Jean Bethke. *Democracy on Trial*. New York: Basic Books, 1995.

Ester, Peter, and Henk Vinken. "Debating Civil Society: On the Fear for Civic Decline and Hope for the Internet Alternative." *International Sociology* 28, no. 4 (2003): 659–80.

Etzioni, Amitai. "The Capabilities and Limits of Global Civil Society." *Millennium—Journal of International Studies* 33 (2004): 341–53.

———. "Communitarianism and the Moral Dimension." In *The Essential Civil Society Reader: The Classic Essays*, edited by Don E. Eberly, 123–39. Lanham, MD: Rowman and Littlefield, 2000.

———. "Law in Civil Society, Good Society, and the Prescriptive State." *Chicago-Kent Law Review* 75 (1999): 355–78.

———. *The Third Way to a Good Society*. London: Demos, 2000.

Fallows, James. *Breaking the News: How the Media Undermine American Democracy*. New York: Vintage Books, 1997.

Febvre, Lucien, and Henri-Jean Martin. *The Coming of the Book: The Impact of Printing 1450–1800*. Translated by David Gerard. London: Verso, 1990.

Fagelson, David. "Perfectionist Liberalism, Tolerance, and American Law." *Res Publica* 8 (2002): 41–70.

Faas, Thorsten, Christian Mackenrodt, and Rüdiger Schmidt-Beck. "Polls That Mattered: Effects of Media Polls on Voters' Coalition Expectations and Party Preferences in the 2005 German Parliamentary Elections." *International Journal of Public Opinion Research* 20, no. 3 (2008): 299–325.

Ferguson, Adam. *An Essay on the History of Civil Society*. 1767. Edited by Fanny Oz-Salzberger. Cambridge: Cambridge University Press, 1995.

Feuer, Lewis. *Spinoza and the Rise of Liberalism*. Rev. ed. New York: Transaction, 1987.

Finnis, J. *Natural Law and Natural Rights*. Oxford: Oxford University Press, 1980.

Fischer, David Hackett. *Albion's Seed: Four British Folkways in America*. Oxford: Oxford University Press, 1989.

Fischer, Frank. *Citizens, Experts, and the Environment: The Politics of Local Knowledge*. 2nd ed. Durham, NC: Duke University Press, 2000.

———. "From Theory to Practice: Confronting 'Wicked Problems.'" *Policy Sciences* 26 (1993): 172–81.

Fontana, Biancamaria, ed. *The Invention of the Modern Republic*. Cambridge: Cambridge University Press, 1994.

Forster, E. M. *Howard's End*. 1921. New York: Penguin, 1992.

Franklin, Benjamin. *Autobiography of Benjamin Franklin*. Edited by Frank Woodworth Pine. Middlesex, England: Echo Library, 2007.

Fritsch, Ahasver. *Die ältesten Schriften für und wieder die Zeitung*. Edited by K. Kurth. Munich: Brünn, 1944.

Frumkin, Peter. *Strategic Giving: The Art and Science of Philanthropy*. Chicago: University of Chicago Press, 2006.

Gagarin, Michael. *Early Greek Law*. Berkeley: University of California Press, 1989.

Galston, William. *The Practice of Liberal Pluralism*. Cambridge: Cambridge University Press, 2005.

———. "Civic Education and Political Participation." *PS: Political Science and Politics* 37, no. 2 (April 2004): 263–66.

Gastil, John, and Peter Levine, eds. *The Deliberative Democracy Handbook: Strategies for Effective Civic Engagement in the Twenty-first Century*. San Francisco: Jossey-Bass, 2005.

Gellner, Ernest. "The Civil and the Sacred." In *The Tanner Lectures on Human Values* 12 (1991), edited Grethe B. Peterson, 301–49. Salt Lake City: University of Utah Press, 1991.

———. *Conditions of Liberty: Civil Society and Its Rivals*. London: Hamish Hamilton, 1994.

Geremek, Bronislaw. *Poverty: A History*. Oxford: Basil Blackwell, 1994.

Geremek, Bronislaw, György Varga, Czeslaw Milosz, Conor Cruise O'Brien, and Eduardo Rabossi. *The Idea of a Civil Society*. Research Triangle Park, NC: The National Humanities Center, 1992.

Giesberg, Judith Ann. *Civil War Sisterhood: The U.S. Sanitary Commission and Women's Politics in Transition*. Boston: Northeastern University Press, 2000.

Godwin, William. *Enquiry Concerning Political Justice*. 1793. Book 8. Edited by K. Codell Carter. Oxford: Oxford University Press, 1971.

Goldsmith, M. M. "Hobbes on Law." In *The Cambridge Companion to Hobbes*, edited by Tom Sorell, 289–98. Cambridge: Cambridge University Press, 1996.

Goode, Luke. *Jürgen Habermas: Democracy and the Public Sphere*. London: Pluto Press, 2005.

Göttler, Christine. "Religiöse Stiftungen als Dissimulation? Die Kapellen der portugiesischen Kaufleute in Antwerpen." In *Stiftungen und Stiftungswirklichkeiten: Vom Mittelalter bis zur Gegenwart*. Vol. 1 of *Stiftungsgeschichten*, edited by Michael Borgolte, 279–305. Berlin: Akademie Verlag, 2000.

Gomez, James. "Think Center: The Internet and Politics in the New Economy." *Asian Journal of Social Science* 30, no. 2 (2002): 304–18.

Gray, John. *Enlightenment's Wake*. London: Routledge, 2005.

Griswold, Charles L., Jr. *Adam Smith and the Virtues of Enlightenment*. Cambridge: Cambridge University Press, 1999.

Grotius, Hugo. *De iure praedae commentarius I*. 1604–08. Translated by Gwladys Williams. New York: Oceana, 1964.

Gross, Robert A. "Giving in America: From Charity to Philanthropy." In *Charity, Philanthropy, and Civility in American History*, edited by Lawrence J. Friedman and Mark D. McGarvie, 29–48. Cambridge: Cambridge University Press, 2003.

Habermas, Jürgen. *The Structural Transformation of the Public Sphere: An Inquiry into a Category of Bourgeois Society*. Translated by Thomas Burger. Cambridge, MA: MIT Press, 1991. Originally published in 1962.

———. "A Reply to My Critics." In *Habermas: Critical Debates*, edited by John B. Thompson and David Held, 280–81. Cambridge, MA: MIT Press, 1982.

Hall, John A. "In Search of Civil Society." In *Civil Society: Theory, History, Comparison*, edited by John A. Hall, 1–31. Cambridge, MA: Polity Press, 1995.

Halfpenny, Peter. "Trust, Charity, and Civil Society." In *Trust and Civil Society*, edited by Fran Tonkiss and Andrew Passey, 132–50. New York: St. Martin's Press, 2000.

Hands, A. R. *Charities and Social Aid in Greece and Rome*. Ithaca, NY: Cornell University Press, 1968.

Hall, Peter Dobkin. "Historical Perspectives on Nonprofit Organizations in the United States." In *Jossey-Bass Handbook of Nonprofit Leadership and Management*, edited by Robert D. Herman and Associates, 3–38. San Francisco: Jossey-Bass, 1994.

———. "An Historical Overview of Philanthropy, Voluntary Associations, and Nonprofit Organizations in the United States, 1600–2000." In *The Nonprofit Sector: A Research Handbook*. 2nd ed., edited by Walter W. Powell and Richard Steinberg, 35–42. New Haven, CT: Yale University Press, 2006.

Hampshire, Stuart. *Spinoza and Spinozism*. Oxford: Oxford University Press, 2005.

Hardin, Garrett. *Exploring New Ethics for Survival: Voyage of the Spaceship Beagle*. Baltimore: Penguin, 1972.

———. "The Tragedy of the Commons." *Science* 162 (1968): 1243–48.

Harline, Craig. *Pamphlets, Printing, and Political Culture in the Early Dutch Republic*. Dordrecht, Netherlands: Martinus Nijhoff, 1987.

Harrington, James. "The Commonwealth of Oceana." 1656. In *The Commonwealth of Oceana and A System of Politics*, edited by J. G. A. Pocock, 1–266. Cambridge: Cambridge University Press, 1992.

Harris, Edward. *Law and Society in Ancient Athens*. Cambridge: Cambridge University Press, 2006.

Harrison, Ross. *Hobbes, Locke, and Confusion's Masterpiece: An Examination of Seventeenth Century Political Philosophy*. Cambridge: Cambridge University Press, 2003.

Heinrich, V. Finn and Lorenzo Fioramonti, eds. *CIVICUS Global Survey of the State of Civil Society*. Vol. 2, Comparative Perspectives. Bloomfield, CT: Kumarian Press, Inc., 2008.

Henderson, John. *Piety and Charity in Late Medieval Florence*. Chicago: University of Chicago Press, 1994.

Hertzgaard, Mark. *On Bended Knee*. New York: Farrar, Straus and Giroux, 1988.

Hess, Charlotte and Elinor Ostrom. "Introduction: An Overview of the Knowledge Commons." In *Understanding Knowledge as a Commons: From Theory to Practice*, edited by Charlotte Hess and Elinor Ostrum, 3–26. Cambridge, MA: MIT Press, 2007.

Hirschman, Albert. *Rival Views of Market Society*. Cambridge, MA: Harvard University Press, 1992.

Holbrook, R. Andrew. "Trust in Government." In *Public Opinion and Polling Around the World: A Historical Encyclopedia*, edited by John Gray Geer, 359–63. New York: ABC-CLIO, 2004.

Hume, David. *Political Essays*. 1752. Edited by K. Haakonssen. Cambridge: Cambridge University Press, 1994.

———. *A Treatise on Human Nature: Being an Attempt to Introduce the Experimental Method of Reasoning into Moral Subjects.* 1739. Part 2, section 2. In *Hume's Ethical Writings*, edited by Alasdair MacIntyre. New York: Collier Books, 1965.

Hundert, E. J. *The Enlightenment's Fable: Bernard Mandeville and the Discovery of Society.* Cambridge: Cambridge University Press, 1994.

Hunter, Ian. *Rival Enlightenments: Civil and Metaphysical Philosophy in Early Modern Germany.* Cambridge: Cambridge University Press, 2001.

Hyde, Lewis. *The Gift: Imagination and the Erotic Life of Property.* New York: Vintage Books, 1979.

Israel, Jonathan, I. *The Dutch Republic: Its Rise, Greatness, and Fall 1477–1806.* Oxford: Clarendon Press, 1995.

———. *Enlightenment Contested: Philosophy, Modernity, and the Emancipation of Man 1670–1752.* Oxford: Oxford University Press, 2009.

———. "The Intellectual Debate about Toleration in the Dutch Republic." In *The Emergence of Tolerance in the Dutch Republic*, edited by C. Berkvens-Stevelick, Jonathan I. Israel, and G. H. M. Posthumus Meyjes, 3–36. Leiden, Netherlands: Brill, 1997.

———. *Radical Enlightenment: Philosophy and the Making of Modernity 1650–1750.* Oxford: Oxford University Press, 2001.

Jacob, Margaret C. *The Origins of Freemasonry: Facts and Fictions.* Philadelphia: University of Pennsylvania Press, 2006.

Jordan, W. K. *Philanthropy in England 1489–1660: A Study in the Changing Pattern of English Social Aspirations.* New York: Russell Sage Foundation, 1959.

Kant, Immanuel. "An Answer to the Question: What Is Enlightenment?" In *What Is Enlightenment? Eighteenth Century Answers and Twentieth Century Questions*, edited and translated by James Schmidt, 58–64. Berkeley: University of California Press, 1996. Originally published as "Beantwortung an der Frage: Was ist Aufklärung?" In *Berlinerische Monatschrift* 4 (1784): 481–94.

Kaul, Inge. "Global Public Goods: What Role for Civil Society?" *Nonprofit and Voluntary Sector Quarterly* 30, no. 3 (September 2001): 588–602.

Kaul, Inge, Isabelle Grunberg, and Marc A. Stern, eds. *Global Public Goods: International Cooperation in the 21st Century.* Oxford: Oxford University Press, 1999.

Kaul, Inge, Pedro Conceição, Katell Le Goulven, and Ronald U. Mendoza. "Why Do Global Public Goods Matter Today?" In *Providing Global Public Goods: Managing Globalization*, edited by Inge Kaul, Pedro Conceição, Katell Le Goulven, and Ronald U. Mendoza, 2–20. Oxford: Oxford University Press, 2003.

Kaviraj, Sudipta, and Sunil Khilnani. *Civil Society: History and Possibilities.* Cambridge: Cambridge University Press, 2001.

Keane, John. *Civil Society: Old Images, New Visions.* Stanford, CA: Stanford University Press, 1998.

———. "Despotism and Democracy: The Origins and Development of the Distinction between Civil Society and the State 1750–1850." In *Civil Society and the State*, edited by John Keane, 35–71. New York: Verso, 1988.

Kempshall, M. S. *The Common Good in Late Medieval Political Thought.* Oxford: Clarendon Press, 1999.

Kennedy, Jane. "Development of Postal Rates: 1845–1955." *Journal of Land Economics* 33, no. 2 (May 1957): 93–112.

Kirner, Guido O. "Polis und Gemeinwohl: Zum Gemeinwohlbegriff in Athen vom 6. bis 4. Jahrhundert v. Chr." In *Gemeinwohl und Gemeinsinn: Historische Semantiken politischer Leitbegriffe*, edited by Herfried Münkler and Harald Bluhm. Vol. 1, 31–63. Berlin: Akademie Verlag, 2001.

Kocka, Jürgen. "Zivilgesellschaft als historisches Problem und Versprechen." In *Europäische Zivilgesellschaft in Ost und West: Begriff, Geschichte, Chancen*, edited by Manfred Hildermeier, Jürgen Kocka, and Cristoph Conrad, 13–39. Frankfurt: Campus Verlag, 2000.

Kossmann, E. H. "Freedom in Seventeenth-Century Dutch Thought and Practice." In *The Anglo-Dutch Moment: Essays on the Glorious Revolution and its World Impact*, edited by Jonathan I. Israel, 281–98. Cambridge: Cambridge University Press, 1991.

Lagemann, Ellen Condliffe. *The Politics of Applied Knowledge: The Carnegie Corporation, Philanthropy, and Public Policy.* Middletown, CT: Wesleyan University Press, 1989.

Lalor, Stephen. *Matthew Tindal, Freethinker: An Eighteenth Century Assault on Religion.* London: Continuum, 2006.

Lasch, Christopher. *The Culture of Narcissism: American Life in an Age of Diminishing Expectations.* Rev. ed. New York: W. W. Norton, 2001.

Levy, Leonard. *Emergence of a Free Press.* Oxford: Oxford University Press, 1985.

Lichty, Lawrence W. "Television in America: Success Story." *The Wilson Quarterly* 5, no. 1 (Winter 1981): 52–65.

Lilla, Mark, Ronald Dworkin, and Robert Silvers, eds. *The Legacy of Isaiah Berlin.* New York: New York Review of Books, 2001.

Lindblom, Charles. *The Market System: What It Is, How It Works, and What to Make of It.* New Haven, CT: Yale University Press, 2002.

Lissak, Rivka Shpak. *Pluralism and Progressives: Hull House and the New Immigrants 1890–1919.* Chicago: University of Chicago Press, 1989.

Locke, John. *The Second Treatise: An Essay Concerning the True Original, Extent, and End of Civil Government.* 1679–81. In *Two Treatises of Government and A Letter Concerning Toleration*, edited by Ian Shapiro. New Haven, CT: Yale University Press, 2003.

Lohmann, Roger. *The Commons: New Perspectives on Nonprofit Organizations and Voluntary Action.* San Francisco: Jossey-Bass, 1992.

Luf, Gerhard. "Zivilgesellschaft und staatliches Rechtsmonopol." In *Das Rechtssystem zwischen Staat und Zivilgesellschaft: Zur Rolle gesellschaftlicher Selbstregulierung und vorstaatlicher Schlichtung*, edited by Jürgen Nautz, Emil Brix, and Gerhard Luf, 55–66. Vienna: Passagen Verlag, 2001.

Lupoi, Maurizio. *The Origins of the European Legal Order.* Translated by Adrian Belton. Cambridge: Cambridge University Press, 2000.

Madison, James. "Letter to George Washington, April 16, 1787." In *The Writings of James Madison*, edited by Gaillard Hunt, vol. 2, 344–52. New York: G. P. Putnam, 1900.

Madison, James. "Vices of the Political System of the United States." In *The Writings of James Madison*, edited by Gaillard Hunt, vol. 2, 361–69. New York: G. P. Putnam, 1900.

Maier, Pauline. *American Scripture: Making the Declaration of Independence*. New York: Alfred A. Knopf, 1997.

Mandeville, Bernard. *The Fable of the Bees*. 1723. In *The Fable of the Bees and Other Writings*, edited by E. J. Hundert, 19–182. Indianapolis: Hackett Publishing, 1997.

Mansbridge, Jane. "On the Contested Nature of the Public Good." In *Private Action and the Public Good*, edited by Walter W. Powell and Elisabeth S. Clemens, 20–35. New Haven, CT: Yale University Press, 1998.

Marres, Noortje. "Net-Work is Format Work." In *Reformatting Politics: Information Technology and Global Civil Society*, edited by Jodi Dean, Jon W. Anderson, and Geert Lovink, 3–18. New York: Routledge, 2006.

Massing, Michael. "A New Horizon for the News." In *The New York Review of Books* 56, no.14 (September 24, 2009): 31–34.

Mathews, David. *For Communities to Work*. Dayton, OH: Kettering Foundation Press, 2002.

———. *Politics for People: Finding a Responsible Public Voice*. Champaign: University of Illinois Press, 1999.

———. *Reclaiming Public Education by Reclaiming Our Democracy*. Dayton, OH: Kettering Foundation Press, 2006.

McCants, Anne E. C. *Civic Charity in a Golden Age: Orphan Care in Early Modern Amsterdam*. Champaign: University of Illinois Press, 1998.

McCarthy, Kathleen. *American Creed: Philanthropy and the Rise of Civil Society, 1700–1865*. Chicago: University of Chicago Press, 2005.

McChesney, Robert W. *Rich Media, Poor Democracy: Communication Politics in Dubious Times*. Champaign: University of Illinois Press, 1999.

McCombs, Maxwell E., and Chaim H. Eyal. "Spending on Mass Media." *Journal of Communication* 30, no. 1 (2006): 153–58.

McGarvie, Mark D. "The Dartmouth College Case and the Legal Design of Civil Society." In *Charity, Philanthropy, and Civility in American History*, edited by Lawrence J. Friedman and Mark D. McGarvie, 91–106. Cambridge: Cambridge University Press, 2003.

McGrade, Stephen. "Ockham and the Birth of Individual Rights." In *Authority and Power: Studies on Medieval Law and Government Presented to Walter Ullmann on His Seventieth Birthday*, edited by Brian Tierney and Peter Linehan, 149–66. Cambridge: Cambridge University Press, 1980.

Miller, Fred D., Jr. "Natural Law, Civil Society, and Government." In *Civil Society and Government*, edited by Nancy L. Rosenblum and Robert C. Post, 187–215. Princeton, NJ: Princeton University Press, 2002.

Miller, Timothy. *The Birth of the Hospital in the Byzantine Empire*. Baltimore: Johns Hopkins University Press, 1997.

Mladinow, Leonard. *The Drunkard's Walk*. New York: Pantheon Books, 2008.

Morone, James. *The Democratic Wish: Popular Participation and the Limits of American Government*. New York: Basic Books, 1990.

Morrall, John B. *Political Thought in Medieval Times*. New York: Harper, 1962.

Myers, Milton L. *The Soul of Modern Economic Man*. Chicago: University of Chicago Press, 1983.

Nie, Norman, and D. Sunshine Hillygus. "The Impact of Internet Use on Sociability: Time-Diary Findings." *ITT and Society* 1, no.1 (Summer 2002): 1–20.

Nord, David Paul. "The Evangelical Origins of Mass Media in America, 1815–1835." *Journalism Monographs* 88 (1984).

Nord, Philip. "Introduction" to *Civil Society Before Democracy: Lessons from Nineteenth-Century Europe*, edited by Nancy Bermeo and Philip Nord, xiii–xxxiii. New York: Rowman and Littlefield, 2000.

Oakley, Francis. "Christian Obedience and Authority, 1520–1550." In *The Cambridge History of Political Thought 1450–1700*, edited by J. H. Burns and Mark Goldie, 159–92. Cambridge: Cambridge University Press, 1991.

O'Connell, Brian. *Civil Society: The Underpinnings of American Democracy*. Hanover, NH: University Press of New England, 1999.

O'Neill, Michael. *Nonprofit Nation: A New Look at the Third America*. San Francisco: Jossey-Bass, 2002.

———. *The Third America: The Emergence of the Nonprofit Sector in the United States*. San Francisco: Jossey-Bass, 1989.

Oestreich, Gerhard. *Strukturprobleme der frühen Neuzeit*. Berlin: Duncker und Humblot, 1980.

Oexle, Otto Gerhard. "Konflikt und Konsens: Über gemeinschaftsrelevantes Handeln in der vormodernen Gesellschaft." In *Gemeinwohl und Gemeinsinn: Historische Semantiken politischer Leitbegriffe*, edited by Herfried Münkler and Harald Bluhm. Vol. 1, 65–84. Berlin: Akademie Verlag, 2001.

Olsen, Mancur. *The Logic of Collective Action: Public Goods and the Theory of Groups*. New York: Schocken, 1965.

Ostrum, Elinor. *Governing the Commons: The Evolution of Institutions for Collective Action*. Cambridge: Cambridge University Press, 1990.

Paine, Thomas. *Common Sense*. 1776. In *The Thomas Paine Reader*, edited by Michael Foot and Isaac Kramnick, 65–115. London: Penguin, 1987.

Parker, Charles. "Poor Relief and Community in the Early Dutch Republic." In *With Us Always: A History of Private Charity and Public Welfare*, edited by Donald T. Critchlow and Charles H. Parker, 13–33. Oxford: Rowman and Littlefield, 1998.

Passey, Andrew, and Fran Tonkiss. "Trust, Voluntary Association and Civil Society." In *Trust and Civil Society*, edited by Fran Tonkiss, Andrew Passey, Natalie Fenton, and Leslie Hems, 31–51. New York: St. Martin's Press, 2000.

Patrizi, Patricia, and Edward Pauly. "Field Based Evaluation as a Path to Foundation Effectiveness." In *Foundations and Evaluation: Contexts and Practices for Effective Philanthropy*, edited by Marc T. Braverman, Norman A. Constantine, and Jana Kay Slater, 185–200. San Francisco: Jossey-Bass, 2004.

Payton, Robert. *Philanthropy: Voluntary Action for the Public Good.* New York: Macmillan, 1988.

Payton, Robert, and Michael Moody. *Understanding Philanthropy: Its Meaning and Mission.* Bloomington: Indiana University Press, 2008.

Pierce, Franklin. "Veto Message, May 3, 1854." In *A Compilation of the Messages and Papers of the Presidents of the United States, 1789–1897*, edited by J. D. Richardson. Vol. 5, 247–56. Washington, DC: United States Congress, 1898.

Popkin, Jeremy D. "Print Culture in the Netherlands on the Eve of the Revolution." In *The Dutch Republic in the Eighteenth Century: Decline, Enlightenment, and Revolution*, edited by Margaret C. Jacob and Wijnand W. Mijnhardt, 273–91. Ithaca, NY: Cornell University Press, 1992.

Popper, Karl. *The Poverty of Historicism.* New York: Harper and Row, 1957.

Porter, Roy. *The Creation of the Modern World: The Untold Story of the British Enlightenment.* New York: W. W. Norton, 2000.

Post, Robert C., and Nancy L. Rosenblum, eds. *Civil Society and Government.* Princeton, NJ: Princeton University Press, 2002.

Postman, Neil. *Amusing Ourselves to Death: Public Discourse in the Age of Show Business.* 20th Anniversary ed. New York: Penguin, 2005.

Pound, Roscoe. "Grotius in the Science of Law." *American Journal of International Law* 19 (1925): 685–88.

Powell, Walter, and Elisabeth S. Clemens, eds. *Private Action and the Public Good.* New Haven, CT: Yale University Press, 1988.

Powell, Walter, and Richard Steinberg, eds. *The Nonprofit Sector: A Research Handbook.* 2nd ed. New Haven, CT: Yale University Press, 2006.

Prewitt, Ken, Mattei Dogan, Steven Heydemann, and Stefan Toepler, eds. *The Legitimacy of Philanthropic Foundations: United States and European Perspectives.* New York: Russell Sage Foundation, 2006.

Price, J. L. *Culture and Society in the Dutch Republic During the Seventeenth Century.* New York: Charles Scribner's Sons, 1974.

———. *The Dutch Republic in the Seventeenth Century.* New York: St. Martin's Press, 1998.

Pullan, Brian. "Good Government and Christian Charity in Early Modern Italy." In *With Us Always: A History of Private Charity and Public Welfare*, edited by Donald T. Critchlow and Charles H. Parker, 77–98. Oxford: Rowman and Littlefield, 1998.

Putnam, Robert D. *Bowling Alone: The Collapse and Revival of American Community.* New York: Simon and Schuster, 2000.

———, ed. *Democracies in Flux: The Evolution of Social Capital in Contemporary Society.* Oxford: Oxford University Press, 2004.

Putnam, Robert D., and Kristen Goss. *Better Together Report of the Saguaro Seminar: Civic Engagement in America.* Cambridge, MA: Saguaro Seminar on Civic Engagement in America at Harvard University's Kennedy School of Government http://www.bettertogether.org/thereport.htm.

Ravitch, Diane, and Joseph P. Viteritti, eds. *Making Good Citizens: Education and Civil Society.* New Haven, CT: Yale University Press, 2001.

Rexroth, Frank. "Stiftungen und die Frühgeschichte von Policey in spätmittelalter-lichen Städten." In *Stiftungen und Stiftungswirklichkeiten: Vom Mittelalter bis zur Gegenwart*, edited by Michael Borgolte, 111–31. Berlin: Akademie Verlag, 2000.

Rheingold, Howard. *Smart Mobs: The Next Social Revolution.* Cambridge, MA: Basic Books, 2002.

Riesman, David, Nathan Glazer, and Reuel Denney. *The Lonely Crowd: A Study of the Changing American Character.* Rev. ed. New Haven, CT: Yale University Press, 2001.

Risse, Guenter B. *Mending Bodies, Saving Souls: A History of Hospitals.* Oxford: Oxford University Press, 1999.

Robbins, Kevin C. "The Nonprofit Sector in Historical Perspective: Traditions of Philanthropy in the West." In *The Nonprofit Sector: A Research Handbook.* 2nd ed. Edited by Walter W. Powell and Richard Steinberg, 13–31. New Haven, CT: Yale University Press, 2006.

Roberts, Suzanne. "Contexts of Charity in the Middle Ages." *In Giving: Western Ideas of Philanthropy*, edited by J. B. Schneewind, 24–53. Bloomington: Indiana University Press, 1996.

Rowen, Herbert H., and Andrew Lossky. *Political Ideas and Institutions in the Dutch Republic.* Pasadena, CA: The Castle Press, 1985.

Rubin, Miri. *Charity and Community in Medieval Cambridge.* Cambridge: Cambridge University Press, 1987.

Salamon, Lester M. *America's Nonprofit Sector: A Primer.* 2nd ed. New York: The Foundation Center, 1999.

———. "The Rise of the Nonprofit Sector: A Global 'Associational Revolution.'" *Foreign Affairs* 74, no. 3 (July/August 1994): 109–24.

Salamon, Lester M., and Helmut Anheier, eds. *Global Civil Society: Dimensions of the Nonprofit Sector.* Baltimore: Johns Hopkins University Press, 1999.

Sandel, Michael. Four Reith Lectures in a series entitled *A New Citizenship.* London: BBC Radio. http://www.bbc.co.uk/programmes/b00kt7rg. Accessed July 16, 2009.

Sandler, Todd. *Collective Action: Theory and Applications.* Ann Arbor: University of Michigan Press, 1992.

Scheller, Benjamin. "Der Streit um den Stiftungsvollzug der Vöhlinschen Prädikatur in Memmingen." In *Stiftungen und Stiftungswirklichkeiten: Vom Mittelalter bis zur Gegenwart*, edited by Michael Borgolte, 257–78. Berlin: Akademie Verlag, 2000.

Schmidt, James. "A Paideia for the 'Bürger als Bourgeois': The Concept of 'Civil Society' in Hegel's Political Thought." In *History of Political Thought* 2, no. 3 (Winter 1981): 469–93.

Schon, Donald. *Beyond the Stable State: Public and Private Learning in a Changing Society.* London: Maurice Temple Smith, 1971.

Schneewind, J. B. "Philosophical Ideas of Charity." In *Giving: Western Ideas of Philanthropy*, edited by J. B. Schneewind, 54–75. Bloomington: Indiana University Press, 1996.

Schwartz, Tony. *The Responsive Chord.* New York: Doubleday, 1974.

Scott, James. *Seeing Like a State: How Certain Schemes to Improve the Human Condition Have Failed*. New Haven, CT: Yale University Press, 1998.

Sealander, Judith. *Private Wealth and Public Life: Foundation Philanthropy and the Reshaping of American Social Policy From the Progressive Era to the New Deal*. Baltimore: Johns Hopkins University Press, 1997.

Seaton, A. A. *The Theory of Toleration under the Later Stuarts*. New York: Farrar, Straus and Giroux, 1972.

Sejersted, Francis. "Democracy and the Rule of Law: Some Historical Experiences of Contradictions in the Striving for Good Government." In *Constitutionalism and Democracy*, edited by Jon Elster and Rune Slagstad, 131–52. Cambridge: Cambridge University Press, 1988.

Seligman, Adam. *The Idea of Civil Society*. Princeton, NJ: Princeton University Press, 1992.

Sellars, John. "Justus Lipsius (1547–1606)." In *The Internet Encyclopedia of Philosophy*. http://www.iep.utm.edu/l/lipsius.htm. Accessed August 10, 2009.

Sennett, Richard. *The Fall of Public Man*. New York: W. W. Norton, 1992.

Shen, Simon. *Redefining Nationalism in Modern China: Sino-American Relations and the Emergence of Chinese Public Opinion in the 21st Century*. New York: Palgrave Macmillan, 2007.

Shils, Edward. *The Virtue of Civility: Selected Essays on Liberalism, Tradition, and Civil Society*. Edited by Steven Grosby. Indianapolis: Liberty Fund, 1997.

Shorto, Russell. *The Island at the Center of the World: The Epic Story of Dutch Manhattan and the Forgotten Colony that Shaped America*. New York: Doubleday, 2004.

Sidorsky, David. "Moral Pluralism and Philanthropy." *Social Philosophy and Policy* 4, no. 2 (Spring 1987): 93–112.

Sievers, Bruce. "Can Philanthropy Solve the Problems of Civil Society?" *Essays on Philanthropy*, no. 16. Indianapolis: Indiana University Center on Philanthropy, 1995.

———. "If Pigs Had Wings." *Foundation News and Commentary* 38, no. 6 (November/December 1997): 44–46.

———. "Philanthropy's Blindspots." In *Just Money: A Critique of Contemporary American Philanthropy*, edited by H. Peter Karoff, 129–50. Boston: TPI Editions, 2004.

Skocpol, Theda. *Diminished Democracy: From Membership to Management in American Civic Life*. Norman: University of Oklahoma Press, 2004.

Smith, Adam. *An Inquiry into the Nature and Causes of the Wealth of Nations*. 1776. Edited by Edwin R. A. Seligman. New York: E. P. Dutton, 1910.

———. *The Theory of Moral Sentiments*. 1790. Reprint of 6th edition published in London by A. Millar. Mineola, NY: Dover, 2006.

Smith, James Allen. "The Evolving Role of American Foundations." In *Philanthropy and the Nonprofit Sector in a Changing America*, edited by Charles T. Clotfelter and Thomas Ehrlich, 34–51. Bloomington: Indiana University Press, 1999.

Smith, James Allen, and Karsten Borgmann. "Foundations in Europe: The Historical Context." In *Foundations in Europe*, edited by Andreas Schulter, 2–33. London: The Directory of Social Change, 2001.

Smith, Steven. *Spinoza, Liberalism, and the Question of Jewish Identity*. New Haven, CT: Yale University Press, 1998.

Sommerville, Johan P. *Thomas Hobbes: Political Ideas in Historical Context*. New York: St. Martin's Press, 1992.

Soros, George. *Open Society: Reforming Global Capitalism*. New York: Public Affairs, 2000.

———. *The Age of Fallibility: Consequences of the War on Terror*. New York: Public Affairs, 2007.

Spaans, Jo. "Early Modern Orphanages between Civic Pride and Social Discipline: Francke's Use of Dutch Models." In *Waisenhäuser in der Frühen Neuzeit, Halleschen Forschungen* 10, edited by Udo Sträter and Josef N. Neumann, 183–96. Tübingen: Max Niemeyer Verlag, 2003.

Spellman, W. M. *European Political Thought 1600–1700*. New York: St. Martin's Press, 1998.

Spinoza, Benedict. *Ethics*. 1677. In *A Spinoza Reader*, edited and translated by Edwin Curley, 85–265. Princeton, NJ: Princeton University Press, 1994.

Spufford, Margaret. "Literacy, Trade, and Religion in the Commercial Centres of Europe." In *A Miracle Mirrored: The Dutch Republic in European Perspective*, edited by Karel Davids and Jan Lucassen, 248–63. Cambridge: Cambridge University Press, 1995.

Starr, Paul. *The Creation of the Media: Political Origins of Modern Communications*. New York: Basic Books, 2004.

Steinberg, Richard. "Economic Theories of Nonprofit Organizations." In *The Nonprofit Sector: A Research Handbook*. 2nd ed. Edited by Walter W. Powell and Richard Steinberg, 119–23. New Haven, CT: Yale University Press, 2006.

Stewart, Dugwald. "Account of the Life and Writings of Adam Smith." In *Adam Smith, Essays on Philosophical Subjects*, edited by W. P. D. Wightman, J. C. Bryce, and I. S. Ross, 269–362. Oxford: Oxford University Press, 1980.

Stillé, Charles J. *History of the United States Sanitary Commission: Being the General Report of Its Work During the War of Rebellion*. New York: Hurd and Houghton, 1868.

Sunstein, Cass. "Das Fernsehen und die Öffentlichkeit." In *Die Öffentlichkeit der Vernunft und die Vernunft der Öffentlichkeit: Festschrift für Jürgen Habermas*, edited by Lutz Wingert and Klaus Günther, 678–701 (my translation). Frankfurt: Suhrkamp, 2001.

Sweetinburgh, Sheila. *The Role of the Hospital in Medieval England: Gift-giving and the Spiritual Economy*. Dublin: Four Courts Press, 2004.

Swenson, David, and Michael Schmidt. "News You Can Endow." *New York Times*, January 27, 2009, national edition.

Tai, Zixue. *The Internet in China: Cyberspace and Civil Society*. Oxford: Routledge, 2006.

Taleb, Nassim Nicholas. *The Black Swan: The Impact of the Highly Improbable*. New York: Random House, 2007.

———. *Fooled by Randomness: The Hidden Role of Chance in the Markets and in Life.* New York: TEXERE, 2001.

Tang, Wenfang. *Public Opinion and Political Change in China.* Stanford, CA: Stanford University Press, 2005.

Taylor, Charles. "Modes of Civil Society." *Public Culture* 3, no. 1 (1990): 95–118.

Taylor, Michael. *Rationality and the Ideology of Disconnection.* Cambridge: Cambridge University Press, 2006.

Thorpe, Francis Newton, ed. "Pennsylvania Constitution of 1776." In *The Federal and State Constitutions, Colonial Charters, and Other Organic Laws* 5:3083. Washington, DC: Government Printing Office, 1909.

Tierney, Brian. *Religion, Law, and the Growth of Constitutional Thought 1150–1650.* Cambridge: Cambridge University Press, 1982.

Titmuss, Richard M. *The Gift Relationship: From Human Blood to Social Policy.* New York: Vintage Books, 1971.

Tocqueville, Alexis de. *Democracy in America.* Vol. 1 1835. Vol. 2 1840. Edited by Alan Ryan. Translated by Francis Bowen. New York: Alfred A. Knopf, Everyman's Library, 1972.

———. Notebook entry, May 29, 1831. Cited in *The Tocqueville Reader: A Life in Letters and Politics*, edited by Oliver Zuna and Alan S. Kahan, 51. Oxford: Blackwell Publishers, 2002.

Trenchard, John, and Thomas Gordon. "Letter No. 15: Of Freedom of Speech." In *Cato's Letters: Or, Essays on Liberty, Civil and Religious.* London: J. Walthoe and T. and L. Longman. 6th ed. 1755. Facsimile reprint edited by Leonard Levy. New York: De Capo Press, 1971.

Tuck, Richard. *Philosophy and Government: 1572–1651.* Cambridge: Cambridge University Press, 1993.

———. "Rights and Pluralism." In *Philosophy in an Age of Pluralism: The Philosophy of Charles Taylor in Question*, edited by James Tully, 159–70. Cambridge: Cambridge University Press, 1994.

Tunstall, Jeremy. *The Media Were American: U.S. Mass Media in Decline.* Oxford: Oxford University Press, 2007.

Ullmann, Walter. *Medieval Political Thought.* New York: Peregrine Books, 1976.

Van der Linden, Marcel, ed. *Social Security Mutualism: The Comparative History of Mutual Benefit Societies.* Bern, Switzerland: Peter Lang AG, 1996.

Van Gelderen, Martin. *The Political Thought of the Dutch Revolt 1555–1590.* Cambridge: Cambridge University Press, 1992.

von Gierke, Otto. *Community in Historical Perspective.* Edited by Antony Black. Translated by Mary Fischer. Cambridge: Cambridge University Press, 1990. Originally published as *Das deutsche Genossenschaftsrecht.* Vol. 1. Berlin: Weidmannsche Buchhandlung, 1868.

Walker, Gary, and Jean Grossman. "Philanthropy and Outcomes: Dilemmas in the Quest for Accountability." In *Philanthropy and the Nonprofit Sector in a Changing America*, edited by Charles T. Clotfelter and Thomas Ehrlich, 449–60. Bloomington: Indiana University Press, 1999.

Walzer, Michael. "A Better Vision: The Idea of Civil Society." *Dissent* 38 (Spring 1991): 296–304.

———. *On Toleration*. New Haven, CT: Yale University Press, 1997.

———. "Socialism and the Gift Relationship." *Dissent* 29 (Fall 1982): 431–41.

———. *Thick and Thin: Moral Argument at Home and Abroad*. Notre Dame, IN: University of Notre Dame Press, 1994.

Waszek, Norbert. *The Scottish Enlightenment and Hegel's Account of Civil Society*. Dordrecht, Netherlands: Kluwer Academic Publishers, 1988.

Weisbrod, Burton. *The Voluntary Sector*. Lexington, MA: Lexington Books, 1977.

Wilson, Renate. "Philanthropy in Eighteenth-Century Central Europe: Evangelical Reform and Commerce." *Voluntas: International Journal of Voluntary and Nonprofit Organizations* 9, no. 1 (1998): 81–102.

Wing, Kennard T., Thomas H. Pollak, and Amy Blackwood. *The Nonprofit Almanac 2008*. Washington, DC: The Urban Institute Press, 2008.

Wing Hung Lo, Carlos, and Sai Wing Leung. "Environmental Agency and Public Opinion in Guangzhou: The Limits of a Popular Approach to Environmental Governance." *The China Quarterly*, no. 163 (September 2000): 677–704.

Winograd, Morley and Michael Hais. *Millennial Makeover: MySpace, YouTube, and the Future of American Politics*. Piscataway, NJ: Rutgers University Press, 2008.

Witteveen, Willem. "Inhabiting Legality: How the Dutch Keep Reconstructing Their 'Rechtstaat.'" In *Understanding Dutch Law*, edited by Sanne Taekema, 75–101. Den Haag: Boom Juridische uitgevers, 2004.

Wittgenstein, Ludwig. *Philosophical Investigations*. 50th Anniversary Edition. Translated by G. E. M. Anscombe. Oxford: Blackwell Publishing, 2001.

Woldring, Henk E. S. "State and Civil Society in the Political Philosophy of Alexis de Tocqueville." *Voluntas: International Journal of Voluntary and Nonprofit Organizations* 9, no. 4 (December 1998): 363–73.

Wolin, Sheldon. *Tocqueville between Two Worlds: The Making of a Political and Theoretical Life*. Princeton, NJ: Princeton University Press, 2001.

Wootton, David, ed. *Republicanism, Liberty, and Commercial Society: 1649–1776*. Stanford, CA: Stanford University Press, 1994.

Zuckert, Michael. *The Natural Rights Republic: Studies in the Foundation of the American Political Tradition*. South Bend, IN: University of Notre Dame Press, 1996.

Zukin, Cliff, Scott Keeter, Molly Andolina, Krista Jenkins, and Michael X. Delli Carpini. *A New Engagement? Political Participation, Civic Life, and the Changing American Citizen*. Oxford: Oxford University Press, 2006.

Index